# MICROSOFT® WORKS FOR WINDOWS™:
## TUTORIAL & APPLICATIONS

# MICROSOFT® WORKS FOR WINDOWS™:
## TUTORIAL & APPLICATIONS

**William R. Pasewark, Sr., Ph.D.**
Professor Emeritus, Texas Tech University
Office Management Consultant

**William R. Pasewark, Jr., Ph.D., C.P.A.**
University of Houston

SOUTH-WESTERN PUBLISHING CO.

ISBN: 0-538-62281-4

1  2  3  4  5  6  7  8  9  JH  99  98  97  96  95  94  93

Printed in the United States of America

| | |
|---|---|
| Editor-in-Chief: | Robert E. First |
| Acquisition Editor: | Janie Schwark |
| Developmental Editor: | Dave Lafferty |
| Consulting Editor: | Cat Skintik |
| Coordinating Editor: | Lisa McClary |
| Production Editor: | Eric Carlson |
| Senior Production Editor: | Jean Findley |
| Senior Designers: | Jim DeSollar (Internal Art) |
| | Elaine St. John-Lagenaur |
| | (Cover/Special Page Art) |
| Electronic Illustration: | Alan Brown/Photonics Graphics |
| Marketing Manager: | Brian Taylor |

This book cover was designed using Strata Inc.'s Stratavision (TM) 3-D imaging software and Adobe Photoshop (TM) image manipulation software. Stratavision allows the creation of three-dimensional shapes and the applications of textures or images to the shapes.

Photo Credit: Courtesy of International Business Machines Corporation, page 5.

Microsoft is a registered trademark and Autosum, Toolbar, and Windows are trademarks of Microsoft Corporation.

# CONTENTS

# PREFACE

This preface has two sections: one for the student and one for the teacher.

## TO THE STUDENT

Computers affect our daily lives. They schedule television programs and advertisements; operate cash registers; print newspapers, books, and documents; keep records of athletic events; control telephone communications; monitor automobile engine performance; and generate high school course schedules and grade reports.

You may already have a working knowledge of computers, or you may have little or no computer experience at all. In either case, *Microsoft*[1] *Works for Windows:*[2] *Tutorial and Applications* will help you develop your level of computer competency.

## Microsoft Works for Windows— An Integrated Software Package

Microsoft Works for Windows is an *integrated* software package, which means that it combines three popular computer applications: word processing, database management, and spreadsheet analysis. These applications can be used for writing letters or research papers (the Works word processor), making lists of names and addresses (the Works database), and recording income and expenses (the Works spreadsheet). You can easily exchange and combine documents and information among the various applications.

Integrated software is commonly used in personal, academic, and career settings to complete routine tasks more quickly and accurately, thus improving efficiency and increasing productivity.

---

[1] Microsoft is a registered trademark of Microsoft Corporation.
[2] Windows is a trademark of Microsoft Corporation.

## Microsoft Works for Windows: Tutorial and Applications— Learn and Apply

The authors planned this book to provide a realistic, complete, and successful learning experience for you. Objectives listed at the beginning of each chapter give you an overview of the chapter. Short segments of text explain new information and tell why it is important. Then activities with numbered steps guide you through computer operations. These activities give you a chance to exercise the concepts you have just learned. The book includes many illustrations and activities to simplify complex concepts and operations. Summaries, short-answer questions, and applications help you review the chapters.

Within *Microsoft Works for Windows: Tutorial and Applications* the authors share with you their enthusiasm about how powerful a tool a computer can be.

# TO THE TEACHER

In today's world, understanding computer concepts, possessing computer skills, and knowing how to apply them are essential. Students enter computer courses with widely varying levels of skill and knowledge. Some may already know several software packages; others may not have been exposed to computers at all.

*Microsoft Works for Windows: Tutorial and Applications* is designed for new and experienced learners as they develop computer competency using an integrated computer software package. The tutorial can be structured for courses of study from 30 to 90 class meetings in length, making it easily adaptable to a variety of curriculum patterns.

## System Requirements

A minimum of an AT-class computer is required to run Works for Windows. This includes the 80286, 80386sx, 80386dx, 80486dx, or higher microprocessor. A full 1 megabyte or more of RAM is recommended. An EGA, VGA, 8514/A, Hercules, or other monitor supported by Microsoft Windows is required. A hard disk is needed. Microsoft Windows 3.0 or later is required and must be purchased separately from Works for Windows. Any Windows-compatible printer will operate with Works.

## Microsoft Works—An Integrated Software Package

Microsoft Works for Windows is an integrated software package. Contained within this single comprehensive program are three different programs:

▶ The Works word processor, with spelling checker and graphics capability

▶ The Works spreadsheet, with charting capability

▶ The Works database, with reporting capability

These programs, also called tools, can be used independently or in any combination. For example, you can easily integrate a chart from the spreadsheet tool into a letter from the word processor tool, or attach a list from the database to a memo created in the word processor.

Integrated computer software packages increase efficiency and productivity and are becoming common in the workplace. Exposure to this type of software package is a definite advantage to students in their academic, personal, and career lives.

## Teaching and Learning Aids

This instructional package is designed to simplify instruction and to enhance learning with a variety of learning and teaching aids, as described in the paragraphs that follow.

**TEXT WORKBOOK—THE TUTORIAL**   The student's text is organized around the following features:

▶ **Learning objectives** listed at the beginning of each chapter give students an overview of the chapter.

▶ **Enumerated step-by-step instructions** for specific operations allow students to progress independently. When the same operations are repeated, instructions are "faded"; that is, fewer specific instructions are included, challenging the student gradually to perform the operations from memory without prompting.

▶ **Computer activities** immediately follow the presentation of new concepts and instructions. The activities give students the opportunity to apply what they have just learned.

▶ The **integration** chapter (Chapter 15) teaches students how to merge the word processing, spreadsheet, and database tools.

▶ **Illustrations** explain complex concepts and serve as reference points as students complete activities.

- ▶ **Chapter summaries** provide quick reviews for each chapter, entrenching the main points in the student's mind.
- ▶ **Short-answer questions** follow each chapter and **computer applications** are provided at the end of Chapters 2–15 to gauge students' understanding of the chapter's information and operations. The applications offer minimal instruction, thus requiring students to apply concepts previously introduced.
- ▶ Two **appendices** cover additional features: Appendix A introduces the WorksWizards. Appendix B includes a brief introduction to modem telecommunications.
- ▶ The **glossary** is a list of common computer terms and definitions.
- ▶ A **comprehensive index** supplies quick and easy accessibility to specific parts of the tutorial.

**THE TEACHER'S MANUAL**   The complete teacher's manual includes a variety of aids for planning the course of study, presenting information, and managing the classroom. All are designed to ensure a successful and enjoyable teaching experience. The manual includes the following features:

- ▶ **Course schedules** suggest ways to use the tutorial for courses from 30 to 90 class meetings in length.
- ▶ Guidelines are provided on **scheduling students** with varying abilities.
- ▶ **General teaching suggestions** include strategies for effective instruction with a minimum of stress.
- ▶ **Specific teaching suggestions** are presented for each chapter.
- ▶ **Reproducible testing materials** include chapter tests and part tests for Parts 2–4. Answers are also provided.
- ▶ **Learning evaluation** can be accomplished using an Application Progress Record, a Grade Record, a Final Grade Record, and an Acceptability Level Grading Chart.

**THE TEMPLATE DISK**   The template data disk contains prekeyed text and selected graphics for activities and applications and may be copied for students. This disk allows students to use class time learning computer operations rather than keying text into the computer.

## THE AUTHORS' COMMITMENT

In writing *Microsoft Works for Windows: Tutorial and Applications*, the authors dedicated themselves to creating a complete and appealing instructional package to make teaching and learning an interesting, successful, and rewarding experience for both teachers and students. The authors assembled in one resource all the materials and aids a teacher needs to create a learning environment in which students can successfully master skills that will serve them in their academic and career endeavors as well as in their personal lives.

## ACKNOWLEDGMENTS

The authors thank Paula Cartwright, W. Allan Evans, and Todd Knowlton for their dedicated and effective contributions to this publication.

# MICROSOFT® WORKS FOR WINDOWS™:

## TUTORIAL & APPLICATIONS

# PART 1

## INTRODUCTION TO WINDOWS AND MICROSOFT WORKS

# MICROSOFT WINDOWS BASICS

## LEARNING OBJECTIVES

**When you complete this chapter, you will be able to:**

1. Understand the background and advantages of a graphical user interface.
2. Start Microsoft Windows from DOS.
3. Perform common mouse operations.
4. Move, resize, scroll through, open, and close windows.
5. Use menus.
6. Use Windows Help.
7. Exit Windows.

## INTRODUCTION TO WINDOWS

When the IBM PC was introduced in 1981, it was not nearly as powerful as today's computers. The operating system, known as DOS, could process a limited number of commands that the user had to key. A simple operation such as copying a file required the user to know the DOS command COPY, to know where the file to be copied was located, and to be able to tell the computer where it should be copied to. This process usually meant typing accurately a number of letters, numbers, and symbols and carefully checking to be sure the file wasn't going somewhere it shouldn't.

As computer *hardware*, the physical components of a computer, became more advanced, computer *software*, the lists of instructions that computers follow to perform specific tasks, did too. IBM PCs and PC compatibles still relied on the DOS operating environment to interpret commands from the user, and users still had to key these commands on a keyboard. But computer programs became easier to use as programmers built in better ways for the user to interact with the computer.

In 1985, the Microsoft Corporation introduced the first version of Windows, a new way for PC users to communicate with their computers. Windows is a *graphical user interface* (*GUI*). This means that the user actually interacts with the computer by means of graphics, or pictures. Instead of having to use the keyboard to enter commands, a user can point at pictures or words that tell the computer to do specific tasks. Recent versions of Windows, like the version you are using, are far more sophisticated than that first version released in 1985.

You can see how a GUI (pronounced "gooey") would be much easier to use. Instead of having to memorize the DOS instructions for opening an application, you can simply point at a pictorial representation of the application and Windows will launch it for you. Sending commands to the computer is no longer a matter of typing the command on the keyboard. Instead, you can select the command from a list and your instructions are carried out instantly.

What is more, all programs designed for Windows' GUI have similar features: Files are opened, saved, and printed in the same way; many commands are the same from program to program; even the screen looks the same from program to program. After you have learned one Windows program, you can easily learn others.

If you have never used Windows before, this chapter will teach you what you need to know to feel comfortable using Microsoft Works for Windows.

## Starting Windows

Depending on how it has been installed on the hard drive, Windows may start automatically when you turn the power on. If Windows does not start automatically, you must start it by keying the command **win** at the DOS prompt. The DOS prompt is DOS's way of asking for a command. The DOS prompt indicates the current disk drive and has a blinking cursor ready to accept your command. For example, C:\_.

**ACTIVITY
1-1**

### Starting Windows

In this activity, you will start your computer and Windows. This activity assumes that Windows is already installed on your hard disk.

1. Turn on the computer. Wait for the computer to go through its ritual of beeps and blinks until DOS is loaded. If your computer automatically starts up in Windows, skip step 2.

2. Key **win** at the prompt. After a few moments, Microsoft Windows will appear.

The first window you see when Windows starts up belongs to the *Program Manager*. The Program Manager organizes your programs and allows you to select a program that you want to run. Later, you will explore the Program Manager. First, you need to make friends with a mouse.

# PARTNERS WITH A MOUSE

**FIGURE 1-1**
A mouse makes using a graphical user interface easier by providing a way to point to and manipulate graphics and text on the screen.

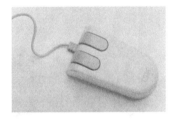

Graphical user interfaces like Microsoft Windows speed the work of the user by teaming the user with a mouse. A *mouse* is a device that rolls on a flat surface and has one or more buttons on it (see Figure 1-1). The mouse allows you to communicate with the computer by pointing to and manipulating graphics and text on the screen.

The four most common mouse operations are point, click, double-click, and drag. These operations are outlined in Table 1-1. Once these operations *click* in your mind, you will see the *point* of using a mouse, and your computer will never again be a *drag* to use.

Figure 1-2 illustrates a typical Program Manager screen. Your screen may vary slightly from the figure. The main features of the window are labeled on the figure and discussed below:

**TABLE 1-1**
Common Mouse Operations

▶ A number of related programs are stored in a *group window*.

▶ The *title bar* tells you the name of the open window. Figure 1-2 shows that the Main group window is open.

▶ Figure 1-2 shows two different types of icons. *Icons* are the small pictures that represent programs or groups of programs. Inside

| Operation | Definition |
|---|---|
| Point | Moving the mouse pointer to a specific item on the screen |
| Click | Pressing the mouse button and quickly releasing it while pointing to an item on the screen (the term *click* comes from the noise you hear when you press and release the button) |
| Double-click | Clicking the mouse twice, quickly, while keeping the mouse still |
| Drag | Pointing to a location on the screen, pressing and holding the mouse button, and moving the pointer while the button is pressed; releasing the button ends the drag operation |

**FIGURE 1-2**

The Program Manager
organizes your programs and
allows you to select a program
that you want to run.

the Main group window are *program icons* for the File Manager, the
Control Panel, and so on. The *group icons* at the bottom of the
Program Manager screen contain other collections of programs.

▶  The *pointer* indicates the *position* of the mouse.

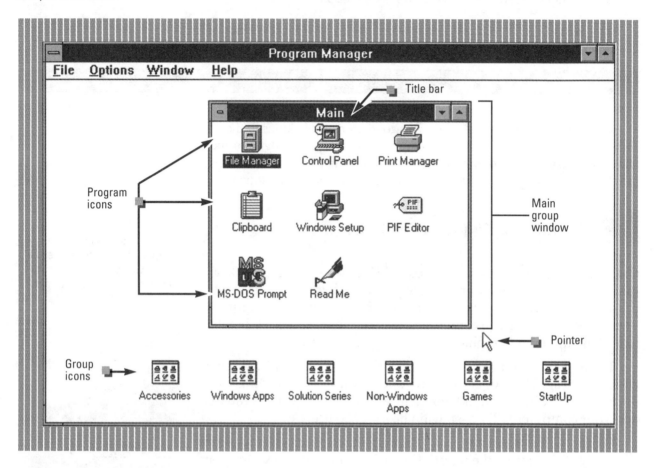

ACTIVITY
1-2

## Using the Mouse to Explore the Program Manager

In this activity, you will practice basic mouse operations while you
explore Windows' Program Manager.

1.    Move the mouse around on your desk and watch the pointer move
      on the screen. Do not press the mouse buttons yet.

2.    Point to the group icon labeled **Main**.

3.    Click. The Main group icon is highlighted, and a menu of choices
      appears above the icon. Do not choose an item from the menu.

4.    Click on the **Accessories** group icon to highlight it.

Activity 1-2 continued

5.  Double-click on the **Main** group icon. The Main group window opens. Inside the window are program icons.

---

*Note: If the window does not appear, double-click again; click faster this time.*

---

6.  To drag the window to a new position, point to the title bar. Press and hold the left mouse button while moving the pointer down about half an inch. Release the mouse button.

## EVERYTHING IS IN A WINDOW

It does not take long to figure out why Microsoft chose to call its graphical user interface "Windows." Almost everything is in a window. Notice that even the Program Manager is in a window. All of these windows share some common features that allow you to change their shapes, sizes, and locations.

### Moving and Resizing Windows

Sometimes you will have several windows on the screen at the same time. In order to work more effectively, you will sometimes need to move or change the size of a window.

**ACTIVITY
1-3**

### Moving and Resizing Windows

In this activity, you will move and resize a window.

1.  In the last activity, you used the mouse to drag the Main group window to a new location. Use the same procedure to drag the Main group window until it appears to be centered on the screen.

2.  Point anywhere on the border at the bottom of the Main group window. The pointer will turn into a vertical two-headed arrow.

3.  While the pointer is a two-headed arrow, drag the bottom border of the window down to enlarge the window.

Activity 1-3 continued

   4.   Point to the border on the right side of the Main group window. The pointer will turn into a horizontal two-headed arrow.

5.   While the pointer is a two-headed arrow, drag the border of the window to the right to enlarge the window.

   6.   It is possible to resize two sides of a window at the same time. Point to the lower right corner of the window border. The pointer becomes a two-headed arrow pointing diagonally.

7.   Drag the border to resize both edges at the same time until the window is only about two inches wide and one inch tall. Scroll bars appear on the window's borders (see Figure 1-3).

**FIGURE 1-3**
Scroll bars appear when there is more to be displayed than the window can show at its current size.

As you can see from the activity you just completed, the pointer is not always the same arrow. The shape of the pointer is an indication of what the computer is doing. Sometimes the pointer will even turn into an hourglass to indicate that the computer is temporarily busy. When the hourglass pointer appears, wait patiently for the pointer to change back.

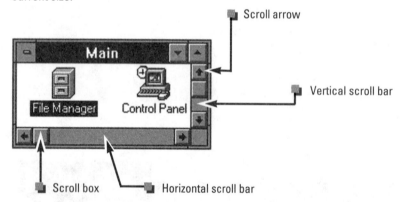

## Scroll Bars

A *scroll bar* appears on the edges of windows any time there is more to be displayed than a window can show at its current size. A scroll bar can appear along the bottom edge and/or along the right side of a window. Scroll bars appeared in the last step of the previous activity because the window was too small to show all the program icons at once.

Scroll bars are a convenient way to move quickly to another part of the window's contents you want to view. On the scroll bar is a sliding box called the *scroll box*. The scroll box indicates your position within the window's contents. When the scroll box reaches the bottom of the scroll bar, you have reached the end of the window's contents. *Scroll arrows* are located at the ends of the scroll bar. Clicking on a scroll arrow moves the window in that direction over the contents of the window.

**ACTIVITY 1-4**

## Scrolling

In this activity, you will practice using the scroll bar, scroll box, and scroll arrows. This activity assumes that the Main group window is open on the screen.

1.  If the Main group window does not have scroll bars on its edges, resize the window until both scroll bars appear (see Figure 1-3).

2.  Click the scroll arrow that points to the right. The contents of the window shift slightly to the left.

3.  Press and hold the mouse button on the same scroll arrow. The contents of the window scroll quickly across the window. Notice that the scroll box moves to the extreme right end of the scroll bar.

4.  You can also scroll by dragging the scroll box. Drag the scroll box on the horizontal scroll bar from the extreme right to the extreme left.

5.  Drag the scroll box on the horizontal scroll bar to the middle of the scroll bar.

6.  Drag the scroll box on the vertical scroll bar to the middle of the scroll bar.

7.  The final way to scroll is to click on the scroll bar. Click the horizontal scroll bar to the right of the scroll box. The contents scroll left.

8.  Click the horizontal scroll bar to the left of the scroll box. The contents scroll right.

## Other Window Controls

Three other important window controls are the Maximize button, the Minimize button, and the Control-menu box (see Figure 1-4). The *Maximize button* enlarges a window to full size. The *Minimize button* shrinks a window back to an icon. The *Control-menu box* is used to close a window. Minimizing and closing a window are sometimes identical operations, but not always.

**FIGURE 1-4**

The Maximize button, Minimize button, and Control-menu box provide efficient window handling.

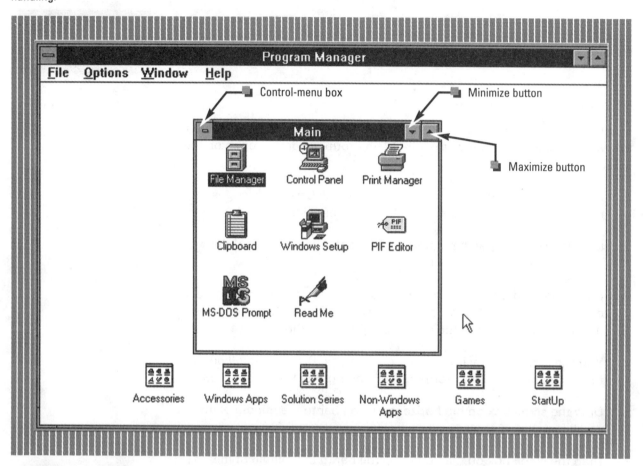

## Maximizing Windows

In this activity, you will use the Maximize button to enlarge a window.

1.  Scroll the Main group window until the horizontal scroll box is at the extreme left of the scroll bar.

2.  Scroll the Main group window until the vertical scroll box is at the top of the scroll bar.

3.  Resize the Main group window until the scroll bars disappear (see Figure 1-4).

4.  Click the **Maximize** button.

When a window is maximized, the Maximize button is replaced by the Restore button (see Figure 1-5). The Restore button restores the window to the size it was before the Maximize button was clicked.

**FIGURE 1-5**

The Restore button returns a maximized window to its regular size.

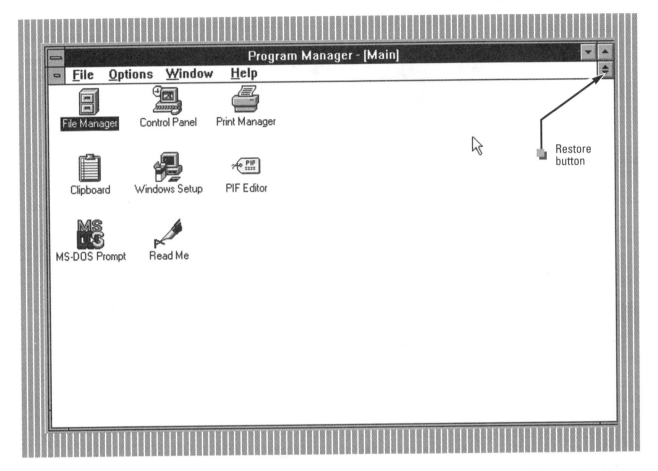

**ACTIVITY
1-6**

## Restoring and Closing Windows

In this activity, you will restore the window that was maximized in the last activity and learn two ways to close a window.

1.  Click the **Restore** button on the Main group window (see Figure 1-5).

2.  Click the **Minimize** button on the Main group window. The window is reduced to an icon.

3.  Double-click the **Main** group icon to open the window again.

4.  Double-click the **Control-menu box** to close the window.

# MENUS

To find out what a restaurant has to offer, you look at the menu. You can also look at a menu on the computer's screen to find out what a computer program has to offer. Menus in computer programs show you what your options are and let you choose one of the options. Menus are accessed from the menu bar (see Figure 1-6).

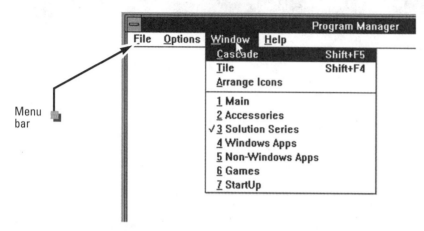

Menu bar

Most restaurants give you only one menu from which to choose. Computers often give you several menus at one time. Each menu's name is in the menu bar. First you choose a menu, then an item from that menu.

## ACTIVITY 1-7

### Using Menus

In this activity, you will practice using menus.

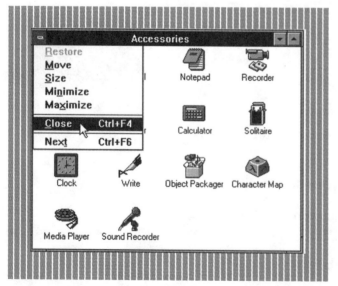

1.   Point to the **Window** menu header in the menu bar.

2.   Click. The menu appears.

3.   Point to **Accessories** in the menu.

4.   Click. The Accessories group window opens. Choosing Accessories from the Window menu has the same result as double-clicking the Accessories group icon.

5.   Click once on the **Control-menu box** of the Accessories group window. A menu appears (see Figure 1-7).

6.   From the **Control** menu, choose **Close**. The window is reduced to an icon.

# THE HELP MENU

**FIGURE 1-8**
The Help menu is a convenient source of information about Microsoft Windows.

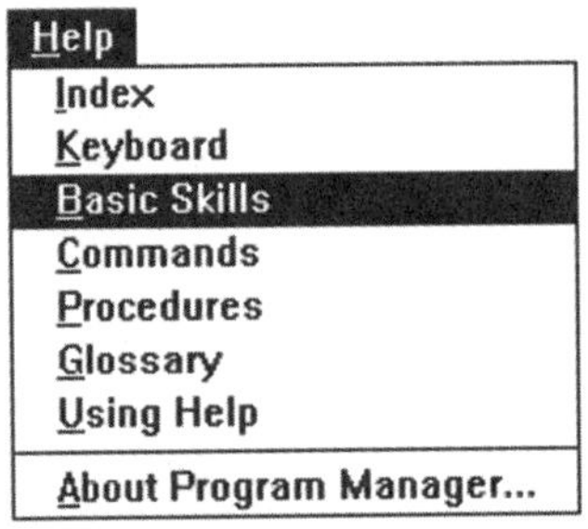

This chapter has covered only a few of the many features of Windows. For additional information, Windows has a tutorial and an easy-to-use help system. The Help menu differs depending on what version of Microsoft Windows you are using. Only version 3.1 offers the tutorial.

| Help |
|------|
| Index |
| Keyboard |
| **Basic Skills** |
| Commands |
| Procedures |
| Glossary |
| Using Help |
| About Program Manager... |

Version 3.0

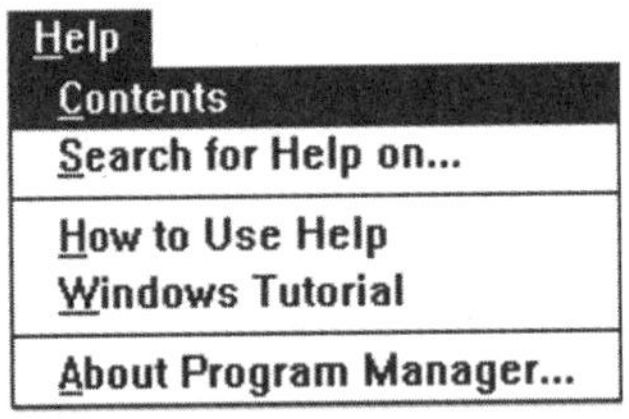

## Windows Help

Use Windows Help as a quick reference when you are unsure about a function. Windows Help is accessed through the Help menu. Figure 1-8 shows the Help menu from versions 3.0 and 3.1. In version 3.0, the topics of Help are available right on the menu. In version 3.1, you can choose either to see the table of contents for Windows Help or to search the help system. In version 3.0, the Using Help command in the Help menu will show you how to use Windows Help. If you need assistance using Windows Help in version 3.1, choose How to Use Help from the Help menu.

| Help |
|------|
| **Contents** |
| Search for Help on... |
| How to Use Help |
| Windows Tutorial |
| About Program Manager... |

Version 3.1

## Windows Tutorial

Microsoft Windows, version 3.1, includes a tutorial that describes all of the features you have seen in this chapter. If you would like to review before moving on, or if you feel you need extra practice, run the tutorial before continuing. To start the tutorial, choose Windows Tutorial from the Help menu. You can exit the tutorial at any time by pressing the Escape key.

# EXITING WINDOWS

The File menu provides the option to exit Windows. Exiting Windows takes you to DOS. Once in DOS, you can turn your computer off.

**ACTIVITY
1-8**

### Exiting Windows

In this activity, you will exit Windows.

1. From the **File** menu, choose **Exit Windows**. A dialog box will appear asking you to confirm that you want to quit. If you are using Windows 3.0, you will have the option of saving changes to Windows. Do NOT save changes.

2. Click **OK**. The computer will return to a DOS prompt.

## Now, ON TO GOOD WORKS

Now that you have learned the basics of Windows, you will get to know Microsoft Works for Windows in the next chapter.

# SUMMARY

Microsoft Works is a graphical user interface (GUI) for IBM and compatible computers. A graphical user interface makes it easier to use a computer. The Program Manager organizes your programs and allows you to select a program you want to run.

In Windows, almost everything on the screen is in a window. These windows can be moved, resized, opened, and closed. If all the contents of a window cannot be displayed in the window's current size, scroll bars appear to allow you to move to the part of the window you want to view. Windows can be maximized to fill the screen or minimized to an icon.

Menus are an important part of Windows. Menus allow you to choose commands to perform different actions. Menus are accessed from the Menu bar near the top of the screen.

Windows Help provides additional information about the many features of Windows. Windows Help defines terms and covers most features of the Program Manager.

# CHALLENGES

## TRUE/FALSE

Circle **T** or **F** to show whether the statement is true or false.

T    F    1.    IBM introduced the first version of Microsoft Windows.

T    F    2.    A graphical user interface makes learning and using a computer easier and more enjoyable to most users.

T    F    3.    When Microsoft Windows starts, the Program Manager allows you to select the program you want to run.

T    F    4.    A mouse makes using a graphical user interface easier.

T    F    5.    Sliding describes the action of holding a mouse button while moving the mouse on a flat surface.

T    F    6.    Double-clicking a group icon opens the group window.

T    F    7.    Scroll bars will not appear if all items in the window are visible.

T    F    8.    Menus can be accessed from the menu bar.

T    F    9.    Windows Help is accessed through the File menu.

T    F    10.   Exiting Windows takes you to DOS.

# COMPLETION

Write the correct answer in the space provided.

1. Name one factor that makes graphical user interfaces easier to use than nongraphical user interfaces, such as DOS.

_____

2. What command is keyed to start Microsoft Windows from DOS?

_____

3. Describe the drag mouse operation.

_____

4. What does it mean when the mouse pointer becomes an hourglass?

_____

5. List three ways to move using the scroll bars.

_____

_____

_____

6. List two ways to close a window.

_____

_____

7. What does the Restore button do?

_____

8. How do you make the Control menu appear for a specific window?

_____

9. What key allows you to exit the Windows Tutorial at any time?

_____

10. What are the steps for exiting Windows?

_____

# WORKS BASICS

## LEARNING OBJECTIVES

**When you complete this chapter, you will be able to:**

1. Understand the concept of an integrated software package.
2. Start Works from Windows.
3. Use the Works Tutorial.
4. Identify the parts of the Works screen.
5. Use menus, dialog boxes, and the Toolbar.[1]
6. Use files and directories.
7. Exit Works.

## INTRODUCTION TO WORKS

Microsoft Works for Windows is an integrated software package. An *integrated software package* is a computer program that combines common tools into one program. Works consists of a word processor tool, a graphics tool, a spreadsheet tool, and a database tool. The word processor enables you to create documents, such as letters and reports. The graphics tool, Microsoft Draw, gives you the ability to add drawings to your documents. The spreadsheet tool works with numbers, and the database tool organizes information, such as addresses or inventory items. Because Works is an integrated program, the tools can be used together. For example, numbers from a spreadsheet can be included in a letter created in the word processor.

## STARTING WORKS

Works is started from the Program Manager in Windows. Chapter 1 showed you how to start Windows. To start Works, double-click the

---

[1] Toolbar is a trademark of Microsoft Corporation.

Microsoft Works icon. The Microsoft Works icon is normally found in the Microsoft Solution Series program group. It is possible that your computer has the Works icon in a different group or in a group with a slightly different name.

## ACTIVITY 2-1

### Starting Works

In this activity, you will start Works. This activity assumes that Windows is already running on your computer and that the Microsoft Works icon is in the Microsoft Solution Series program group.

**FIGURE 2-1**

The Startup dialog box gives you the chance to choose a tool.

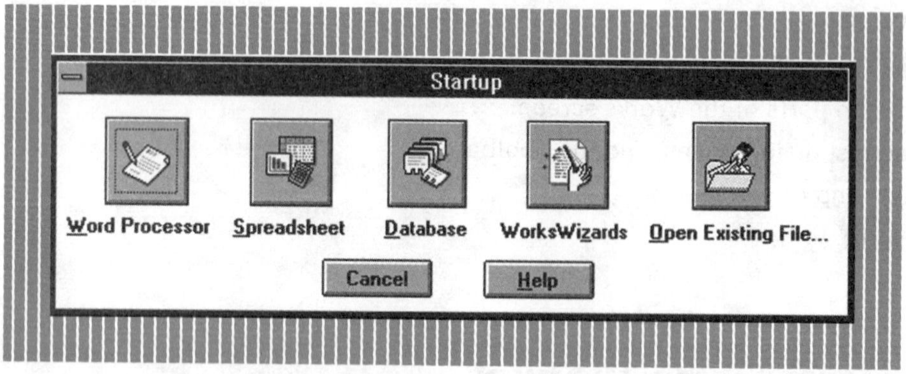

1.  Double-click the **Microsoft Solution Series** icon. The Microsoft Solution Series group window appears.

2.  Double-click the **Microsoft Works** icon. Works starts. The Startup dialog box appears (see Figure 2-1). Each tool has a corresponding button in the Startup dialog box.

3.  Click **Cancel**. Now Works is running, but no tool is in use.

## USING THE WORKS TUTORIAL

Works includes a tutorial that describes everything from computer fundamentals to integrating the Works tools. In the next several activities, you will use the Works Tutorial to learn the basic concepts of Works.

## ACTIVITY 2-2

### Using the Works Tutorial

In this activity, you will start the Works Tutorial and select the first topic.

1.  From the **Help** menu, choose **Tutorial**. The Works Tutorial welcome screen appears.

Activity 2-2 continued

2. Click the left mouse button anywhere on the screen. The tutorial's main menu appears (see Figure 2-2).

**FIGURE 2-2**
The Works for Windows Tutorial has six topics.

3. Click **2   Starting with Works**. The menu for the selected topic appears, as in Figure 2-3. (If you accidentally choose the wrong topic, click **Main Menu:M** to return to the tutorial's main menu.)

4. Click **A   Introducing Works for Windows**. The first screen of the lesson appears. Near the bottom of the screen are three buttons (see Figure 2-4).

5. Click **Instructions:Ctrl+I**. Read the screen to learn how to use the tutorial (see Figure 2-5). Press any key or click the mouse when you have read the screen.

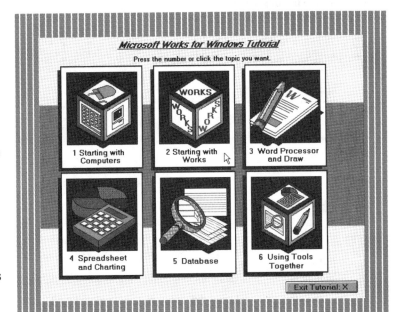

**FIGURE 2-3**
Each topic in the tutorial has a menu.

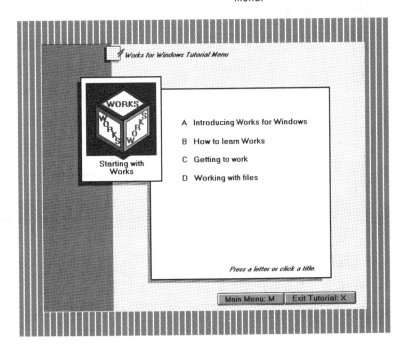

Activity 2-2 continued

**FIGURE 2-4**
The flow of the tutorial is
controlled by the buttons at the
bottom of the tutorial's screen.

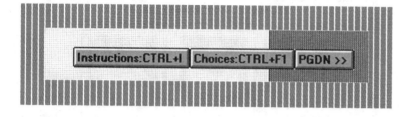

**FIGURE 2-5**
The Works Tutorial is easy to
use.

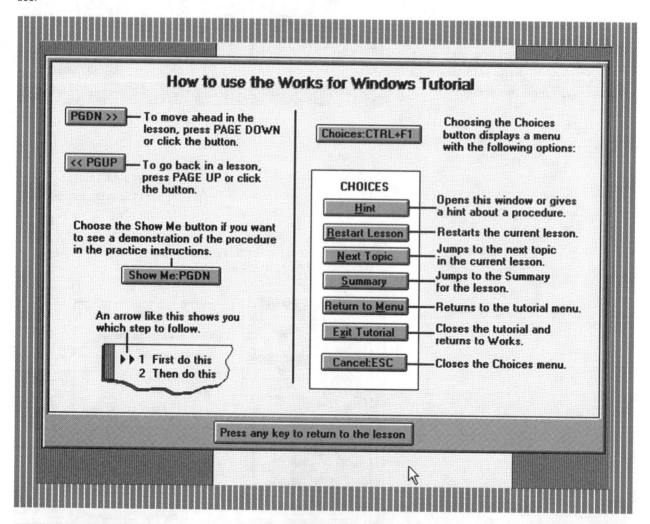

## Exploring the Tutorial on Your Own

In this activity, you will use the tutorial on your own to learn about Works for Windows and working with files.

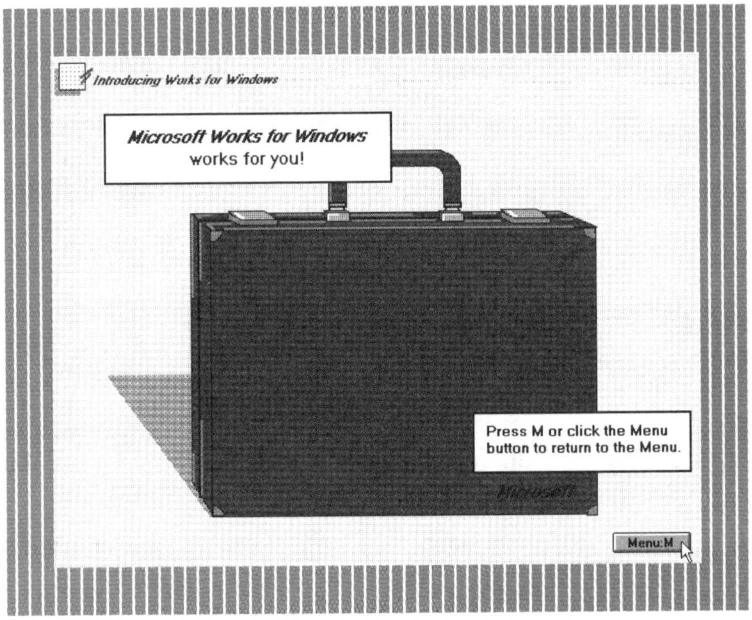

1.  Click **PGDN>>** (or press **Page Down**) to move to the next screen. Read the screens as they are presented. Continue to click **PGDN>>** and read each screen until the screen shown in Figure 2-6 appears. This lesson will take about 5 minutes.

2.  Click **Menu:M** to return to the menu.

3.  Click **C    Getting to work** from the Starting with Works menu. Read the screens as you did in the previous lesson. In this lesson, you will have the chance to try some of the features yourself. The tutorial will not let you make a mistake, so relax and enjoy the tour. If the tutorial asks you to do something you don't understand, click the **Show Me:PGDN** button and the computer will do it for you.

4.  Click **PGDN>>** to move from one screen to the next and follow the directions presented until the lesson is complete. This lesson will take about 20 minutes.

5.  Complete lesson **D    Working with files** from the Starting with Works menu. This lesson will take about 20 minutes.

6.  When you reach the summary of the lesson, click **Menu:M**. The menu for the topic appears.

7.  Click **Exit Tutorial**. The blank Works screen appears.  No tool is currently in use.

**FIGURE 2-6**
At the end of a tutorial lesson, click Menu:M to return to the tutorial menu.

## WORKING WITH FILES

In all of the Works tools, you *open, save,* and *close* files in the same way. Opening a file is the process of loading a file from a disk onto your screen. Saving is done two ways. The Save command saves a file on a disk using the current name. The Save As command saves a file on a disk using a new name. The Save As command can also be used to save a file in a new location. Closing a file removes it from the screen.

The tutorial showed you how files are opened and saved in Works. To be an expert with files, however, you need to know more about filenames, directories, subdirectories, and paths.

## Filenames

A filename may contain up to eight characters and may not include any spaces. Works will automatically provide a three-letter extension to the end of the filename depending on the tool you are using: word processor (wps), spreadsheet (wks), or database (wdb). For example, *bankacct.wks* is a spreadsheet document. The filename can include most characters found on the keyboard but must start with either a letter or a number. Characters that cannot be used in a filename are shown in Table 2-1.

**TABLE 2-1**

Characters That Cannot Be Used in Filenames

Name a file with a descriptive name or one that will remind you of what the file contains. Because a filename is limited to only eight characters, it is sometimes hard to think of a name that describes the document. One way to help overcome this problem is to group your documents. In the next section, you will learn how to group documents on your disks.

| Character | Character Name | Character | Character Name |
|-----------|----------------|-----------|----------------|
| \         | backslash      | .         | period         |
| [ ]       | brackets       | ;         | semicolon      |
| :         | colon          | /         | slash          |
| ,         | comma          | "         | quotation mark |
| =         | equal sign     | \|        | vertical bar   |

## Directories and Subdirectories

Because computer disks have such a large capacity, it is not unusual for a floppy disk to contain dozens of files or for a hard disk to contain hundreds or thousands of files. To organize its files, a disk can be divided into directories and subdirectories. A *directory* groups files that have something in common. For example, your hard disk has a directory that holds the program files necessary to run Works. You can also create directories for your documents. A *subdirectory* is a directory within a directory. For example, you could create a directory to group all of the files with which you are currently working. Within that directory, you could have several subdirectories that group different projects.

When you open a file, you must tell Works where the file is. In the same way, when you save a file, you must tell Works where you want to save the file. You specify the location of a file by giving Works a *pathname*, or *path*. The path consists of the disk drive letter and the directory. For example, if the file you want to open is in a directory named *letters* on a floppy disk in the A drive, the path is *a:\letters*. To indicate a subdirectory in a path, you just extend the path with another backslash and the name of the subdirectory. For example, within the *letters* directory you can have a subdirectory for each of the people to whom you frequently write letters. If within the *letters* directory there is a *gabriel* subdirectory, the path to the files in the *gabriel* subdirectory is *a:\letters\gabriel*.

The colon appears in a path to separate the drive letter from the rest of the path. The backslash is used to separate directories, subdirectories, and files in a path. Many times you will see a specific filename at the end of a path. For example, *c:\reports\finance\may.wks* specifies the location of a file named *may.wks*, on drive C, in the *reports* directory, in the *finance* subdirectory.

When you choose Open Existing File from the File menu, the Open dialog box appears (see Figure 2-7). The Open dialog box enables you to open a file from any available disk and directory. The Drives box, near the bottom of the dialog box, is where you select the disk drive that contains the file you want to open. The Directories box shows you what directories are on the disk using pictures of folders. A folder is an appropriate way to show a directory or subdirectory graphically, because, like a folder, a directory groups files that have something in common.

**FIGURE 2-7**
The Open dialog box can open a file from any available disk and directory.

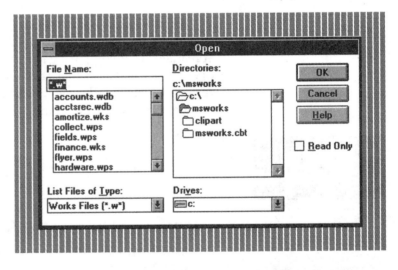

**ACTIVITY 2-4**

## Changing Disk Drives and Directories

In this activity, you will practice navigating through directories on disk.

1. From the **File** menu, choose **Open Existing File**. The Open dialog box appears.

2. Insert your template disk into drive A.

3. Click on the arrow in the Drives box to display the available disk drives.

4. Click **a:**. The Directories box should be similar to Figure 2-8.

**FIGURE 2-8**
The Directories box provides a graphical representation of the current directory.

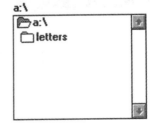

Activity 2-4 continued

---

**FIGURE 2-9**

Within the letters directory are several subdirectories.

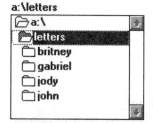

Directories:

a:\letters

5.  Double-click the **folder** in the Directories box named *letters*. The subdirectories within the letters directory will appear (see Figure 2-9).

6.  Double-click the **gabriel** folder. The File Name box displays the names of the files in the gabriel subdirectory.

7.  Click on **skitrip.wps** in the File Name box.

8.  Click **OK** to open the file.

9.  Leave the file open for the next activity.

---

You can see how directories can help organize and identify documents. In the same subdirectory as the letter to Gabriel is a spreadsheet for comparing ski trip options. In the next activity, you will open the spreadsheet that goes with the letter. Notice that Works remembers the subdirectory where you are currently working. Therefore, opening the second file in the gabriel subdirectory is quick and easy.

## ACTIVITY 2-5

### Opening a File from the Current Directory

In this activity, you will open the spreadsheet that is mentioned in the ski trip letter to Gabriel.

1.  From the **File** menu, choose **Open Existing File**. The path is still set to drive A and the gabriel subdirectory (a:\letters\gabriel).

2.  From the **File Name box**, click on **skicost.wks**.

3.  Click **OK** to open the spreadsheet.

4.  From the **File** menu, choose **Close**. *Skicost.wks* closes.

5.  From the **File** menu, choose **Close**. *Skitrip.wps* closes.

---

### Shortcut for Loading Recently Used Files

At the bottom of the File menu are the paths and filenames of the four most recently opened documents. The filename with the number 1 beside it is the most recently opened document. When a new file is opened, each filename moves down to make room for the new number 1 file. To load one of the files, you simply choose it as if it were a menu selection. If the document you are looking for is not in the File menu, use Open Existing File to load it from the disk.

## Ending Your Works Session

As you saw in the tutorial, the File menu provides the option to exit Works. Exiting Works takes you back to the Windows Program Manager. Always remove your data or template disks before turning off the computer.

**ACTIVITY 2-6**

## Exiting Works

In this activity, you will exit Works and return to the Program Manager.

1.  Pull down the **File** menu. Notice the files listed at the bottom of the menu. These are the four most recently used files mentioned in the previous section.

2.  Choose **Exit Works**. Works will close and the Program Manager will appear on the screen.

## If You Do Not Finish before the End of Class

If you need to exit Works while working on an activity or application, save your work on your data disk and exit Works. When you have the opportunity to finish, open the document from your data disk and continue.

## Consider Repeating the Tutorial

You may find it helpful to repeat the tutorial (or parts of it) so you feel confident before launching into the rest of the chapters. The concepts presented in the parts of the tutorial you have just completed are very important and will be applied throughout this book.

# SUMMARY

Microsoft Works is an integrated software package. Works consists of a word processor tool, a graphics tool, a spreadsheet tool, and a database tool. The documents of an integrated software package can be used together.

Works is started from the Program Manager by double-clicking the Microsoft Works icon. The Works Tutorial is started by choosing Tutorial from the Help menu.

No matter which tool you are using, files are opened, saved, and closed the same way. Filenames may contain up to eight characters and may not include any spaces. A three-letter extension is added to the filename to identify what type of document it is. Files can be saved in groups on a disk, called directories. The location of a file is specified using a pathname. Recently used files can be opened quickly by choosing the filename from the bottom of the File menu. To exit works, choose Exit Works from the File menu.

# CHALLENGES

## TRUE/FALSE

Circle **T** or **F** to show whether the statement is true or false.

T   F   1. An integrated software package is a computer program that combines common tools into one program.

T   F   2. Works is started from the Program Manager.

T   F   3. The Works Tutorial is started from the File menu.

T   F   4. The menu bar contains the names of Works menus.

T   F   5. A dimmed command in a menu is the recommended choice.

T   F   6. Only one check box at a time can be chosen.

T   F   7. The Toolbar provides buttons as shortcuts to choosing commands from menus.

T   F   8. When a file is open, the copy on the disk remains safely stored.

T   F   9. The Save As command saves a document as a different type of document.

T   F   10. To exit Works, click the Exit button on the Toolbar.

# COMPLETION

1. List the three primary tools that make up Works.

_____

_____

_____

2. What part of the screen allows you to move to different parts of a document?

_____

3. Where is the name of a document shown?

_____

4. What part of the screen gives a brief description of commands?

_____

5. What does an ellipsis (. . .) after a command in a menu indicate?

_____

6. What makes option buttons different from check boxes?

_____

_____

7. Name one command that can be accessed quickly from the Toolbar.

_____

8. When is using the Save command more convenient than using the Save As command?

_____

9. After a document is saved, what command (other than Exit) can be used to remove the document from the screen?

_____

10. What appears on the screen after you exit Works?

_____

APPLICATIONS

# APPLICATION 2-1

Refer to Figure 2-10 and match the letter of the screen item with the name of the item below.

_____ 1. scroll bar

**FIGURE 2-10**
The Works Document Window

_____ 2. Toolbar

_____ 3. title bar

_____ 4. menu bar

_____ 5. Minimize button

_____ 6. Maximize button

_____ 7. scroll box

_____ 8. Control-menu box

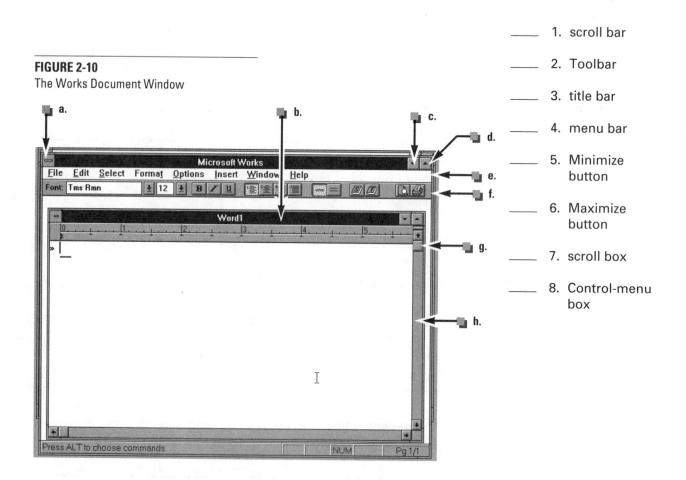

## APPLICATION 2-2

Write the path and filename for each of the following items:

Example: A file named *readme.wps* in the *notes* directory on drive C.

Path: *c:\notes\readme.wps*

1.  A file named *address.wdb* on drive A.

Path: _____

2.  A file named *camp.wps* in the *kirk* subdirectory in the *letters* directory on drive B.

Path: _____

# PART 2

# WORD PROCESSING

# WORD PROCESSING BASICS

## CONCEPTS OF WORD PROCESSING

*Word processing* is the use of computer software to enter and edit text. In the past, typewriters were the most common way to put text on paper. If you have ever used a typewriter, you know that it is not always an easy process. Using word processing software, such as the word processor in Works, you can create and edit documents much more easily than you could using a typewriter.

For example, if you make a mistake while keying text on a typewriter, you usually have to fix it using correction tape or liquid. If you leave out a sentence, you may have to rekey the entire document. But the same kinds of mistakes are easy to fix when you're using a word processor. This is because words keyed on a word processor are stored in the computer's memory or on a disk. You don't print the text on paper until after you have edited your document on the screen.

In this chapter, you will learn basic features of the word processor, such as entering text, saving your work on a disk to open and revise later, and printing a document. These features will help you to create letters, reports, or term papers in the future.

## STARTING THE WORD PROCESSOR

As you learned in Chapter 2, Microsoft Works for Windows is an integrated software package. This means it incorporates several tools into one program. You have already seen that, when you start Works, you can choose which tool to work with, or you can choose to open an existing file. No matter which of the tools you decide to work with, the process of starting Works and creating a new file is the same.

### Starting Works and Creating a New Word Processing Document

As you have already learned, you start Works from the Program Manager by clicking on the Microsoft Works icon. If you need a reminder about the Program Manager and its group icons, review Chapter 1. When the Startup dialog box appears, you can click the button that corresponds to the tool you want to work with. Works will open a new document screen.

## ACTIVITY 3-1

### Starting Works and Creating a New Word Processing Document

In this activity, you will start Works and create a new word processing document.

1. From the **Program Manager** window, double-click the **Microsoft Solution Series** icon. The Microsoft Solution Series group window appears. Your computer may have the Microsoft Works icon in a different group or in a group with a slightly different name.

2. Double-click the **Microsoft Works** icon. The Startup dialog box appears.

3. Click the **Word Processor** button. The document window appears with *Word1* in the title bar.

4. Leave the document window on the screen for the next activity.

## Creating a New File

One of the most useful features of Works is its ability to open more than one document at a time. While you are working on one document, you can create a new document and work on them both simultaneously. Suppose, for example, you are creating a résumé in one document. While the résumé document is on the screen, you can create a new document in which to type the cover letter you will send with the résumé. If you want to send two different cover letters, you can even open a third document in which to type the second cover letter. All the tools in Works will let you open new documents while you are working on other documents, as you will see later in this book.

Opening a new document is very simple: You choose Create New File from the File menu, and Works displays the new document on top of the document that is already open. The new document window becomes the *active window*. You can determine this because the title bar of the active window is a different color or intensity from the title bar of the inactive window. It is very simple to move back and forth between documents: Just click on the title bar of the document you want to work on, and it will become the active window and come to the front of the screen. You can also choose a document you want to become active in the Window menu. You can only enter text in an active window.

> **ACTIVITY
> 3-2**

## Creating a New File

In this activity, you will create a new word processing document from within the word processor and learn to switch between documents.

1. From the **File** menu, choose **Create New File**. The Create New File dialog box appears containing several tools, as in Figure 3-1.

2. Click the **Word Processor** button. Another word processing window appears on top of the *Word1* document with *Word2* in the title bar. Notice that the title bar of the *Word2* document is a different color from the title bar of the *Word1* document. This means it is the active window.

   Although you chose to create a new word processor file here, you could also have chosen to open a new database or spreadsheet file. You can access any Works tool from any application.

**FIGURE 3-1**
The Create New File dialog box allows you to choose the type of document you want to create.

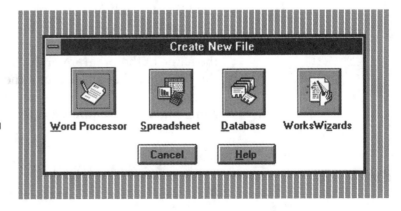

Activity 3-2 continued

3.   Click on the **Word1** title bar and notice that it becomes the active window. *Word2* disappears from the screen because it is now behind *Word1*.

4.   To bring *Word2* to the front again, click on the **Window** menu. At the bottom of the menu, you will see your two documents listed, with a check mark beside *Word1*. Click on **Word2**.  The menu will close and *Word2* will once again be the active window.

5.   From the **File** menu, choose **Close**. The *Word2* window closes and the *Word1* window remains on the screen.

6.   Leave the *Word1* window on the screen for the next activity.

## WORD PROCESSOR WINDOWS

If you look closely at your screen, you will see that you really have two windows on the screen: the Microsoft Works window and the window containing *Word1*. The window containing Microsoft Works is called the *application window*. No matter which tool you choose to use in Works, you will always see this window on your screen. The *Word1* window is called the *document window*. This is the window where you will actually do your work. In the word processor, the first document window that appears on your screen is called *Word1*. In the database, the first document window is called *Data1*, and in the spreadsheet, the first document window is called *Sheet1*. All these document windows share some features that will make your work easier, as shown in Figure 3-2.

### Identifying Parts of the Screen

In Chapter 2, you learned the names of some of the parts of the screen from the tutorial. As you look at your screen, you will see the features you learned plus some additional features that appear only in the word processor.  A *title bar* is located at the top of every window. It contains the name of the program or document in the window. The *menu bar* is the horizontal bar at the top of the application window that contains menu titles from which you can choose a variety of word processing commands. The *Toolbar*, located directly below the menu bar, contains

**FIGURE 3-2**
The document window is located within the application window.

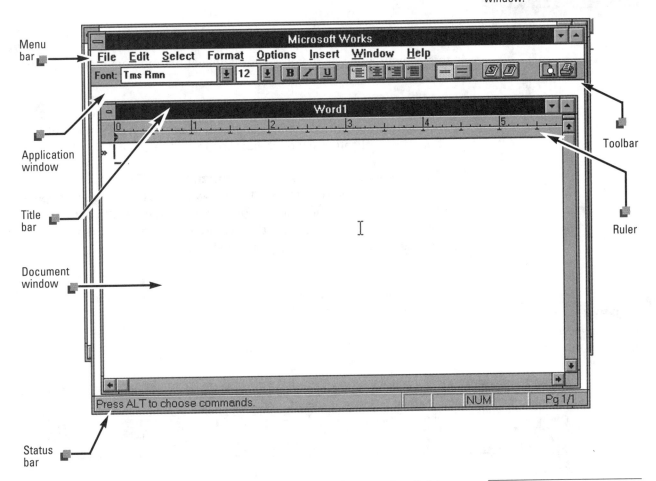

Menu bar

Application window

Title bar

Document window

Status bar

Toolbar

Ruler

common word processing commands you can use by simply clicking the correct button. Using the *ruler*, located directly below the Toolbar, you can quickly change indentions, tabs, and margins. Located at the bottom of the application window is a one-line ***status bar***. The message in the status bar gives you directions on how to access menus and briefly summarizes the actions of commands that you choose.

## Changing the Size of the Windows

When you start Works, the application window and document window do not fill the screen. As you learned in Chapter 1, you can maximize the windows to take advantage of the entire screen. Figure 3-3 will remind you where to find the Maximize and Minimize buttons.

**FIGURE 3-3**
The Maximize button changes the size of a window while the Minimize button reduces a window to an icon.

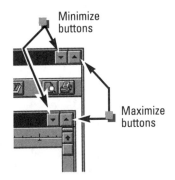

Minimize buttons

Maximize buttons

**ACTIVITY
3-3**

## Maximizing the Windows

In this activity, you will maximize the application and document windows.

1.  Click the application window's **Maximize** button. Remember that the application window is the one with *Microsoft Works* in the title bar. The application window expands to fill the screen.

2.  Click the document window's **Maximize** button. The document window expands to fill the application window. The windows appear as in Figure 3-4. Notice that the document window's title bar has disappeared, and the application window's title bar now reads *Microsoft Works - [Word1]* to let you know what document you are in.

3.  Leave the *Word1* document window on the screen for the next activity.

**FIGURE 3-4**
The document window and application window appear maximized.

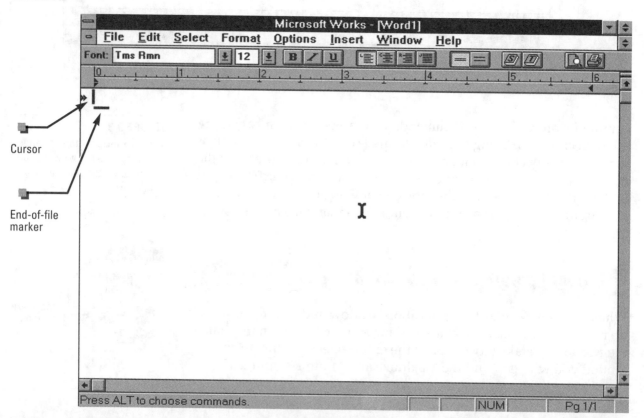

Cursor

End-of-file marker

## ENTERING TEXT

Look again at Figure 3-4 or at your screen. The vertical blinking line in the document window is called the *cursor*, or *insertion point*. The cursor marks your place in the text and indicates where the next character you key will appear. The horizontal line is called the *end-of-file marker*. It moves down as you enter a new line of text and marks the end of the document. The cursor cannot be moved below the end-of-file marker.

When you begin to enter text, you will notice that the cursor moves to the right in front of each letter you key. As you reach the right side of the window, the cursor automatically moves to the next line. This feature is called *wordwrap*. It is one feature that sets word processors apart from typewriters, on which you must manually return each time you wish to type a new line.

It is easy to make typographical errors while keying text. If you make a mistake while keying the paragraph in Activity 3-4, press the Backspace key to delete characters to the left of the cursor and then continue keying the paragraph.

## ACTIVITY 3-4

### Entering Text

In this activity, you will key a paragraph of text.

1. Key the following text. As you key, watch what happens to the words as you reach the end of the line. Your screen should resemble Figure 3-5 when you have finished.

   **In 1961, NASA launched the first chimpanzee into space. This chimp, named Ham, traveled a total distance of 422 miles at a top speed of 1,200 miles per hour. Ham helped pioneer safe space travel during the infancy of the United States Space Program.**

2. The text you entered wrapped at the end of each line to start a new line. Your cursor is now to the right of the last character, and the end-of-file marker appears directly below the text, as in Figure 3-5. Press **Enter** to move the cursor down one line.

3. Leave the *Word1* document window on the screen for the next activity.

Activity 3-4 continued

**FIGURE 3-5**
Letters appear to the left of the
cursor as you key.

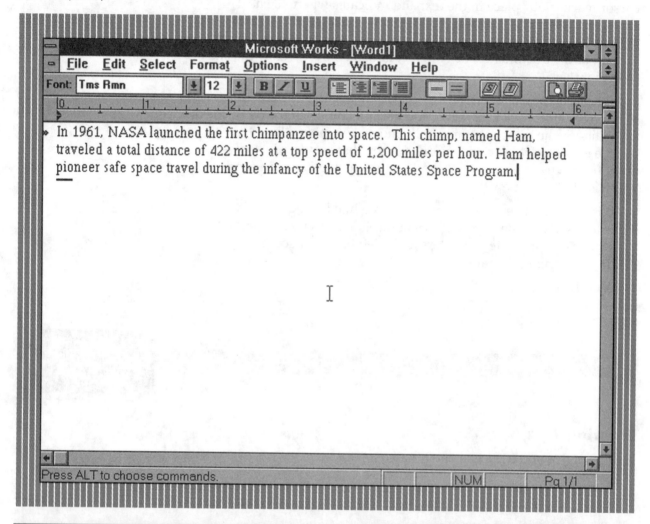

## SAVING YOUR WORK

Saving is one of the most important features of any computer program.
You can store files you have created on a floppy disk or on the
computer's hard drive. It is a good idea to get in the habit of saving
often. An electrical failure can cause you to lose a document you have
not yet saved, and if that document was long and tedious, you are
really out of luck!

All Windows applications give you two ways to save a file: with
the Save and with the Save As commands. The first time you save a

file, you will not have to choose between these two commands: When you select Save from the File menu, Works will automatically present you with the Save As dialog box. In this dialog box, you can type the name you wish to give your file and the destination where you want Works to save it. Works will then store the file in that location under the name you have supplied and return you to your document.

The next time you want to save your document, you again choose Save. This time, you will not see a dialog box, and Works will save the current document by overwriting the previous version of it. You won't see the saving process on the screen, but the status bar tells you that Works is saving your file to disk.

If you wish to give your existing file a different name or save it to a new location, you can choose Save As from the File menu. Once again, you will see the Save As dialog box. Type in the new name or destination for the file, and Works will store a new copy of the file according to your directions.

## ACTIVITY 3-5

## Saving a Document

In this activity, you will save the document you created in the previous activity under a specific name. You will also key an additional paragraph and save it in the same file.

1. From the **File** menu, choose **Save**. The Save As dialog box appears, as shown in Figure 3-6.

2. In the box under **File Name** notice that *Word1* is highlighted. This means that you won't have to delete this name. As soon as you press a key, the name *Word1* disappears and your keystroke appears in the File Name box. Key **space** as the filename of the document.

3. Place your data disk in drive A. In the **Drives** box, choose **a:** to select your floppy disk drive.

4. Click **OK**. Works saves the document and automatically assigns the filename extension *.wps* to indicate the document type.

5. Press **Enter** to create a blank line.

6. Key this additional paragraph:

   **The Soviet Union was the first country to send a female into orbit. Her name was**

**FIGURE 3-6**
The Save As dialog box allows you to save a document with a specific name or in a specific drive or directory.

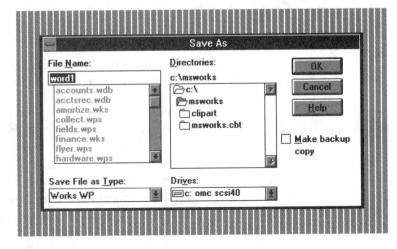

Activity 3-5 continued

Valentina Tereshkova. **Sally Ride was the first American woman to travel in space. Ride's job on the mission was to help recover a stranded satellite.**

**FIGURE 3-7**

The additional text is saved with the original text.

7.  From the **File** menu, choose **Save**. The file is saved under the name *space.wps* and now includes the additional text you entered, as shown in Figure 3-7.

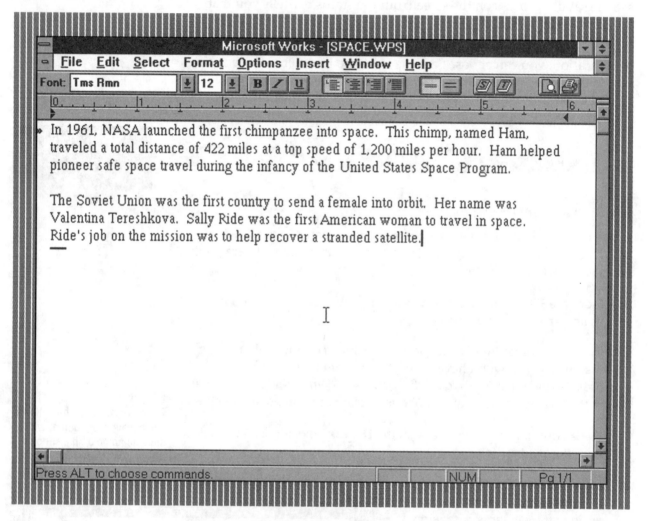

8.  Now select the **File** menu again and look at the Save command. Notice that at the right side of the menu are the letters *Ctrl+S.*

    This series of letters is called a *key combination.* A key combination always contains a plus sign, which indicates that you are to press two keys at the same time. To use a key combination, hold down the first key while you press the second. Key combinations are often used as shortcuts for commands. In this case, Ctrl+S is the shortcut for the Save command. Pressing Ctrl+S will save your file just as if you had selected the Save command. As you use menus in Works, be alert to the key combinations that offer you keyboard shortcuts for commands.

9.  From the **File** menu, choose **Close**. *Space.wps* closes and the application window remains.

## OPENING A SAVED DOCUMENT

Sometimes you may be unable to finish an entire document at one time. If you have to quit a document before you are done with it, you can save it according to the instructions in the previous section. Then, when you are ready to work on the document again, you simply choose Open Existing File from the File menu. You have already done this once in Chapter 2, so this activity is just a reminder.

**ACTIVITY 3-6**

### Opening an Existing File

In this activity, you will open the file you created in the previous activity.

1.  From the **File** menu, choose **Open Existing File**. The Open dialog box appears.

2.  In the **File Name** box, click the name of the file you want to open: **space.wps**.

3.  Click **OK**. The file appears in the document window.

4.  Leave the document on the screen for the next activity.

## MOVING THE CURSOR

Before you can learn how to edit text, you need to learn how to move the cursor through a document. Works offers two different methods of moving the cursor: the mouse and keyboard commands.

For short documents, you may find it faster to move the cursor using the mouse pointer. As you move the mouse pointer through the document window, it assumes the shape of an *I-beam*. To move the cursor, place the I-beam where you want the cursor to be and then click the left mouse button. The blinking cursor will appear.

**TABLE 3-1**
Keyboard Shortcuts for Moving the Cursor

If you are working with a long document, you may find it tedious to use the mouse pointer to move the cursor. Scrolling through a document of several pages using the mouse can take a long time. In this case, it will be faster to use the keyboard to move your cursor. Table 3-1 shows the keys you can press to move your cursor both short and long distances.

| Press | To Move the Cursor |
|---|---|
| Right Arrow | Right one character |
| Left Arrow | Left one character |
| Down Arrow | To the next line |
| Up Arrow | To the previous line |
| End | To the end of a line |
| Home | To the beginning of the line |
| Page Down | To the next screen |
| Page Up | To the previous screen |
| Ctrl+Right Arrow | To the next word |
| Ctrl+Left Arrow | To the previous word |
| Ctrl+End | To the end of the document |
| Ctrl+Home | To the beginning of the document |

**ACTIVITY 3-7**

**Moving the Cursor**

In this activity, you will move the cursor by using the mouse and the keyboard. *Space.wps* should be open, and the cursor should be blinking in the upper left corner.

1. Move the mouse pointer to the end of the first line in the first paragraph. Click once. The cursor moves to the end of the line.

2. Press **Ctrl+End** to move the cursor to the end of the document.

3. Move the mouse pointer to the left of the first word in the document. Click once.

4. Press **Ctrl+Right Arrow** four times to move to the word *launched* in the first line.

5. Leave the document on the screen for the next activity.

# EDITING TEXT

Editing text with a pencil, paper, and typewriter is often a long, tedious process. And, once you have edited your document, you then have to rekey it. When you use a word processor, however, you can edit your document on the screen and only print the final copy when you are completely satisfied with it.

In this section, you will learn the most basic forms of editing your document: inserting, selecting, and deleting text and moving and copying blocks of text.

## Inserting Text

You already know one way to insert text: Move the cursor to the place you want the text and begin typing. You can also use the Overtype option to insert text. *Overtype* does just what its name says. It replaces the characters on the screen with new characters as you type them. You turn Overtype on and off by pressing the Insert key, which, on most keyboards, is located in the group of six keys above the arrow keys. The Overtype option can also be turned on through the Options menu. Be careful not to replace more characters than you intend to when using Overtype. Overtype allows you to type over not only characters but also spaces between words.

**ACTIVITY 3-8**

## Inserting Text

In this activity, you will insert text in a document. *Space.wps* should be on your screen.

1. Move the cursor to one space after the word *female* in the first line of the second paragraph. Key **astronaut**. Remember to leave one space before and after *astronaut*.

2. Move the cursor before the word *orbit* in the first line of the second paragraph. Press **Insert** to toggle the Overtype option on. The letters *OVR* should appear in the bottom right corner of your screen.

3. Key **space**. The word *orbit* disappears.

4. Press **Insert** to toggle the Overtype option off.

5. Press **Ctrl+S** to choose Save from the File menu. The file is saved and includes the changes you made.

6. Leave the document on the screen for the next activity.

## Selecting Text

*Selecting* means highlighting a block of text. The block can be as small as one word or as large as an entire document. Once you have selected a block of text, you can edit the entire block at once. This speeds operations such as large deletions and changes to line spacing.

**ACTIVITY
3-9**

### Selecting Text

In this activity, you will select text using the mouse. *Space.wps* should be on your screen.

1. Move the mouse pointer before the first word in the first paragraph.

2. Press the left mouse button and drag the mouse pointer to the end of the last word of the first sentence.

3. Release the mouse button. The first sentence of the first paragraph should appear highlighted. Click to remove the highlighting.

4. Move the mouse pointer before the first word of the second paragraph. Drag the mouse pointer down until the paragraph appears highlighted. Release the mouse button. Click to remove the highlighting.

5. Leave the document on the screen for the next activity.

## Deleting Text

No matter how good a typist you are, you are bound to make typographical errors while keying text. One of the first editing skills you must master, therefore, is how to delete text. Works gives you two different ways to delete characters. You can use either the *Backspace key* or the *Delete key*. Pressing the Backspace key deletes the character to the left of the cursor; pressing the Delete key removes the character to the right of the cursor. If you hold down either of these keys, it will continue to remove characters until you release the key. This is an easy way to remove a whole line of text.

## Using the Backspace and Delete Keys

In this activity, you will delete text with the Backspace and Delete keys. *Space.wps* should be on your screen.

1. Place the cursor before the word *on* in the phrase *on the mission* in the last line of the second paragraph.

2. Hold down the **Delete** key until the words *on the mission* disappear. Remember to leave one blank space between the remaining words.

3. Place the cursor after the word *stranded* in the last line of the second paragraph.

4. Hold down the **Backspace** key until the word *stranded* disappears. Again, leave one blank space between the remaining words. Your document should appear similar to Figure 3-8.

**FIGURE 3-8**
The Delete and Backspace keys are useful for deleting phrases.

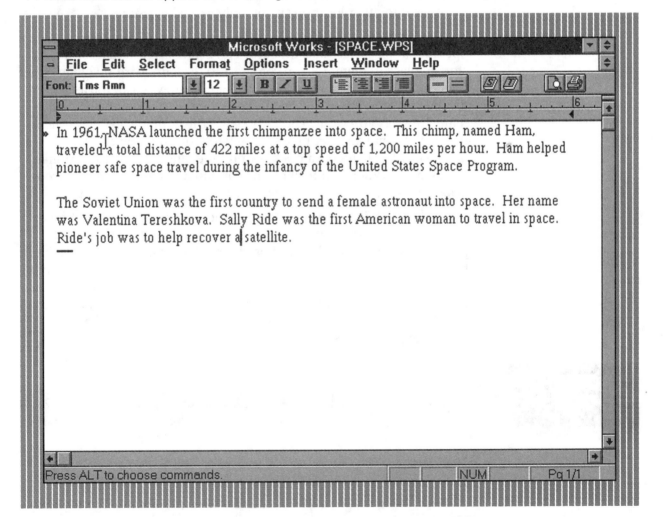

Microsoft Works - [SPACE.WPS]

File   Edit   Select   Format   Options   Insert   Window   Help

Font: Tms Rmn        12        B   /   U

In 1961, NASA launched the first chimpanzee into space. This chimp, named Ham, traveled a total distance of 422 miles at a top speed of 1,200 miles per hour. Ham helped pioneer safe space travel during the infancy of the United States Space Program.

The Soviet Union was the first country to send a female astronaut into space. Her name was Valentina Tereshkova. Sally Ride was the first American woman to travel in space. Ride's job was to help recover a satellite.

Press ALT to choose commands.                          NUM        Pg 1/1

5.   Save the document.

6.   Leave the document on the screen for the next activity.

## Using the Clipboard to Move and Copy Text

At some point when you are editing a document, you will probably wish you had put a certain paragraph last or a specific sentence first. If you were working on a typewriter, you would either have to retype your entire document to reorder those items or accept the poor organization of your first draft. A word processor, of course, gives you much more control over the organization of your document. If you do not like where a paragraph is, a couple of simple steps can move it to a better location. If you especially like the way that a sentence reads, you can copy it to other locations using only a few keystrokes.

The Works feature that makes these moving and copying operations so easy is the Clipboard. The *Clipboard* is a temporary storage place in memory. You send text to the Clipboard by using either the Copy command or the Cut command. Then, you can retrieve that text by using the Paste command. You can paste the Clipboard text as many times as you want. The Clipboard will store the text you send to it until you send another block of copy to it or until you clear the Clipboard. The Clipboard does not provide long-term storage, unlike saving a file. When you turn off the computer, the text in the Clipboard is lost.

**MOVING TEXT**   When you want to move text from one location to another, you use the Cut and Paste commands. The Cut command places selected text on the Clipboard. The Paste command recalls the text from the Clipboard and pastes it at the location of the cursor in the word processing document. If this sounds like the kind of editing you used to do with scissors, you're right. This operation is often referred to simply as *cutting and pasting*. But it is far easier to do it on the screen than with paper, scissors, and glue.

## ACTIVITY 3-11

## Moving Text

In this activity, you will cut text from a document and paste it to a different location within the document. *Space.wps* should now be on the screen.

Activity 3-11 continued

1.  Beginning with the first word of the first paragraph, drag the mouse to highlight the entire paragraph.

2.  From the **Edit** menu, choose **Cut**. The paragraph you selected disappears from the screen. It has been placed on the Clipboard.

3.  Press the **Delete** key to delete the extra space above the remaining paragraph.

4.  Place the cursor after the period following the last word of the last sentence in the paragraph. Press **Enter** twice to create a blank line.

5.  From the **Edit** menu, choose **Paste**. The paragraph reappears, as shown in Figure 3-9.

6.  Save the document.

7.  Leave the document on the screen for the next activity.

**FIGURE 3-9**
The Cut and Paste commands allow you to move entire paragraphs from one place to another in a document.

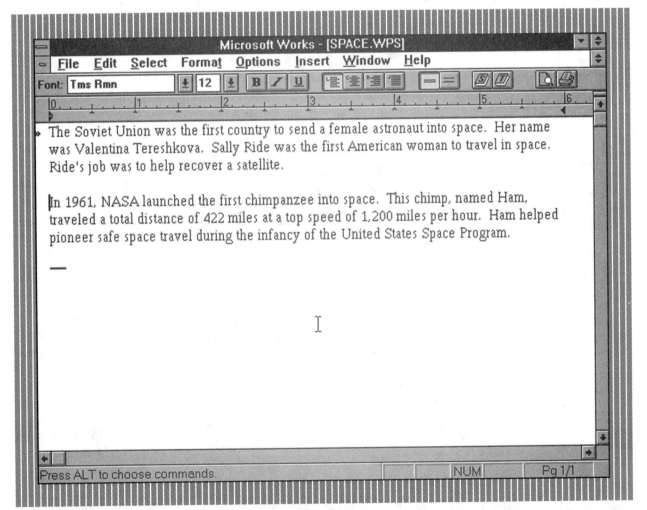

The Soviet Union was the first country to send a female astronaut into space. Her name was Valentina Tereshkova. Sally Ride was the first American woman to travel in space. Ride's job was to help recover a satellite.

In 1961, NASA launched the first chimpanzee into space. This chimp, named Ham, traveled a total distance of 422 miles at a top speed of 1,200 miles per hour. Ham helped pioneer safe space travel during the infancy of the United States Space Program.

COPYING TEXT   The Copy command is similar to the Cut command. When you choose the Copy command, however, a copy of your highlighted text is placed on the Clipboard while the original text remains on the screen. You use the Paste command, as before, to retrieve the copied text from the Clipboard.

## ACTIVITY 3-12

### Copying Text

In this activity, you will copy text from a document and paste it in a different location within the document. *Space.wps* should now be on the screen.

1.  Using the mouse, highlight the paragraph that begins with *The Soviet Union*.

2.  From the **Edit** menu, choose **Copy**. A copy of the text you selected is placed on the Clipboard. Notice that the highlighted text remains on the screen.

**FIGURE 3-10**

The first paragraph has been copied and pasted below the second paragraph.

3.  Place the cursor after the period following the last sentence of the second paragraph. Press **Enter** twice.

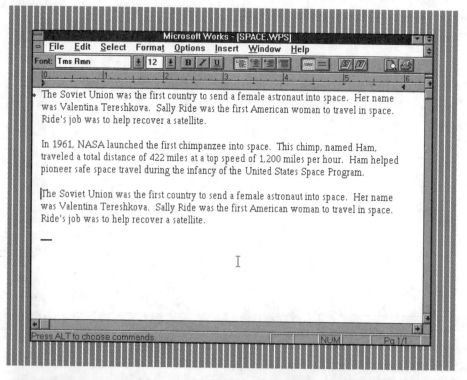

4.  From the **Edit** menu, choose **Paste**. A copy of the paragraph reappears. The original text remains at the top of the document, as shown in Figure 3-10.

5.  Highlight the last paragraph of the document. Press the **Delete** key.

6.  Save the document.

7.  Leave the document open for the next activity.

# PREVIEWING YOUR DOCUMENT

The Print Preview command enables you to look at a document as it will appear when printed. The command allows you to zoom in and out to help find mistakes before you print your document. Zoom In enlarges the document while Zoom Out reduces the size of the document in Print Preview. The Print Preview button is located on the Toolbar.

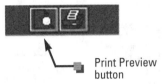

Print Preview button

**ACTIVITY 3-13**

## Previewing Your Document

In this activity, you will preview the document you have created. *Space.wps* should be on your screen.

1.   Click the **Print Preview** button on the Toolbar. The document you created appears with the entire page visible, as in Figure 3-11.

2.   Click the **Zoom In** button. The document enlarges.

3.   Click the **Zoom In** button again. The document enlarges to an even greater size.

**FIGURE 3-11**
Print Preview allows you to look at a document before you print it.

4.   Point to the right scroll arrow. Click several times to view the entire document.

5.   Click **Zoom Out** twice to view the document again with the entire page visible.

6.   Click the **Cancel** button. The document window reappears.

7.   Leave the document on the screen for the next activity.

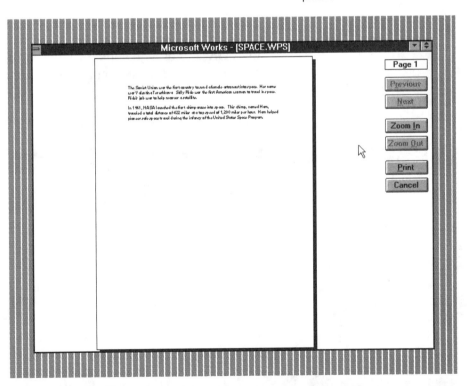

# PRINTING YOUR DOCUMENT

The Print command enables you to print your document on paper.
After you choose the Print command, the Print dialog box, shown in
Figure 3-12, will appear showing the printing options. The Works
default is set to print an entire document. You can, however, print
multiple copies of a document or print specific pages. For example, if
you wanted to print pages 5, 6, and 7 in a ten-page document, you
would choose Pages, key 5 in the From box, key 7 in the To box, and
click OK. The Print button is located on the Toolbar and provides a
shortcut to printing a document from the File menu.

Print
Preview
button

Print
button

## ACTIVITY 3-14

### Printing Your Document

In this activity, you will print the document you have created. *Space.wps*
should be on your screen.

1. Click the **Print** button on the Toolbar. The Print dialog box appears.

2. Click **OK**. A message appears showing the status of the printing
   document. In a few moments, the document should start printing.
   Wait for the page to print.

3. From the **File** menu, choose **Close**.

# SUMMARY

Word processing involves the use of computer software designed to manipulate text. Text can be edited without rekeying the entire document. This is an advantage of word processing over typewriters.

The application window and the document window can be maximized and minimized to take full advantage of the screen. The menu bar, the Toolbar, the ruler, and the status bar are features of the word processor that make working with a document easier.

Words keyed on the word processor will appear after the cursor, or insertion point. The end-of-file marker marks the end of the document. Wordwrap moves text nearing the end of a line to the next line and eliminates the need to press Enter at the end of every line.

Documents can be saved under a designated name with the Save As command and updated with the Save command. Files can be opened after being saved.

Editing text with Works is a much easier process than pencil-and-paper editing. The cursor may be moved in the document window with the mouse or the keyboard. Features such as delete, insert, cut, copy, and paste speed editing.

The Print Preview command allows you to see your finished document as it will appear when printed. The Print command produces a hard copy of your document on a printer.

# CHALLENGES

## TRUE/FALSE

Circle **T** or **F** to show whether the statement is true or false.

| | | | |
|---|---|---|---|
| T | F | 1. | Word processing involves the use of a computer program to enter and edit text. |
| T | F | 2. | The Create New File command is accessed through the File menu. |
| T | F | 3. | The Toolbar is located directly above the menu bar. |
| T | F | 4. | The cursor cannot be moved past the end-of-file marker. |
| T | F | 5. | When entering text in the word processor, you must press Enter at the end of every line. |
| T | F | 6. | You can choose Save or Save As the first time you save a file. |
| T | F | 7. | The Open Existing File command is accessed through the File menu. |
| T | F | 8. | The cursor can be moved only with the mouse. |
| T | F | 9. | Pressing the Insert key turns the Overtype option on or off. |
| T | F | 10. | The Print Preview command may be used to help find mistakes before printing. |

# COMPLETION

Write the correct answer in the space provided.

1. Describe an advantage of word processing over manual typewriting.

_____

_____

_____

2. List three parts of the word processor window discussed in this chapter.

_____

_____

_____

3. What feature allows you to key text without pressing Enter at the end of every line?

_____

4. Describe the differences between the two types of Save commands.

_____

_____

5. When you open an existing file, in which box are the filenames listed?

_____

6. What does the mouse pointer change to when moved through the document window?

_____

7. How do you move the cursor to the end of a document using the keyboard?

_____

8. What is the advantage of using the Print Preview command?

_____

_____

9. Describe the steps in printing a document.

_____

_____

_____

10. Name the two buttons on the Toolbar used in this chapter.

_____

_____

_____

# APPLICATIONS

## APPLICATION 3-1

In the blank space, write the letter of the keystroke that matches the cursor movement.

| Cursor Movement | Keystroke |
|---|---|
| ____ 1. To the next screen | a. Right Arrow |
| ____ 2. To the end of the document | b. Left Arrow |
| ____ 3. Right one character | c. Down Arrow |
| ____ 4. To the end of a line | d. Up Arrow |
| ____ 5. To the next line | e. End |
| ____ 6. To the previous line | f. Home |
| ____ 7. Left one character | g. Page Down |
| ____ 8. To the previous word | h. Page Up |
| ____ 9. To the beginning of the line | i. Ctrl+Right Arrow |
| ____ 10. To the beginning of the document | j. Ctrl+Left Arrow |
| ____ 11. To the next word | k. Ctrl+End |
| ____ 12. To the previous screen | l. Ctrl+Home |

# APPLICATION 3-2

1. Open *app3-2.wps* from your template disk.
2. Insert an *f* in the word *effective* in the first sentence of the document.
3. Delete the word *can* in the second sentence of the document.
4. Delete the comma and the word *meaningless* before the word *words* in the third sentence.
5. Insert the sentence *Use correct punctuation.* before the word *Correct* in item number 3. Remember to add two spaces after the period.
6. Save the corrected document to your data disk as *writing*.
7. Preview the document. Zoom in to check your corrections.
8. Print the finished document.
9. Close the document.

# APPLICATION 3-3

1. Open *app3-3.wps* from your template disk.
2. Key the words **Student Housing** before the word *orientation* in the last sentence of the first paragraph.
3. Insert an *m* in the word *roommate* in the first sentence of the second paragraph.
4. Delete the room number *607* in the third paragraph and key **425**.
5. Delete the words *Junior and Senior students* in the third paragraph and key **entering freshmen**.
6. Cut the fourth paragraph and paste it two spaces after the period following the word *studying* in the last sentence of the second paragraph. Delete any extra spaces that remain between the paragraphs.
7. Save the revised document to your data disk as *housing*.
8. Preview the document. Zoom in to check your revisions.
9. Print the finished document.
10. Close the document.

# STRENGTHENING WORD PROCESSING SKILLS

## LEARNING OBJECTIVES

**When you complete this chapter, you will be able to:**

1. Change margins, indents, and spacing in a document.
2. Understand and choose fonts.
3. Use the Undo command.
4. Set tabs and justify text.
5. Insert page breaks.
6. Use the Spellchecker and Thesaurus.

In Chapter 3, you learned basic word processing operations such as entering text, making simple formatting changes, and printing a document. This chapter will further strengthen your word processing skills and teach you how to use more of the word processor's commands and features.

Many of the topics discussed in this chapter deal with changing the appearance of a document. Changing a document's margins, spacing, or fonts are a few of the options you have to make a document look different.

## MARGINS

A *margin* is the amount of space between the edge of a page and the printed or written text in a document. Works provides default margins for a page. This means that Works will always set the margins at a specified place. You might, however, want to change the default margins to suit a particular type of document. For example, a document to be placed in a three-ring spiral notebook might require more white space on the left edge and, therefore, a wider left margin.

## ACTIVITY 4-1

### Adjusting a Document's Margins

In this activity, you will change a document's margins. Before starting the activity, view the document in Print Preview and observe the existing margins.

1. Start Works if it is not already running on your computer.

**FIGURE 4-1**
The Page Setup & Margins dialog box contains the document's default margins.

2. Open *act4-1.wps* from your template disk.

3. From the **File** menu, choose **Page Setup & Margins**. The Page Setup & Margins dialog box appears showing the default margins, as shown in Figure 4-1.

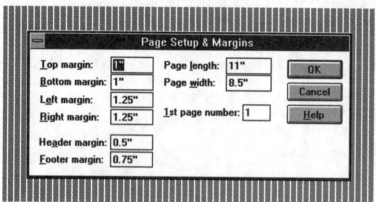

4. The cursor appears in the Top margin box. Key **1.25**.

5. Press **Tab** to move to **Bottom margin**. Key **1.25**.

6. Press **Tab** to move to **Left margin**. Key **1.5**.

7. Click **OK**. The top and bottom margins are now set at 1.25 inches. The right margin is set at 1.25 inches, and the left margin is set at 1.5 inches. Use Print Preview to view the changes that you have made.

8. Save the document on your data disk as *mountain*. Leave the file open for the next activity.

## INDENTING

An *indent* is the space you place between text and a document's margin. You can indent text from either the left or the right margin, or from both margins. Indents can be used to make text more readable or to set off some parts of the text from the rest of it. For example, it is common to indent the first line of a paragraph to make the text easier to read.

In Works, you can indent text by using either the indent markers on the ruler or the Indents & Spacing command from the Format menu. Figure 4-2 shows the indent markers on the ruler. The first-line indent marker sits on top of the left-indent marker at the left edge of the ruler, and the right-indent marker is at the right side of the ruler. To indent text, you simply drag one of these markers to the desired point on the ruler.

**FIGURE 4-2**
The indent markers are located on the ruler.

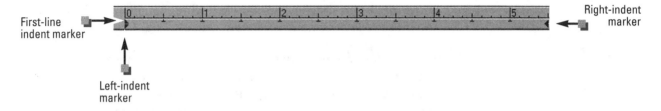

First-line indent marker

Left-indent marker

Right-indent marker

## First-Line Indents

Changing the first-line indent gives you many different ways to vary the look of your text. Using the first-line indent marker along with the left-indent marker lets you automatically indent paragraphs as you type your text or create hanging indents in which the first full line of text is followed by indented lines. This feature is useful for bibliographies and lists.

Because the first-line indent and the left indent are often used together, they sometimes move at the same time. If you drag the first-line indent to the right, for example, the left-indent marker will not move. But when you drag the left-indent marker, the first-line indent marker will also move. You must use care when pointing at these markers to be sure you drag the one you want.

**ACTIVITY**
**4-2**

## Changing First-Line Indents

In this activity, you will change the first-line indents of paragraphs. *Mountain.wps* should now be on the screen.

1. Place the cursor before the first word of the first paragraph.

2. Drag the left-indent marker to the right. Refer to Figure 4-2 to be sure you drag the correct marker. Notice that the first-line indent marker moves with the left-indent marker. Release the mouse button at the ½-inch mark on the ruler.

3. Now, drag the first-line indent marker to the left. Be sure to position the pointer over the correct marker. Release the mouse button at the 0-inch mark on the ruler. The first line of text begins at the

Activity 4-2 continued

0-inch mark and the remaining lines are indented ½ inch. This is called a ***hanging indent***.

4.   Drag the first-line indent marker to the right. Release the mouse button at the 1-inch mark on the ruler. You have created a ***paragraph indent***. Any text you key when you have a paragraph indent set will automatically indent the first line.

5.   Drag the left-indent mark to the left. Release the mouse button at the 0-inch mark on the ruler. Notice that the first-line indent marker also moves, so your paragraph is still indented. The first line is indented ½ inch and the remaining lines are against the left margin.

6.   Drag the first-line indent mark to the left. Release the mouse button at the 0-inch mark on the ruler.

7.   Verify that the cursor is in front of the first word in the first paragraph.

8.   Press the down scroll arrow to move to the end of the document.

9.   Place the mouse pointer after the last word in the sixth paragraph, the paragraph that ends with the word *world*.

10.  Hold down the **Shift** key and press the mouse button. The six paragraphs appear highlighted. This method of selecting is an alternative way to select a large amount of text without having to scroll through the entire document.

11.  Drag the first-line indent marker to the right. Release the mouse button at the ½-inch mark on the ruler. The six paragraphs appear with a first-line indent of ½ inch. Click the mouse button to turn off the highlight.

12.  Press **Ctrl+Home** to return to the beginning of the document.

13.  Save the document. Leave the file open for the next activity.

## Indenting from Both Margins

As discussed above, you can indent from either the left or right margin, or both. Indenting from both margins is useful for setting off paragraphs from the main body of the text. This is commonly done for long quotations or for setting lines of poetry or equations. You can indent from both margins using the left- and right-indent markers or the Indents & Spacing command from the Format menu.

## Indenting from Both Margins

In this activity, you will indent a paragraph from both margins.
*Mountain.wps* should now be on the screen.

1.  Place the cursor before the first word in the fifth paragraph, the
    paragraph that begins with *An orangy.*

2.  Drag the first-line indent marker to the left. Release the mouse
    button at the 0-inch mark on the ruler.

3.  Drag the left-indent marker to the right. Release the mouse button at
    the 1-inch mark on the ruler.

4.  Drag the right-indent mark to the left. Refer back to Figure 4-2 if
    necessary to locate the right-indent marker. Release the mouse
    button at the 5-inch marker.

5.  Save the document. Leave the file open for the next activity.

## SPACING

*Spacing* refers to the distance between lines of text or paragraphs.
Works allows you to single-space text or to add any amount of space
between lines of text. If you wish, Works will also insert space between
paragraphs.

By default, Works single-spaces text. This means that there is no
extra space between lines of text. Single-spaced text is commonly used
in business letters. You might also use single-spaced text in newsletter
articles and for parts of long documents, such as footnotes,
bibliographies, or long quotations.

To make text more readable, you can choose to add space between
lines of text. Double-spaced text has a full blank line between each line
of text. Usually reports and term papers are double-spaced. Speeches
are often typed using triple-spaced text, with two full blank lines
between lines of text so that a speaker can easily keep his or her place
in the speech while looking back and forth between the notes and
audience.

Works offers two ways to change the line spacing of your
document. You can use the Single- or Double-space buttons on the
Toolbar, or you can choose Indents & Spacing from the Format menu to
add any amount of line space you want.

Single-space        Double-space
button              button

Another way to increase the readability of a page of text is to add spaces between the paragraphs. Works lets you add space before or after a paragraph, and you can decide how much space to add in each place. To add space around paragraphs, you must use the Indents & Spacing command from the Format menu.

**ACTIVITY 4-4**

## Adjusting the Spacing

In this activity, you will adjust the spacing in a document. *Mountain.wps* should now be on the screen.

1. Place the cursor before the first word in the first paragraph.

2. Highlight the six paragraphs in the document, including the table.

3. Click the **Double-space** button on the Toolbar. The text in the document becomes double-spaced.

4. Place the cursor anywhere in the fifth paragraph. Click the **Single-space** button on the Toolbar. The paragraph becomes single-spaced.

5. Again, highlight the six paragraphs in the document, including the table.

6. From the **Format** menu, choose **Indents & Spacing**. The Indents & Spacing dialog box appears, showing indents and spacing options, as in Figure 4-3.

7. Place the cursor in the **Space after paragraph** box. Key **2**.

**FIGURE 4-3**
The Indents & Spacing dialog box contains several indents and spacing options.

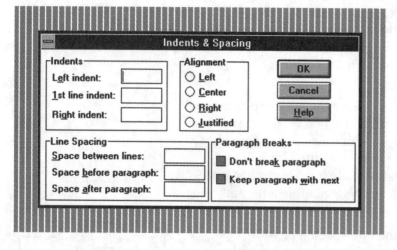

8. Click **OK**. Works places two blank lines after each paragraph. Click the **Print Preview** button on the Toolbar. Click **Zoom In** to observe the blank lines between the paragraphs, as shown in Figure 4-4. Click **Cancel** to return to the document.

9. From the **Format** menu, choose **Indents & Spacing**. Place the cursor in the **Space after paragraph** box. Key **0**.

10. Click **OK**. Works deletes the two blank lines between each paragraph. Use Print Preview to make sure that the changes you made are correct. Click the mouse button to turn off the highlighting.

Activity 4-4 continued

11. Place the cursor after the colon following the word *wrote* in the fourth paragraph.

12. From the **Format** menu, choose **Indents & Spacing**. Place the cursor before the zero in the **Space after paragraph** box.

13. Press **Delete** to delete the zero. Key **1**.

14. Click **OK**. Works places a blank line after the fourth paragraph.

15. Save the document. Leave the file open for the next activity.

**FIGURE 4-4**
Works places two blank lines after each paragraph.

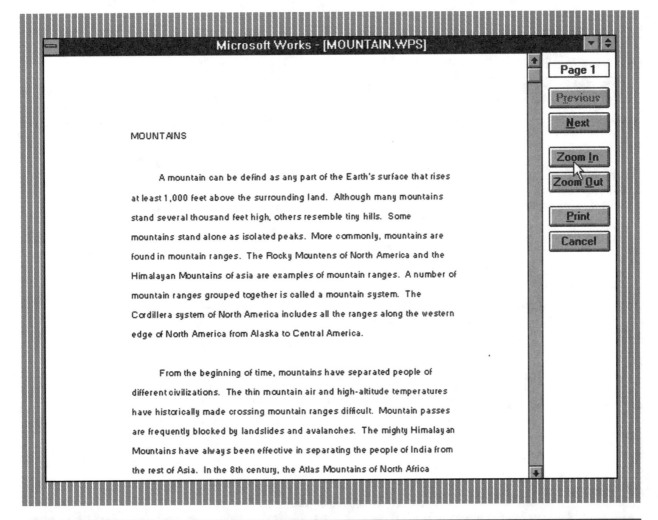

# FONTS

The term *font* refers to the shape of the characters belonging to a particular family of type. A font is also called a *typeface*. Works gives

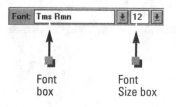

Font
box

Font
Size box

**FIGURE 4-5**
Fonts can give text very
different appearances.

> This font is called Arial.
>
> This font is called Courier.
>
> *This font is called Zapf Chancery.*
>
> This font is called Times New Roman.

**FIGURE 4-6**
Small lines added to the ends
of characters are called serifs.

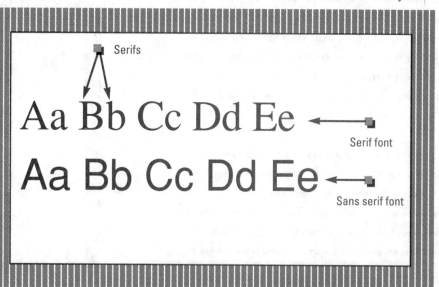

you two ways to change the font and font size of your document. You can use the Font box and the Font Size box located on the Toolbar. You can also choose a font by selecting Font & Style from the Format menu.

## Choosing a Font

Just as clothing comes in different designs, fonts have different designs. Like clothing, type can be dressy or casual. When you are creating a document, you should consider what kind of impression you want the text to make. Do you want your document to look as if it has been typed on a typewriter? Or do you want it to look as if it has been set by a commercial typesetter? The fonts shown in Figure 4-5 would result in four very different looking documents.

If you look closely at the first line in Figure 4-6, you can see small lines at the ends of the characters. These lines are called *serifs*. If a font has these serifs, it is called a *serif font*. If a font does not have serifs, it is called a *sans serif font*. Serif fonts are generally considered to be "dressier" than sans serif fonts, and are often used for the text portion of a document. Sans serif fonts are considered to be harder to read, so they are often used for titles, headings, and page numbers.

## Changing the Font

You can change the font of text by using the Toolbar or the Font & Style choice in the Format menu. You might want to change the font of the title of a document, for example, to set it apart from the body of the document.

**ACTIVITY
4-5**

## Changing the Font

In this activity, you will change the font of the text in a document. *Mountain.wps* should now be on the screen.

1.  Press **Ctrl+Home** to return to the beginning of the document.

2.  Works provides a quick way to highlight an entire document: From the **Select** menu, choose **All**. The entire document becomes highlighted.

3.  Click the arrow to the right of the Font box. A list of fonts appears, as shown in Figure 4-7. Your Font box may differ in the types of fonts it contains.

4.  Choose **Times New Roman**. You may have to use the scroll bar to locate this font. The document will appear in the Times New Roman font.

5.  Click in the document to remove the highlight, then highlight the title of the document, *MOUNTAINS*.

6.  From the **Format** menu, choose **Font & Style**. The Font & Style dialog box appears, as shown in Figure 4-8.

7.  Choose **GillSans**. If GillSans is not available on your computer, choose a font other than Times New Roman. Click **OK**. The title appears in the selected font, as shown in Figure 4-9. Click the mouse button to turn off the highlight.

8.  Save the document. Leave the file open for the next activity.

**FIGURE 4-7**
The Font box contains a list of available fonts.

**FIGURE 4-8**
The Font & Style dialog box contains options for changing the font.

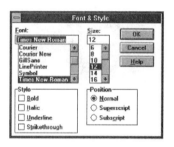

**FIGURE 4-9**
Thè title appears in GillSans.

» MOUNTAINS

## Style

Changing fonts is one way to alter the appearance of your text. Another way to emphasize text is to change the style of the font. *Type style* refers to certain standard changes in the appearance of a font. Common styles are boldface, italic, and underline. These styles can be applied to change the appearance of any font.

When you begin keying a document in the word processor, you are using a normal style. This is the style you will most likely use for the body of your document. However, you will probably want to use other styles for particular features in your document. For example, you may want to make your title stand out by applying a bold style to it. Titles

**FIGURE 4-10**

Fonts can appear in different styles, such as the default normal, bold, italic, underline, and strikethrough.

of books and magazines should appear in italic style. Headings will show up more clearly if you key them using underline style. As you are editing your document, you may want to use a strikethrough style to indicate sentences or passages you are thinking of removing. Figure 4-10 illustrates these different type styles.

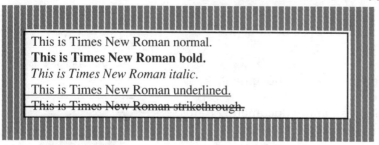

This is Times New Roman normal.
**This is Times New Roman bold.**
*This is Times New Roman italic.*
This is Times New Roman underlined.
~~This is Times New Roman strikethrough.~~

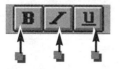

Bold button    Italic button    Underline button

Works allows you to change type style using either the Toolbar or the Font & Style dialog box. You should note, however, that the Toolbar shows only three of the four style options: bold, italic, and underline.

## ACTIVITY 4-6

### Changing the Type Style

In this activity, you will change the type style. *Mountain.wps* should now be on the screen.

1.  Highlight the title of the document.

2.  Click the **Bold** button on the Toolbar. The title becomes bold.

3.  Highlight the word *mountain* in the first sentence of the first paragraph. Click the **Italic** button on the Toolbar. The word *mountain* appears in italics.

4.  Highlight the word *Earth's* in the first line of the first paragraph.

5.  From the **Format** menu, choose **Font & Style**. The Font & Style dialog box appears.

6.  Choose **Strikethrough** in the **Style** box. Click **OK**. The word *Earth's* appears in strikethrough style.

7.  Again, from the **Format** menu, choose **Font & Style**. Choose **Strikethrough** to turn off the strikethrough style. Click **OK**.

8.  Save the document. Leave the file open for the next activity.

## Size

Type size is determined by measuring the height of characters in units called *points*. There are 72 points in an inch. A common type size is 12 point because this is approximately the size of lettering from a typewriter. Figure 4-11 illustrates the Arial font in 10, 12, and 24 point. You can change type size by using the Font Size box or by using the Font & Style dialog box.

**FIGURE 4-11**
Different sizes can be selected within the same font.

This is Arial 10 point.

This is Arial 12 point.

# This is Arial 24 point.

**ACTIVITY
4-7**

### Changing the Type Size

In this activity, you will change the type size. *Mountain.wps* should now be on the screen.

1. Select the title of the document. Highlight only the word *MOUNTAINS*. Do not highlight the space after it.

2. Click the arrow to the right of the Font Size box. A list of font sizes appears.

3. Choose **14** point. The title appears in 14 point size. Click the mouse button to turn off the highlighting.

4. Save the document. Leave the file open for the next activity.

## UNDO

When editing a document, you will sometimes delete text accidentally or change your mind about a deletion immediately after you have pressed the Delete key. This is when the Undo command is useful. The *Undo* command will reverse a previous command to delete text. It will also restore formatting changes and editing changes that you have previously deleted or changed. Undo will also reverse changes made using the Spellchecker, the Thesaurus, and the Replace command. The Undo command, however, will only reverse the most recent change.

## ACTIVITY 4-8

### Using the Undo Command

In this activity, you will use the Undo command to restore deleted text. *Mountain.wps* should now be on the screen.

1.  In the second line of the document, highlight the words *above the surrounding land*.

2.  Press **Delete** to delete the words.

3.  From the **Edit** menu, choose **Undo**. The words that you deleted will reappear. Leave the file open for the next activity.

## TABS

**FIGURE 4-12**

Use tabs to align columns in a table or list.

*Tabs* mark the place the cursor will stop when the tab key is pressed. Tabs are useful for creating tables or aligning numbered items. Default tab stops in Works are set every half inch. Text can be aligned, however, with decimal, left-aligned, right-aligned, or centered tabs, as shown in Figure 4-12. Numbers can be aligned by using a decimal tab. Notice that different tab symbols appear over the different types of tab settings.

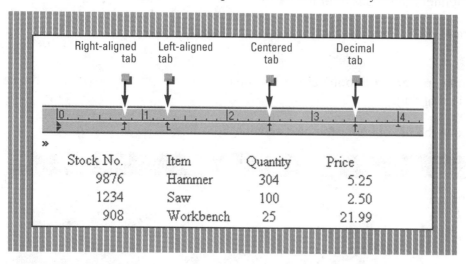

## ACTIVITY 4-9

### Setting Tabs

In this activity, you will set different tab stops. *Mountain.wps* should now be on the screen.

1. Place the cursor after the period following *27,923 ft.* in the table. Press **Enter**. Notice the tab markers on the ruler. These markers indicate that the tabs in the table have already been preset. You will now key the last entry in the table.

2. Press **Tab**. The cursor moves to the decimal tab stop at 0.8 inches. Key **5**. Remember to key a period after the *5.*

3. Press **Tab**. The cursor moves to the left-aligned tab stop at 1.2 inches. Key **Makalu 1**.

4. Press **Tab**. Again, the cursor moves to a left-aligned tab stop at 2.4 inches. Key **Nepal/China**.

5. Press **Tab**. The cursor moves to the right-aligned tab stop at 4.2 inches. Key **27,824 ft.** Remember to key a period after *ft.*

6. Now, you will insert your own tab stops to create column headings for the table. Place the cursor after the period following the sixth paragraph of the text.

7. Press **Enter**.

8. From the **Format** menu, choose **Tabs**. The Tabs dialog box appears, as in Figure 4-13. The Tabs dialog box allows you to specify exactly where you want each column head to begin.

**FIGURE 4-13**
The Tabs dialog box allows you to specify exactly where you want your tab stops to appear.

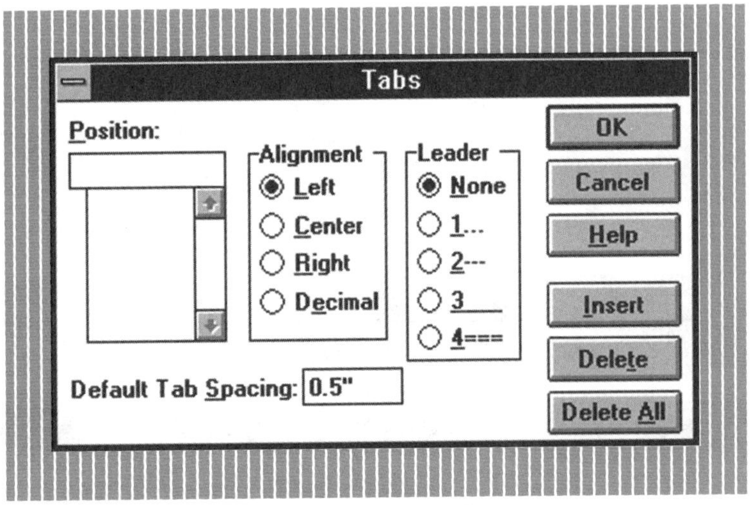

9. Insert tab stops following these steps:

   a. In the box under Position, key **1.2**. Click **Insert**. Works inserts a left-aligned tab stop on the ruler.

   b. Key **2.9**. Choose **Center** in the Alignment box. Click **Insert**. Works inserts a centered tab stop on the ruler.

   c. Key **4.2**. Choose **Right** in the Alignment box. Click **Insert**. Works inserts a right-aligned tab stop on the ruler. Click **OK**.

10. Create the column headings following these steps:

   a. Press **Tab**. Press the **Underline** button on the Toolbar. Key **Mountain**. Press the **Underline** button to discontinue using the underline style font. Remember that selecting an option

Activity 4-9 continued

that is already on will turn that option off. If you do not turn Underline off, it will trail across the screen to the next tab.

b.   Press **Tab**. Press the **Underline** button on the Toolbar. Key **Location**. Press the **Underline** button again.

c.   Press **Tab**. Press the **Underline** button on the Toolbar. Key **Height**. Press the **Underline** button to turn Underline off.

11.   You will notice that the column headings are not centered over the columns. Works allows you to drag tab markers to fine-tune the alignment of text. Drag the left-aligned tab marker to the right until the *Mountain* column heading appears centered over the column.

**FIGURE 4-14**

Works allows you to fine-tune alignment by dragging tabs.

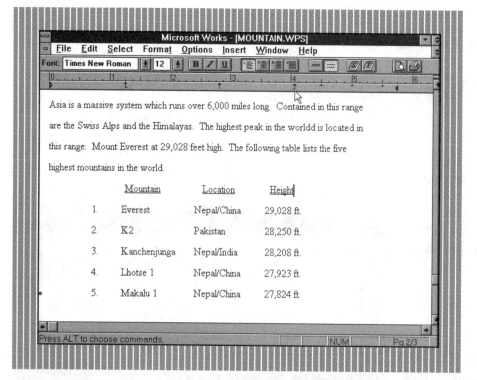

12.   Drag the centered tab stop to fine-tune the alignment of the *Location* column heading.

13.   Drag the cursor to the left until the *Height* column heading appears centered over the column. The table should now include an added entry and underlined column headings centered above the columns, as in Figure 4-14.

14.   Save the document. Leave the file open for the next activity.

## JUSTIFICATION

*Justification* determines how text is aligned at the margins. Justification can be set in one of the following ways:

1.   Left-justified text lines up at the left edge of the page and has a ragged right edge. Left-justified text is easy to read because your eye has a smooth edge of text to return to after reading a line.

2.   Centered text is centered in the middle of a page. Centering is useful for positioning headings and titles.

3. Right-justified text lines up at the right edge of the page and has a ragged left edge. Right-justified text is often used to align small amounts of text, such as a page number or a date.

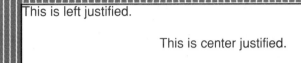

**FIGURE 4-15**
Text can be left-, center-, right-, or full-justified.

4. Full-justified text lines up on both sides of a page. Works inserts extra space between words in full-justified text to form smooth edges. This gives it the appearance of a newspaper column. Figure 4-15 illustrates the different types of justification.

This is left justified.

This is center justified.

This is right justified.

This is full justified because text at both the left and right margins are aligned. This is full justified because text at both the left and right margins are aligned. This is full justified because text at both the left and right margins are aligned. This is full justified because text at both the left and right margins are aligned. This is full justified because text at both the left and right margins are aligned.

You can justify text by clicking the buttons on the Toolbar or by choosing the Indents & Spacing command from the Format menu.

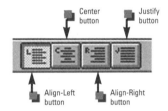

Center button    Justify button

Align-Left button    Align-Right button

**ACTIVITY 4-10**

## Justifying Text

In this activity, you will justify text in a document. *Mountain.wps* should now be on the screen.

1. Press **Ctrl+Home** to move the cursor to the beginning of the document.

2. Highlight the title of the document.

3. Press the **Center** button on the Toolbar. The title becomes centered.

4. Place the cursor anywhere in the first paragraph. Press the **Align-Right** button on the Toolbar. The paragraph appears right-justified.

5. Press the **Justify** button on the Toolbar. The paragraph appears full-justified.

6. From the **Format** menu, choose **Indents & Spacing**. Choose **Left** in the box under Alignment. This is an alternative to using the Align-Left button on the Toolbar.

Activity 4-10 continued

7.   Click **OK**. The paragraph appears left-justified.

8.   Save the document. Leave the file open for the next activity.

## PAGE BREAKS

When a document has more text than will fit on one page, Works must select a place in the document to end one page and begin the next. The place where one page ends and another begins is called a *page break*. Works automatically inserts page breaks where they are necessary. You may also insert a page break manually. An example of when you would want to insert a page break manually is when an automatic page break separates a heading from the text that follows it. To insert a page break manually, select Page Break from the Insert menu or press Ctrl+Enter.

An automatic page break is indicated by a small symbol at the left side of the screen, >>. This symbol points to the first line of the next page. A page break that is inserted manually is indicated with a dotted line across the screen.

**ACTIVITY
4-11**

### Inserting Page Breaks

In this activity, you will insert a page break. *Mountain.wps* should now be on the screen.

1.   Place the cursor after the period following the last word in the sixth paragraph of the document.

2.   From the **Insert** menu, choose **Page Break**. The dotted line indicates that a page break has been inserted, as shown in Figure 4-16. The table is now on page 3 of the document.

3.   Save the document. Leave the file open for the next activity.

Activity 4-11 continued

FIGURE 4-16
A dotted line across the screen indicates that a page break has been inserted manually.

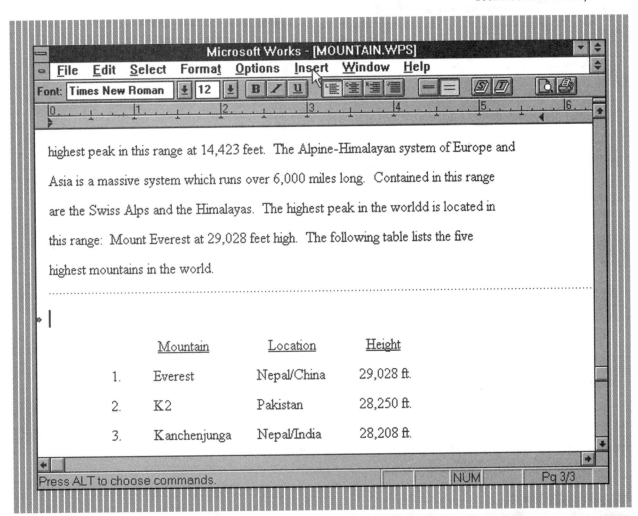

highest peak in this range at 14,423 feet. The Alpine-Himalayan system of Europe and Asia is a massive system which runs over 6,000 miles long. Contained in this range are the Swiss Alps and the Himalayas. The highest peak in the worldd is located in this range: Mount Everest at 29,028 feet high. The following table lists the five highest mountains in the world.

| | Mountain | Location | Height |
|---|---|---|---|
| 1. | Everest | Nepal/China | 29,028 ft. |
| 2. | K2 | Pakistan | 28,250 ft. |
| 3. | Kanchenjunga | Nepal/India | 28,208 ft. |

## USING THE SPELLCHECKER

Works contains a dictionary of 120,000 words to check the spelling of words in your document. You can check an entire document or portions of the document by using the Spelling button on the Toolbar or by using the Check Spelling command in the Options menu.

Spelling button

The Spelling dialog box shown in Figure 4-17 contains options that allow you to check the spelling of words, ignore words, change misspelled words, or add words to your own custom dictionary. Table 4-1 explains each of the available options. The dictionary is capable of checking spelling only. It will not find grammatical errors.

**FIGURE 4-17**

The Spelling dialog box
contains several options for
spellchecking a document.

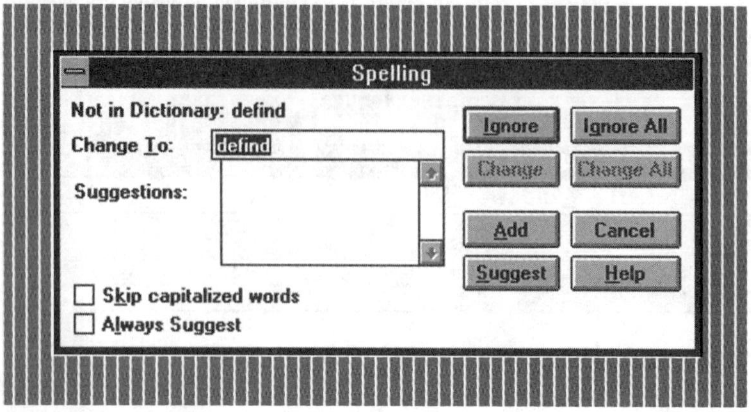

**TABLE 4-1**

Spelling Dialog Box Options

| Option | Action |
|---|---|
| Ignore | Ignores only the highlighted word |
| Ignore All | Ignores all instances of the same word |
| Change | Changes only the highlighted word |
| Change All | Changes all instances of the same word |
| Add | Adds the highlighted word to the custom dictionary |
| Suggest | Displays a list of proposed spellings |

**ACTIVITY
4-12**

### Checking a Document's Spelling

In this activity, you will check your document for spelling errors.
*Mountain.wps* should now be on the screen.

1.   Press **Ctrl+Home** to move the cursor to the beginning of the
document.

2.   Press the **Spelling** button on the Toolbar.

3.   The word *defind* is highlighted in the text and the Spelling dialog
box appears. Note that the misspelled word also appears in the

Activity 4-12 continued

Change To box. Click **Suggest**. A list of suggestions appears in the Suggestions box. Choose **defined**. Click **Change**. Works replaces the misspelled word and continues spellchecking.

4.  The word *Mountens* is highlighted. Click **Suggest**. A list of suggestions appears in the Suggestions box. Choose **Mountains**. Click **Change**. Works replaces the misspelled word and continues spellchecking.

5.  The word *Himalayan* is highlighted. If you click Suggest, Works offers *Malayan* as an option. This means that Himalayan is not in the dictionary. The word is spelled correctly here and throughout the remaining text. Click **Ignore All** to skip future occurrences of this word.

6.  The word *asia* is highlighted and the Spelling dialog box notes that this is an irregular capitalization error. Click **Suggest**. Choose **Asia**. Click **Change**. Works replaces the error and continues spellchecking.

7.  Several proper names will appear that are not in the Spellchecker dictionary. They are all spelled correctly. Click **Ignore All** after each one until the next spelling error appears.

8.  The word *worldd* is highlighted. You can easily fix this misspelling in the Change To box. Press the **left arrow** key to turn off the highlight. Press **Delete** to delete the extra *d*. Click **Change**. Works replaces the error and continues spellchecking.

9.  Press **Ignore All** to ignore each of the remaining proper names.

10.  A message will appear indicating that Works has finished checking for spelling errors. Click **OK**. The cursor returns to the beginning of the document.

11.  Save the document. Leave the file open for the next activity.

# USING THE THESAURUS

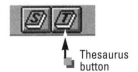

Thesaurus button

The 190,000-word Works *Thesaurus* is a useful feature for finding a *synonym*, or a word with a similar meaning, for a word in your document. The Thesaurus button is located on the Toolbar.

# ACTIVITY
## 4-13

## Using the Thesaurus

In this activity, you will find a synonym using the Works Thesaurus. *Mountain.wps* should now be on the screen.

**FIGURE 4-18**
The Thesaurus dialog box contains a list of meanings and synonyms for a selected word or phrase.

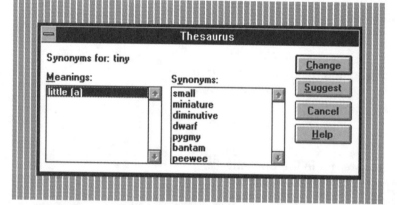

1. Place the cursor on the word *tiny* in the second sentence in the first paragraph.

2. Click the **Thesaurus** button on the Toolbar. The Thesaurus dialog box appears, as in Figure 4-18. The box under Meanings contains a list of the meanings of *tiny*. The box under Synonyms contains a list of synonyms for *tiny*.

3. Choose **small** in the Synonyms box.

4. Click **Change**. Works replaces the word *tiny* with *small*.

5. Save the document.

6. Close the file.

# SUMMARY

Although Works provides default margins for a page, margins can be changed to suit a particular type of document you are creating. Indenting the first line or the left and right sides of a paragraph can alter the paragraph's appearance. Indents can be changed by moving the indent markers on the ruler or by using the Indents & Spacing command in the Format menu. Text can be spaced in different ways. Line spacing can be adjusted to leave no space, one space, or a specified amount of space between lines of text. Paragraph spacing can be adjusted to change space between paragraphs of text.

The term *font* refers to the shape of the characters belonging to a particular family of type. Fonts can be chosen by using the Toolbar or the Font & Style command in the Format menu. Fonts can appear in a number of standard type styles, such as bold, italic, or underline.

The Undo command is useful for restoring text, formatting changes, and editing changes that have been previously deleted or altered. Undo will only restore the most recent change made.

Tabs are useful for creating tables and aligning numbered items. Text in Works can be left-, center-, right-, or full-justified. Manual page breaks are inserted to separate text or keep text together.

Works contains a dictionary of 120,000 words. The Works Check Spelling command corrects capitalization and spelling errors. The Check Spelling command, however, will not correct grammatical errors. The Works Thesaurus is a useful synonym finder for a variety of words.

# CHALLENGES

## TRUE/FALSE

Circle **T** or **F** to show whether the statement is true or false.

T  F  1. The Page Setup & Margins dialog box is accessed through the File menu.

T  F  2. The style and size of a document's fonts can be changed only by using the Toolbar.

T  F  3. The Undo command can only correct the most recent change you have made to your document.

T  F  4. The Tabs dialog box contains four options for aligning tabs.

T  F  5. Full-justified text is ragged on the right margin.

T  F  6. A page break can be inserted by pressing Ctrl+Insert on the keyboard.

T  F  7. Work's Check Spelling command is useful for checking grammatical errors involving word usage.

T  F  8. The Check Spelling command is found on the Options menu.

T  F  9. Pressing the Ignore All button in the Spelling dialog box tells Works to ignore all remaining occurrences of a word.

T  F  10. The Works Thesaurus command is found on the Insert menu.

# COMPLETION

Write the correct answer in the space provided.

1. What term describes a space you set between text and a document's margins?

_____

2. What are the units of measurement that determine type size?

_____

3. Through which menu is the Undo command accessed?

_____

4. Name four types of tab alignments.

_____

_____

_____

_____

5. Name four ways that text can be justified.

_____

_____

_____

_____

6. Through which menu is the Page Break command accessed?

_____

7. Name two ways to start the Work's Check Spelling command.

_____

8. Which button, located in the Spelling dialog box, is used to list possible correct spellings for a word?

_____

9. What is the purpose of the Change button in the Spelling dialog box?

_____

10. What type of word is the Works Thesaurus useful for finding?

_____

APPLICATIONS

## APPLICATION 4-1

Refer to Figure 4-19 and match the letter of the Toolbar or ruler part with the name of the item given below.

**FIGURE 4-19**
The Toolbar and the Ruler

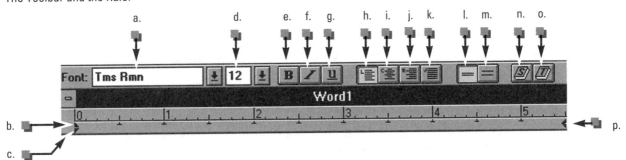

____ 1. Font box

____ 2. Bold button

____ 3. Thesaurus button

____ 4. Right-indent marker

____ 5. Font Size box

____ 6. Double-space button

____ 7. Align Right button

____ 8. Spelling button

____ 9. Left-indent marker

____ 10. Single-space button

____ 11. Italic button

____ 12. Center button

____ 13. First-line indent marker

____ 14. Underline button

____ 15. Align Left button

____ 16. Justify button

# APPLICATION 4-2

In this application, you will change the font and font size in a document.

1.  Open *app4-2.wps* from your template disk.
2.  Select the upper-case and lower-case characters.
3.  Change the font to the first font in the Font box.
4.  Set the font to the largest size available in the Font Size box.
5.  Look closely at the font to determine if it is a serif or sans serif font. Record the name of the font and whether it is serif or sans serif on a sheet of paper.
6.  Repeat for each font available in the Font box.
7.  Close the document. Do not save the document.

# APPLICATION 4-3

In this application, you will format a document from your template disk.

1.  Open *app4-3.wps* from your template disk.
2.  Change the font of the document to Times New Roman. If Times New Roman is not available on your computer, choose another serif font.
3.  Change the left and right margins to 1.5 inches.
4.  Center the title of the document: *Briarcliff High School Update*. Change the size of the font to 16 point. Use italic and bold styles for the title.
5.  Place the cursor after the words *Briarcliff High School* below the title. Set a center-aligned tab at 3 inches and a right-aligned tab at 5½-inches.
6.  On the same line as the words *Briarcliff High School*, key **Volume 4, No. 7** at the 3-inch tab stop. Key **April 10, 19--** at the 5½-inch tab stop.
7.  Use bold style for each paragraph heading.
8.  Left-justify the first paragraph.
9.  Check the spelling of the document.
10. Save the finished document on your data disk as *update*.
11. Preview and print the document.

# MICROSOFT DRAW

## LEARNING OBJECTIVES

**When you complete this chapter, you will be able to:**

1. Understand the concept of graphics in documents.
2. Perform the necessary steps to add graphics to documents.
3. Use the tools and features of Draw to create drawings.
4. Use Draw to import art.

## GRAPHICS IN THE WORD PROCESSOR

The word processor allows you to enhance documents by adding graphics. *Graphics* are pictures that help illustrate the meaning of the text or that make the page more attractive or functional. Works includes a drawing program, Microsoft Draw, to enable you to add drawings to your documents. Draw is accessible only from the word processor. You can use Draw to create drawings or to import art from other sources. Graphics that are already drawn and available for use in documents are called *clip-art*.

Figure 5-1 shows two documents created with Works. The letter from Baker's Bikeworks takes on a more professional appearance with the addition of a letterhead that includes a bicycle created in Draw. The poster about a Washington, D.C., trip includes an imported graphic to grab the reader's attention.

## DRAW BASICS

Microsoft Draw is simple to learn and easy to use. Even if you aren't very talented at drawing, Draw gives you the option of importing graphics created by people who *are* talented.

**FIGURE 5-1**

You can draw your own graphics or import graphics from other sources.

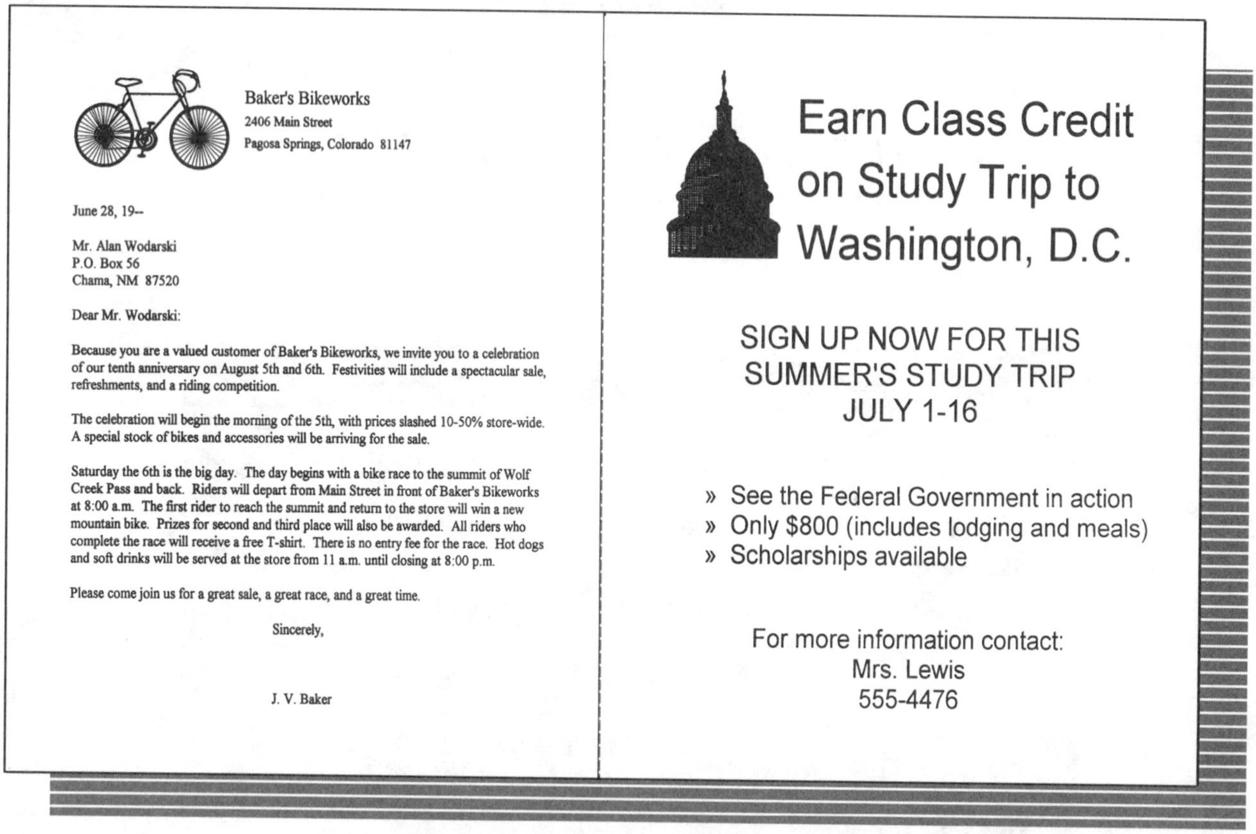

Baker's Bikeworks
2406 Main Street
Pagosa Springs, Colorado 81147

June 28, 19--

Mr. Alan Wodarski
P.O. Box 56
Chama, NM 87520

Dear Mr. Wodarski:

Because you are a valued customer of Baker's Bikeworks, we invite you to a celebration of our tenth anniversary on August 5th and 6th.  Festivities will include a spectacular sale, refreshments, and a riding competition.

The celebration will begin the morning of the 5th, with prices slashed 10-50% store-wide.  A special stock of bikes and accessories will be arriving for the sale.

Saturday the 6th is the big day.  The day begins with a bike race to the summit of Wolf Creek Pass and back.  Riders will depart from Main Street in front of Baker's Bikeworks at 8:00 a.m.  The first rider to reach the summit and return to the store will win a new mountain bike.  Prizes for second and third place will also be awarded.  All riders who complete the race will receive a free T-shirt.  There is no entry fee for the race.  Hot dogs and soft drinks will be served at the store from 11 a.m. until closing at 8:00 p.m.

Please come join us for a great sale, a great race, and a great time.

Sincerely,

J. V. Baker

# Earn Class Credit on Study Trip to Washington, D.C.

### SIGN UP NOW FOR THIS SUMMER'S STUDY TRIP JULY 1-16

» See the Federal Government in action
» Only $800 (includes lodging and meals)
» Scholarships available

For more information contact:
Mrs. Lewis
555-4476

## Starting Draw

Draw can only be started from the word processor. Before you start Draw, you need to place the cursor at the location that you want the finished graphic to appear. This is because you will actually leave the word processor document window, create the graphic in the Draw window, and then return to the word processor window. The graphic you create will automatically appear at the cursor location. For example, if you want the graphic to appear at the top of the document, move the cursor to the left of the first character in the document. If you want the graphic inserted between two paragraphs, place the cursor on a blank line between them. When you are ready to create your graphic, select Drawing from the Insert menu.

## ACTIVITY 5-1

### Starting Draw

In this activity, you will create a new document, position the cursor, and start Draw.

Activity 5-1 continued

1. Start Works if it is not already running.

2. Create a new word processor document.

3. Key **This is above the drawing**.

4. Press **Enter** twice.

5. Key **This is below the drawing**.

6. Position the cursor on the blank line between the two lines of text.

7. From the **Insert** menu, choose **Drawing**. A Draw window similar to that shown in Figure 5-2 appears. On your screen, the Draw window may appear in a different size or position than in Figure 5-2.

8. Leave the Draw window open for the next activity.

**FIGURE 5-2**
The Draw window appears over your document.

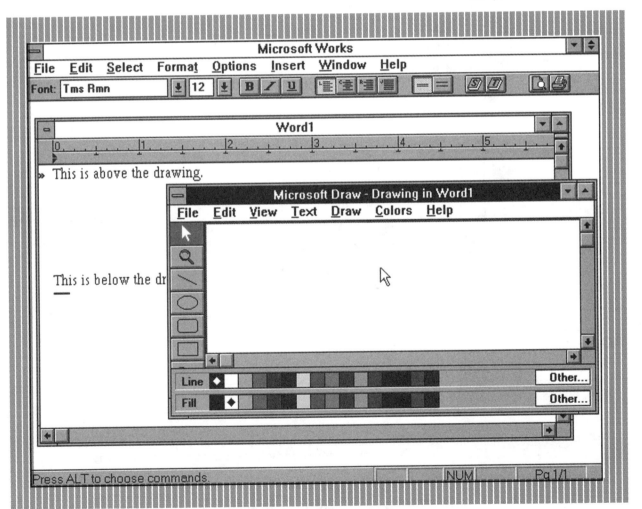

## The Draw Window

Figure 5-3 illustrates the parts of the Draw window. The Toolbox holds tools for drawing lines, rectangles, circles, and more. At the bottom of the window is a color palette that you can use to add color to the shapes you draw. Across the top of the window are menus that provide other options. You'll explore these options further in the activities in this chapter.

Table 5-1 summarizes the drawing tools that appear in the Toolbox.

**FIGURE 5-3**

The Draw window provides the tools for drawing or importing graphics.

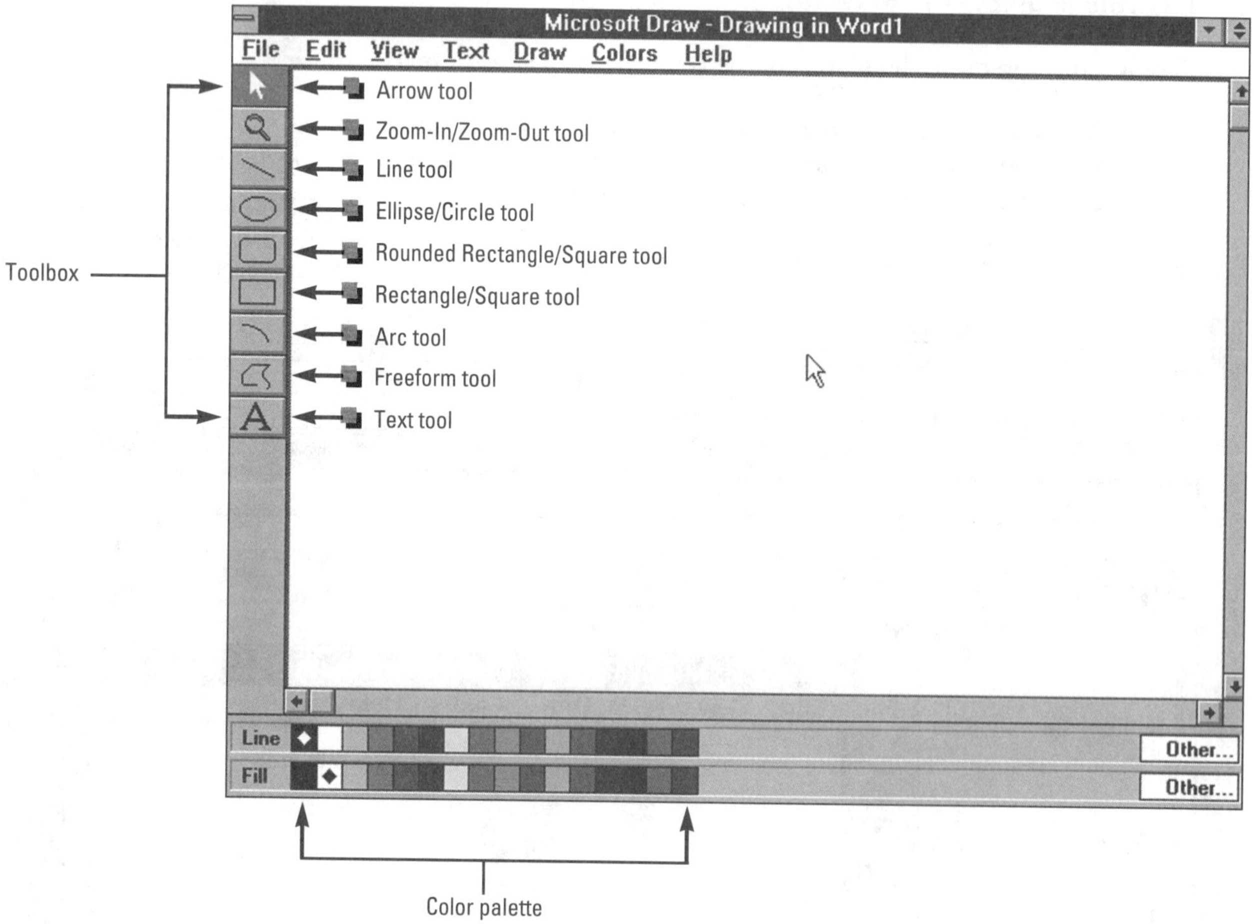

**TABLE 5-1**

Drawing Tools

| Tool Name | Function |
| --- | --- |
| Arrow tool | Lets you select and manipulate objects. To use, click on the arrow. The cursor will assume the pointer shape. |
| Zoom In/Zoom Out tool | Changes the magnification of a drawing. To use, click on the magnifying glass and drag it to the area of your drawing you want to enlarge. Clicking while holding down the Shift key will reverse the magnification. |

**TABLE 5-1**
Drawing Tools (*continued*)

| Tool Name | Function |
|-----------|----------|
| Line tool | Draws straight lines. To use, position the pointer where you want the line to begin, then click and hold the mouse button and drag to where you want the line to end. |
| Ellipse/Circle tool | Draws ellipses and circles. To use, click and hold the mouse button, then drag to draw the ellipse or circle. To force the object to be a perfect circle, hold down the Shift key as you drag. |
| Rounded Rectangle/Square tool | Draws rectangles and squares with rounded corners. To use, click and hold the mouse button, then drag to draw. To force the object to be a perfect square, hold down the Shift key as you drag. |
| Rectangle/Square tool | Draws rectangles and squares. To use, click and hold the mouse button, then drag to draw. To force the object to be a perfect square, hold down the Shift key as you drag. |
| Arc tool | Draws arcs. To use, click and hold the mouse button, then drag to draw. |
| Freeform tool | Draws polygons and freehand objects. To draw straight sections, click at each endpoint or vertex. To draw freehand, drag. You can mix straight sections and freehand drawing in the same object. |

**ACTIVITY
5-2**

## Drawing a Graphic

In this activity, you will create a simple drawing.

1.   Click the **Rectangle/Square tool**.

2.   Move the pointer to the center of the work area.

3.   Press and hold the mouse button and drag to draw a rectangle about 1 inch tall and 2 inches wide. Release the mouse button when you're satisfied with your rectangle.

4.   Click the **Ellipse/Circle tool**.

5.   Move the pointer to the left of the rectangle you just drew.

6.   Draw a circle with a diameter of about 1 inch.

7.   Leave the Draw window open for the next activity.

## Editing the Graphic

Now that you have drawn several objects, you need to learn a bit more about how to manipulate the images on your screen. Before you can proceed to more complicated graphics, you should know how to select and resize objects.

**SELECTING AN OBJECT**   When you first drew the objects in Activity 5-2, you probably noticed the little squares that appeared at the edges of the graphic when you released the mouse. These small squares are called *handles*. They indicate that the object is selected and allow you to manipulate the selected object in some way. As soon as you choose another tool, the selection handles around an object disappear. Before you can copy, move, delete, or otherwise manipulate the object, you will have to select it again so that the handles show.

To select an object, you use the Arrow tool. If you are using another tool, choose the Arrow tool from the Toolbox. When the cursor becomes an arrow pointer, click on the object you want to select. The selection handles appear around the object, and you can then perform the desired operation.

To deselect an object, click on another object or anywhere in the drawing window.

**RESIZING AN OBJECT**   Handles do more than indicate that an object is selected. They also allow you to resize an object. Often during the process of creating a drawing, you will realize that the line, rectangle, or circle you just drew isn't quite the right size. Resizing is an easy process. You simply select the object to make the handles appear and then drag the handles inward or outward to make the object smaller or larger.

# ACTIVITY
# 5-3

## Selecting, Resizing, and Moving Objects

In this activity, you will select and resize the objects you drew in Activity 5-2.

1.  Click the **Arrow tool** and select the rectangle.

2.  Drag the upper right handle of the rectangle to enlarge it until it measures about 2 inches tall and 3 inches wide.

3.  Select the circle. To move the circle into the rectangle, place the Arrow pointer anywhere inside the circle, hold down the mouse button, and drag the circle to its new position. When you release the mouse button, the selection handles will reappear.

Activity 5-3 continued

4. By dragging the circle's handles, resize it until it becomes an ellipse that fits snugly inside the rectangle.

5. Leave the Draw window open for the next activity.

## Returning to the Word Processor

When you are satisfied with your graphic, exit Draw and return to the word processor. Works will ask you if you want to update your word processor file. If you say yes, your graphic will appear at the cursor position in your document.

**ACTIVITY
5-4**

## Returning to the Word Processor

In this activity, you will exit Draw and return to the word processor.

1. From the **File** menu, choose **Exit and Return to Word1**. A dialog box appears asking if you want to update your document.

2. Click **Yes**. The Draw window closes. Your document should look similar to Figure 5-4.

3. Save the file on your data disk as *mydraw*.

4. Close the file.

**FIGURE 5-4**
When you exit Draw, the graphic is inserted in your document.

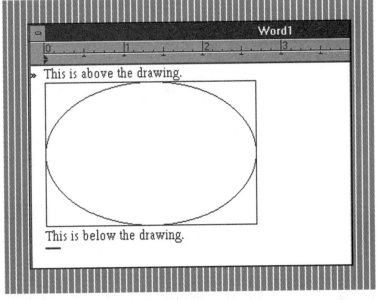

# WORKING WITH A DRAWING

**FIGURE 5-5**

Even complex drawings, like this locomotive, can be created with Draw.

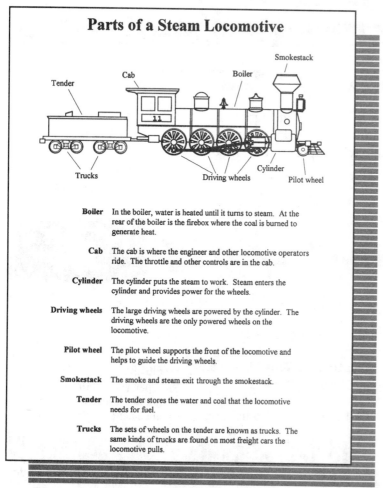

**Parts of a Steam Locomotive**

| | |
|---|---|
| **Boiler** | In the boiler, water is heated until it turns to steam. At the rear of the boiler is the firebox where the coal is burned to generate heat. |
| **Cab** | The cab is where the engineer and other locomotive operators ride. The throttle and other controls are in the cab. |
| **Cylinder** | The cylinder puts the steam to work. Steam enters the cylinder and provides power for the wheels. |
| **Driving wheels** | The large driving wheels are powered by the cylinder. The driving wheels are the only powered wheels on the locomotive. |
| **Pilot wheel** | The pilot wheel supports the front of the locomotive and helps to guide the driving wheels. |
| **Smokestack** | The smoke and steam exit through the smokestack. |
| **Tender** | The tender stores the water and coal that the locomotive needs for fuel. |
| **Trucks** | The sets of wheels on the tender are known as trucks. The same kinds of trucks are found on most freight cars the locomotive pulls. |

Drawings created in Draw can be made up of one or more objects. Each time you use a tool to add to your drawing, you create another object. The locomotive shown in Figure 5-5 is an example of a relatively complex drawing made up of well over 100 objects, all of which were created with the tools in Draw. To learn about Draw's capabilities and practice using the drawing tools, you will start with an unfinished version of the locomotive and complete it in the activities in this section.

## Using Undo in Microsoft Draw

Using Undo in Draw is like using Undo anywhere else in Works. The Undo command in the Edit menu will cancel the last drawing operation. Undo can reverse only the most recently made change.

## Zooming In and Out

When you are drawing a complex graphic, like the locomotive in Figure 5-5, you will find it helpful to be able to view your drawing at different sizes. You need a close-up view for the small details and an overall view to see how the parts of the graphic fit together. Microsoft Draw borrows the term *zoom* from photography to describe what happens when you change the size of the image on your screen.

Zooming in makes the drawing appear larger. Zooming out makes the drawing appear smaller. Zooming does not actually change the size of your drawing; it just provides you with different views.

There are two ways to zoom in and out: the Zoom In/Zoom Out tool and the View menu.

**THE ZOOM IN/ZOOM OUT TOOL**   The Zoom In/Zoom Out tool gives you the most control over zooming. To use this tool, select it from the Toolbox. Position the pointer over the area on which you wish to zoom in and click. Each time you click, the view will zoom in further until the maximum magnification is reached. Holding down the Shift key will reverse the zooming and cause the view to zoom out each time you click.

**THE VIEW MENU**   The View menu lets you choose the degree of magnification directly from a menu. The disadvantage of the View menu is that it does not give you control over the area that becomes magnified.

### ACTIVITY 5-5

## Changing Views

In this activity, you will open a document and use the Zoom In/Zoom Out tool and the View menu to change views.

1.  Open *act5-5.wps* from your template disk. A document will appear showing a graphic of a locomotive. The locomotive drawing is not yet complete.

2.  Maximize both the application window and the document window by clicking the **Maximize** buttons of each window.

    Because there is already a Draw graphic in the document, you can use a shortcut method to start Draw.

3.  Double-click the graphic of the train to start Draw. The Draw window appears. It may take several seconds for Draw to activate.

4.  Click the **Zoom In/Zoom Out tool**. The pointer becomes a magnifying glass (see Figure 5-6).

5.  Click the magnifying glass on the pilot wheel at the front of the locomotive. (Look at the labels on Figure 5-5 if you need to know exactly which wheel is the pilot wheel.) The locomotive is redrawn larger.

6.  Click the same wheel two more times. The drawing increases to the maximum magnification.

**FIGURE 5-6**

The Zoom In/Zoom Out tool lets you view your drawing at different sizes.

7.  Hold down the Shift key. Notice how the pointer changes to show a minus sign (-) in the center of the magnifying glass.

8.  With the Shift key pressed, click the wheel. The magnification decreases.

9.  With the Shift key still pressed, click five more times. The drawing will reach the minimum magnification. Release the Shift key.

10. From the **View** menu, choose **Full Size**. The View menu is an alternative to the Zoom In/Zoom Out tool. Because the View menu does not give you control over the area that is magnified, you may need to use the scroll bars to get the locomotive back in view.

11. Leave the Draw window open for the next activity.

## Selecting More Than One Object

Sometimes you will want to select more than one object. Works gives you two ways to select more than one object. The first is called shift-clicking. The second method is to draw a selection box around a group of objects.

**SHIFT-CLICKING**   To shift-click, hold down the Shift key and click each of the objects you want to select. Use shift-clicking when you need to select objects that are not close to each other or when the objects you need to select are near other objects you do not want to select. If you select an object unintentionally, click it again to remove it from the group.

**DRAWING A SELECTION BOX**   Using the Arrow tool, you can drag a box around a group of objects. Objects that are included in the selection box will be selected. Use a selection box when all of the objects you want selected are near each other and can be surrounded with a box. Be sure your selection box is large enough to enclose all the selection handles of the various objects. If you miss a handle, that item will not be selected.

**COMBINING METHODS**   You can also combine these two methods. First use the selection box, then shift-click to include objects that the selection box may have missed.

## Grouping Objects

As your drawing becomes more complex, you will find it necessary to "glue" objects together into groups. Grouping objects allows you to work with a group of objects as though it were one object. The locomotive you are working with already has many grouped objects. For example, all the pieces in each wheel are grouped to create a wheel object that can be moved, copied, and aligned as a unit.

To group objects, select the objects you want to group and choose Group from the Draw menu. Objects can be ungrouped using the Ungroup command.

## Grid Snap

One of the most difficult parts of drawing with a computer drawing program is aligning and sizing objects. To help with this problem, Draw provides an invisible grid on your screen. Objects automatically align to the nearest grid line. This feature is called *grid snap*. This makes it easy, for example, to draw three lines that are an equal distance apart. You can place each line one grid distance from the next. The result is lines that are perfectly spaced.

There will be times, however, that you will want to be able to place an object more precisely. For example, when you are drawing the details on your graphic, grid snap may not allow you to place two objects as close together as you would like. To allow for more precise alignment, the program provides a way to turn grid snap off. The Draw menu has a command called Snap to Grid. Choosing the Snap to Grid command will toggle grid snap on or off. If the command has a check mark by it when you pull down the menu, grid snap is on.

## ACTIVITY 5-6

### Selecting and Grouping Objects and Turning Grid Snap On and Off

In this activity, you will practice selecting and grouping objects and turning grid snap on and off.

1. Zoom in on the bell one level of magnification. Your screen should look similar to Figure 5-7.

2. Pull down the **Draw** menu and make sure that Snap to Grid is checked. (If there is no check mark next to Snap to Grid, choose **Snap to Grid**.)

3. Click the **Arrow tool**.

4. Position the arrow above and to the left of the bell and drag a selection box around the bell, as shown in Figure 5-8. The objects that make up the bell will be selected.

Activity 5-6 continued

**FIGURE 5-7**
Zooming in on part of a
drawing gives you more control
over details.

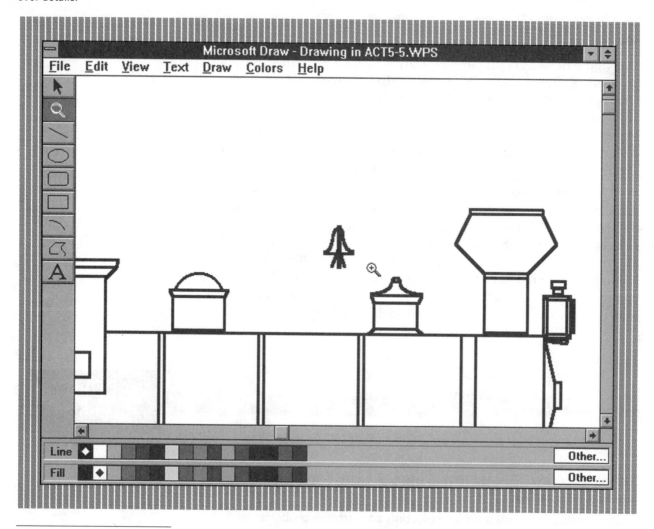

**FIGURE 5-8**
Dragging a selection box
around a group of objects
selects every object within the
box.

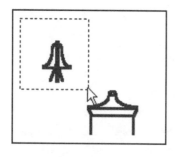

5.  From the **Draw** menu, choose **Group**. The objects that make up the
    bell will be grouped into one object. One set of handles will
    surround the bell.

6.  Drag the bell down to the boiler, as shown in Figure 5-9. Because
    grid snap is on, the bell cannot be positioned properly on the boiler.
    The bell snaps to a position that is either too high or too low.

7.  Choose **Snap to Grid** from the **Draw** menu to turn grid snap off.

8.  Position the bell properly on the boiler, as shown in Figure 5-10.

Activity 5-6 continued

9.   From the **View** menu, choose **Full Size**. Center the drawing on
     your screen using the scroll bars.

10.  Leave grid snap off and the Draw window open for the next activity.

**FIGURE 5-9**
Grid snap sometimes prevents
precise alignment.

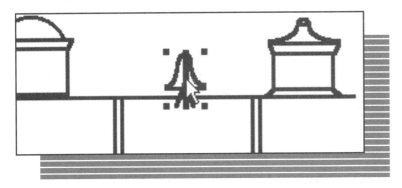

**FIGURE 5-10**
With grid snap off, the bell can
be aligned precisely.

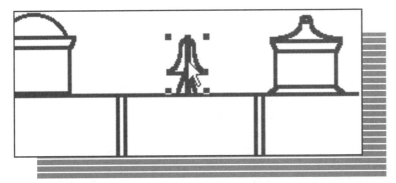

## Layering

In Draw, each object you create can be changed, moved, or deleted at
any time. This is an advantage of drawing on a computer rather than
on paper. The computer will allow you to lift your mistakes right off
the screen and try again. The objects you create with Draw are laid on
top of each other. When you create an object, it is placed on top of other
objects that have already been drawn. Sometimes you will need to
rearrange the order in which objects are layered. Draw provides two
commands for doing this: Send to Back and Bring to Front. Both
commands are in the Edit menu. The Send to Back command moves
the selected object or objects to the bottom layer. The Bring to Front
command moves the selected object or objects to the top layer.

### Cutting, Copying, Pasting, and Deleting Objects

Objects can be cut, copied, and pasted like text. The Cut and Copy commands place a copy of the selected image on the Clipboard. Pasting an object from the Clipboard places the object in the Draw window. You can then move it into position.

Deleting an object is most easily done by selecting the object you want to delete and pressing the Delete key.

**ACTIVITY 5-7**

### Copying and Moving an Object

In this activity, you will copy and paste the truck on the locomotive's tender, group the tender into one object, and move it into position behind the locomotive. Refer to Figure 5-5 to find the locations of these objects.

1.  Click the **Arrow tool**.

2.  Turn grid snap on.

3.  Locate the tender on your screen. You may have to use the scroll bars. Click the truck on the tender. Handles will appear around the object to show that it has been selected.

4.  From the **Edit** menu, choose **Copy**. The object is copied to the Clipboard.

5.  From the **Edit** menu, choose **Paste**. A copy of the object appears in the workspace.

6.  The newly pasted truck is already selected. Drag it into position under the tender (see Figure 5-11).

7.  Select the body of the tender. From the **Edit** menu, choose **Bring to Front**. The truck will appear to be in the proper position underneath the tender.

8.  Move the pointer slightly above and to the left of the tender. Drag a selection box around the entire tender, selecting all of the objects that make up the tender.

9.  From the **Draw** menu, choose **Group**. The tender becomes a single object.

**FIGURE 5-11**

After the new truck is pasted on your drawing, drag it to the correct position.

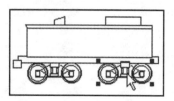

Activity 5-7 continued

10.  Drag the tender into position behind the locomotive. If necessary, turn grid snap off to properly align the tender. Your screen should look similar to Figure 5-12.

11.  Leave the Draw window open for the next activity.

**FIGURE 5-12**
Position the tender behind the locomotive.

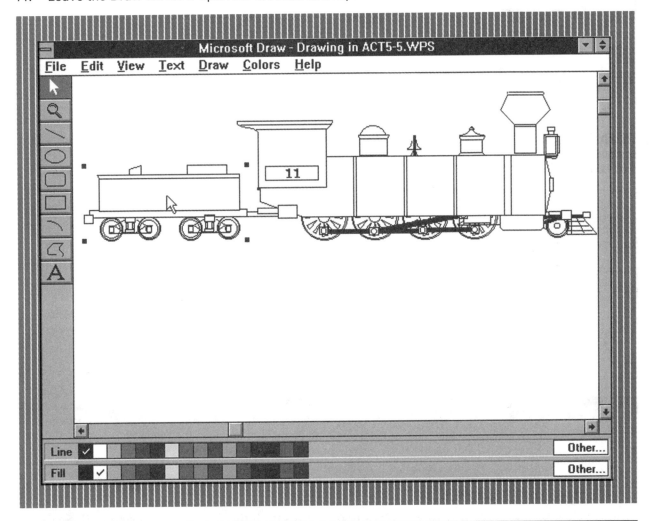

**ACTIVITY 5-8**

## Finishing Touches

In this activity, you will use the Line tool, the Rectangle/Square tool, and the Ellipse/Circle tool to add windows and some finishing touches to your locomotive.

Activity 5-8 continued

**FIGURE 5-13**
The Line tool can be used to add details to a drawing.

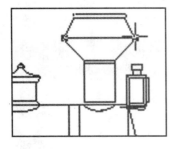

**FIGURE 5-14**
Drawing a circle is easy with the Ellipse/Circle tool.

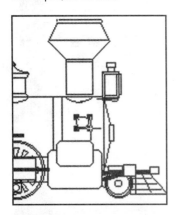

1.  Select the boiler of the locomotive. (Refer back to Figure 5-5 if you do not remember where the boiler is.)

2.  From the **Edit** menu, choose **Send to Back**. The driving wheels are now visible.

3.  Click the **Line tool**.

4.  Draw a line across the smokestack, as shown in Figure 5-13.

5.  Click the **Rectangle/Square tool**.

6.  Draw two windows in the cab of the train, as shown in Figure 5-5. You can draw both windows with the Rectangle/Square tool or draw one window, then copy and paste.

7.  Draw the small circle near the front of the boiler, as shown in Figure 5-14. Concentrate on drawing the circle the correct size. Then move it into position if necessary using the Arrow tool.

8.  Leave the Draw window opened for the next activity.

## Text in Drawings

You can add text to drawings with the Text tool. Working with text in Draw is similar to working with text in the word processor. Draw provides a Text menu that lets you choose the typeface, size, and style.

### ACTIVITY 5-9

### Adding Text

In this activity, you will use the Text tool to add a name to the locomotive's tender.

Activity 5-9 continued

1. If necessary, use the scroll bars to adjust the drawing so that the tender is visible.

2. Click the **Arrow tool**.

3. From the **Text** menu, choose **Center**.

4. Click the **Text tool**.

5. Click the center of the tender, as shown in Figure 5-15.

6. Key your name or another name of your choice.

7. Using the Text menu, experiment with various typefaces, styles, and sizes until you achieve the right look.

8. From the **File** menu, choose **Exit and Return to Act5-5.wps**. Click **Yes** when asked if you would like to update the document.

9. Save the document on your data disk as *mytrain*.

10. Close the file.

**FIGURE 5-15**
Click the Text tool in the place you want to add text.

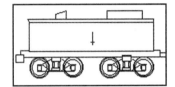

## OTHER FEATURES IN DRAW

Draw provides other features that allow you to do things like add color or patterns to objects, and rotate and flip objects.

### Using Colors and Patterns

Draw allows you to draw in color and to fill objects with patterns and colors. Most printers will not print in color. Therefore, it is best to use color in drawings that will be viewed on the screen. Patterns, however, can be printed and are a good way to enhance a drawing. If you have a monochrome monitor, you can use shades of gray instead of colors.

COLOR   Draw provides a color palette at the bottom of the Draw screen that allows you to choose colors for your drawing. Notice that the color palette has two areas of colors. The top one is marked *Line* and the bottom one is marked *Fill. Line* refers to the outline of the object, the line that is created when you use a tool. *Fill* is the area inside the outline. When you select color for an object, you can choose different colors for the line and the fill.

Coloring an object is a two-step process. First select the object you want to color. Then select the colors you want from the color palette. Works marks your selections with diamonds in the color palette.

**ACTIVITY
5-10**

## Coloring Objects

In this activity, you will color objects to make the flag of Sweden.

1.  Open *act5-10.wps* from your template disk.

2.  Double-click the drawing to activate Draw.

3.  Click the **Arrow tool** to deselect the objects. Select only the large rectangle.

4.  Click the lighter blue color (or the darkest shade of gray) in the Fill color palette and in the Line color palette.

5.  Select the long, narrow, horizontal rectangle.

6.  Click the color yellow (or the lightest shade of gray) in the Line color palette and in the Fill color palette.

7.  Select the rectangle that is still white.

8.  Click the color yellow (or the lightest shade of gray) in the Line color palette and in the Fill color palette.

9.  Exit Draw and update the document. When you return to the word processor, the colors of the flag will be different until the drawing is deselected.

10.  Save the document as *swedflag* on your data disk. Close the file.

**PATTERNS**    As mentioned above, most printers will not print color images. You can still make an impact with your drawings by using patterns to fill objects. Works includes a palette of patterns located under the Pattern command in the Draw menu.

To use a pattern, first select the object you want to fill with the pattern. Then choose Pattern from the Draw menu and select a pattern. Your object will fill with that pattern.

You can also combine patterns with color to create interesting effects on your screen. You can fill an object with a pattern and then change the color of the pattern using the Line color palette.

## Rotating and Flipping Objects

Draw allows you to rotate and flip objects. The ability to flip objects is especially useful when what you are drawing is symmetrical, as you will see in the next activity.

**ACTIVITY
5-11**

### Flipping Objects

In this activity, you will use flipping to draw a symmetrical object.

1.  Open *act5-11.wps* from your template disk.

2.  Double-click the drawing to start Draw.

3.  Click the mouse to deselect the image, then select the jagged line. Use Copy and Paste to duplicate it.

**FIGURE 5-16**
Flipping can help you quickly create symmetrical objects.

4.  Make sure that one of the duplicated objects is selected.

5.  Pull down the **Draw** menu and click **Rotate/Flip** to activate the Rotate/Flip submenu.

6.  From the **Rotate/Flip** submenu, choose **Flip Horizontal**.

7.  Drag the flipped object to form a leaf, as shown in Figure 5-16.

8.  Drag the arc under the leaf to serve as a stem.

9.  Select all three of the objects with a selection box and group them.

10. Leave the Draw window open for the next activity.

**ACTIVITY
5-12**

### Rotating and More Flipping

In this activity, you will make a leaf collection from the leaf you drew in the last activity.

Activity 5-12 continued

**FIGURE 5-17**
Rotating and flipping make a
variety of arrangements
possible.

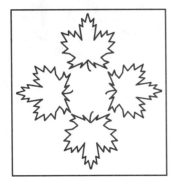

1.   Select the leaf. From the **Edit** menu, choose **Copy**.

2.   From the **Edit** menu, choose **Paste**. Another leaf appears.

3.   Move the leaf so that it does not overlap the other leaf. From the **Rotate/Flip** submenu, choose **Rotate Right**.

4.   From the **Edit** menu, choose **Paste**. Another leaf appears.

5.   Move the leaf so that it does not overlap the other leaves. From the **Rotate/Flip** submenu, choose **Rotate Left**.

6.   From the **Edit** menu, choose **Paste**. Another leaf appears.

7.   Move the leaf so that it does not overlap the other leaves. From the **Rotate/Flip** submenu, choose **Flip Vertical**.

8.   Arrange the leaves to match Figure 5-17.

9.   Exit Draw and update the document.

10.  Save the document as *leaves* on your data disk. Close the file.

## Exploring Draw on Your Own

Other features are available when you are creating your own drawings. You may want to experiment with the menu commands not presented in this chapter. Use the Help menu if you need some extra help.

## IMPORTING ART

You may sometimes want to use art from another source rather than do the drawing yourself. Clip-art libraries offer artwork of common objects that can speed up and possibly improve the quality of your work.

To import a graphic, start Draw as you normally do. Choose Import from the File menu. Choose the graphic file you want to import from the dialog box that appears. The image will be read into Draw and will appear on your screen.

**ACTIVITY
5-13**

## Importing Clip-Art

In this activity, you will import a piece of clip-art from your template disk.

1.   Create a new word processor document.

2.   From the **Insert** menu, choose **Drawing**. The Draw window
     appears.

3.   From the **File** menu, choose **Import Picture**. The Import Picture
     dialog box appears.

4.   Choose **act5-13.pcx** from your template disk. The clip-art appears
     after the file is read.

5.   Exit Draw. Update the document.

6.   Save the document on your data disk as *key*.

7.   Close the document.

# SUMMARY

Graphics can enhance documents by illustrating text or making the page more attractive or functional. Microsoft Draw is a program that adds graphics to word processor documents. Graphics can be created in Draw or imported from an existing file.

Graphics are added to a document by positioning the cursor, starting Draw, drawing or importing the graphic, and returning to the word processor.

Graphics created in Draw are made up of one or more objects. Draw provides a Toolbox of tools, such as lines, rectangles, ellipses, and more, for drawing objects. The menus in Draw provide many options for working with graphic objects.

# CHALLENGES

## TRUE/FALSE

Circle **T** or **F** to show whether the statement is true or false.

| | | | |
|---|---|---|---|
| T | F | 1. | Microsoft Draw adds graphics to a word processor document. |
| T | F | 2. | Microsoft Draw can only be started from the word processor. |
| T | F | 3. | Zooming in can be used to enlarge your printouts. |
| T | F | 4. | Selection boxes are small squares that appear around a selected object. |
| T | F | 5. | Grid snap causes objects to align to the nearest object. |
| T | F | 6. | Draw creates objects in layers. |
| T | F | 7. | Graphic objects can be cut, copied, and pasted. |
| T | F | 8. | The Freeform tool allows you to draw using straight lines and freehand drawing. |
| T | F | 9. | Flipping can be used to create symmetrical graphics. |
| T | F | 10. | Importing graphics is a way to utilize graphics created previously. |

## COMPLETION

Write the correct answer in the space provided.

1. What is the name for a graphic that is predrawn and available for use in your documents?

2. What are five steps involved in drawing a graphic using Draw?

_____

_____

_____

_____

_____

3. What is the advantage of using the Zoom In/Zoom Out tool instead of the View menu?

_____

_____

4. What kind of box is created when you drag a box using the Arrow tool?

_____

5. Imagine you have just created five objects that are assembled to form a single object. What command can you use to make the five objects work together as one?

_____

6. What command would you use to move an object to the bottom layer?

_____

_____

7. How can you force the Rectangle/Square tool to draw a perfect square?

_____

8. Explain how you would resize a rectangle.

_____

_____

_____

9. When you color an object, for what two parts of an object can you specify a color?

_____

10. From what menu in Draw do you import graphics?

_____

# APPLICATIONS

## APPLICATION 5-1

Add labels to identify the parts of the locomotive you completed in the activities. Refer to Figure 5-5.

1.   Open *mytrain.wps* from your data disk.

2.   Center the heading *Parts of a Steam Locomotive* in a large font at the top of the page.

3.   Add labels to the drawing using Draw and the Text tool. Use the Line tool to draw the diagonal lines.

4.   Save the document on your data disk as *locolabl.*

## APPLICATION 5-2

Draw a flag using color or patterns. You can design your own flag or draw an actual flag, such as your state flag or the flag of another country. Do not choose a flag with complex insignias or unusual shapes. Choose one that includes stripes, lines, circles, or even text. Save the document as *myflag* on your data disk.

## APPLICATION 5-3

Open *app5-3.wps* from your template disk and follow the instructions in the document to complete the three exercises. Print the document when you complete the third exercise. Save the document as *ans5-3* on your data disk.

## APPLICATION 5-4

Follow the instructions below to practice creating various graphic objects.

1.   Create a new word processor document.

2.   Start Draw.

3.   Draw a perfect circle about 1 inch in diameter.

4.   Directly below the circle, draw an ellipse about 1 inch tall and 2 inches wide.

5.   Enclose the circle and the ellipse in a rounded rectangle. Send the rounded rectangle to the back.

6.   Draw an arc inside the rounded rectangle.

7.  Draw a diagonal line about 1 inch long in the rounded rectangle.

8.  Draw a perfect square inside the ellipse. Make the square small enough to fit comfortably in the ellipse.

9.  With the Freeform tool, draw a triangle beside the square, but inside the ellipse.

10. Exit Draw, update your document, print it, and save it on your data disk as *objects*.

---

## APPLICATION 5-5

Design a letterhead for a business. You can use a real or a fictitious business. Include graphics of some kind. You can use a drawing, like the bicycle in Figure 5-1, or create a design using the drawing tools. You can even import a graphic if you like. Remember to include the company name and address. Save the finished document on your data disk as *letthead*.

# ADVANCED WORD PROCESSOR OPERATIONS

## LEARNING OBJECTIVES

**When you complete this chapter, you will be able to:**

1. Open and save a document as text.
2. Work with multiple and multipage documents.
3. Find specific data and replace it with other data.
4. Insert headers, footers, special characters, footnotes, and bookmarks.
5. Use the Border and Show All Characters commands.
6. Print documents in Portrait and Landscape orientation.

In Chapter 4, you learned features of the word processor that strengthened your word processing skills. Chapter 5 introduced you to the Draw feature. In this chapter, you will learn advanced word processing operations, such as opening and saving text documents, finding and replacing data, and inserting headers, footers, special characters, footnotes, and bookmarks. You will also learn how to use the Border and Show All Characters commands and learn how to print a document in Portrait and Landscape orientation.

## OPENING AND SAVING A DOCUMENT AS TEXT

Suppose you and a classmate are working together on a project that requires you both to use a word processing program. You intend to use Works, but your friend has another word processing application. Will you be able to use her files?

The answer is yes. The Works word processor can open documents created by other applications in a form called a *text file*. A text file is a document that does not contain any of the codes that control fonts, font size, and type style. Works uses a file format called *ASCII* when opening a file created by another type of word processor. ASCII is an acronym for American Standard Code for Information Interchange. The ASCII format was developed to provide a standard for communication between different types of programs. In ASCII format, each alphabetical character, number, or symbol has a specific value that is the same no matter what program the file has been created in. For example, the letter *d* has an ASCII value of 100, whereas *D* has a value of 68. This system makes it easy for different applications to share the same information. Text files are commonly saved with the extension .TXT to indicate they contain only ASCII characters.

When a document is opened in Works as text, it will not contain any of the formatting codes inserted in the original document, such as codes to control font choice, font size, margins, and so on. This is because these codes are not ASCII characters. After you have opened a text file, you can insert these codes yourself to format the document.

To open a document as text, choose Open Existing File from the File menu. If the document has a .TXT filename extension, choose Text in the List Files of Type box. If the file you want to open doesn't have a .TXT extension, then select the document in the File Name box. After you click OK, Works will open the document. You can then edit it in the same way you would edit any other word processing document.

You can save a document as text by choosing Save As from the File menu. Choose Text in the Save File As Type box. A message will appear asking if you want to save the document without formatting. Click OK. Works saves the document and supplies the filename extension .TXT. Remember that you will lose all codes that control formatting, such as fonts, font sizes, and margins, when you save a document as text.

**ACTIVITY
6-1**

## Opening a Text Document

In this activity, you will open a text document. Works should be running and the application window should be maximized.

1.   From the **File** menu, choose **Open Existing File**. The Open dialog box appears.

2.   Choose **a:** from the **Drives** box.

3.   Click the **List Files of Type** box arrow. A list of file types appears.

Activity 6-1 continued

**FIGURE 6-1**

You can open a text file in the word processor, spreadsheet, or database by clicking the appropriate button in the Open File As dialog box.

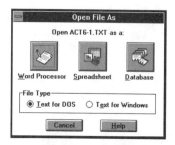

4. Choose **Text (\*.txt)** as the file type. The filename *act6-1.txt* appears in the File Name box.

5. Choose **act6-1.txt**. Click **OK**. The Open File As dialog box appears, as shown in Figure 6-1.

6. Click the **Word Processor** button. The file appears in the document window.

## WORKING WITH MORE THAN ONE DOCUMENT

As you learned in Chapter 3, Works allows you to have more than one document open at a time. This is useful when you want to move or copy text between two documents. Opening more than one document is as easy as opening a single document. The Create New File and the Open Existing File commands are available in the File menu even when you have another document open. You can have as many as eight files open at one time.

In Chapter 3, you also were introduced to the two ways to switch between documents. You will remember that the quickest way is to click in the window or on the title bar of the document with which you want to work. The window is brought to the front and becomes the active window. The other way to switch is to use the Window menu. At the bottom of the Window menu are the names of the documents that are currently open. Choosing one of these documents from the Window menu will make that document active and bring it to the front.

**ACTIVITY 6-2**

### Switching between Documents

In this activity, you will review opening an additional document and switching between documents.

Activity 6-2 continued

1. From the **File** menu, choose **Open Existing File**. The Open dialog box appears.

2. Choose **act6-2.wps** in the File Name box. Click **OK**. The *act6-2.wps* document appears over the *act6-1.txt* document, as shown in Figure 6-2. You can see that *act6-2.wps* is the active document because the title bar is darkened and it appears on top of the *act6-1.txt* document.

3. Click the title bar of the *act6-1.txt* document. The window is brought to the front and becomes the active window.

4. From the **Window** menu, choose **act6-2.wps**. The document again moves to the front and becomes active.

**FIGURE 6-2**
In Works, two documents can be open at the same time.

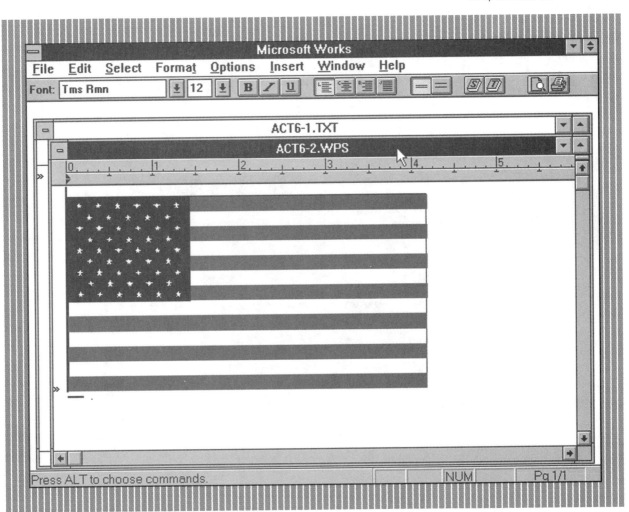

## Arranging Windows

When you have more than one document open on your screen, it can become tedious to switch among them. Some operations, such as moving or copying text between documents, would be easier if you could rearrange the document windows on your screen.

One way to arrange windows on your screen is to resize and move the windows manually. Any window that is not maximized can be resized and moved. As you learned in Chapter 2, you can use the mouse to drag the entire window to a new location. Dragging an edge or corner of a window resizes it.

But you don't have to arrange your windows manually. Most Windows programs, including Works, provide two ways to automatically arrange windows on the screen: cascading and tiling.

**CASCADE**   The Cascade command in the Window menu overlaps the windows and arranges them so that the titles are visible, as shown in Figure 6-3. An active cascaded window will appear in front of the other windows and will have a darkened title bar. Up to six windows can be cascaded on the screen and still have their titles visible.

**FIGURE 6-3**
The Cascade command overlaps document windows.

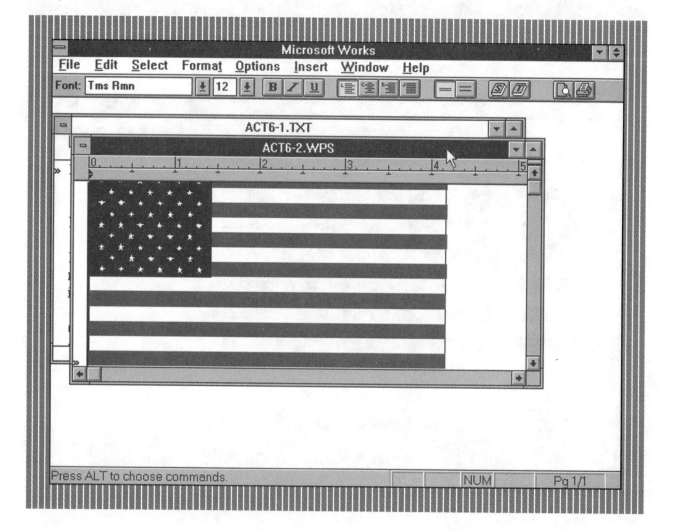

**TILE**   The Tile command in the Window menu arranges windows so that they do not overlap each other. The Tile command will place windows side by side as shown in Figure 6-4. An active tiled window will appear with a darkened title bar. If more than three windows are opened, the Tile command will stack them. Up to eight windows can be tiled on the screen at one time.

**FIGURE 6-4**
The Tile command places windows side by side.

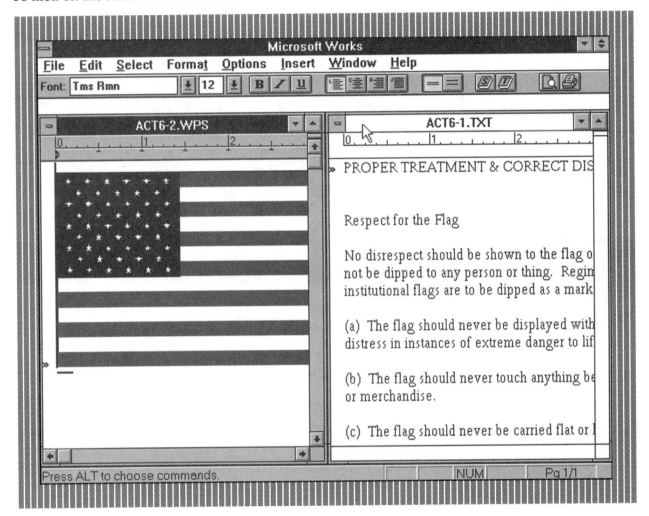

ACTIVITY
6-3

## Arranging Windows with Cascade and Tile

In this activity, you will arrange windows using the Cascade and Tile commands. *Act6-1.txt* and *act6-2.wps* should be on your screen. *Act6-2.wps* should be the active window.

1.   From the **Window** menu, choose **Cascade**. The windows are resized and cascaded, as in Figure 6-3.

2. From the **Window** menu, choose **Tile**. The windows are placed side by side, as in Figure 6-4.

3. Leave the files open for the next activity.

## Copying and Moving Text between Documents

Just as you can copy or move text within a document, you can copy or move data from one document to another. For example, you might copy a paragraph from one document to another, or you might move a whole section from one report to another. It is easiest to transfer text between two documents while the documents are tiled or cascaded.

**ACTIVITY 6-4**

### Copying and Moving Text between Documents

In this activity, you will copy and move text between two documents. *Act6-1.txt* and *act6-2.wps* should be tiled on your screen.

1. Click anywhere in *act6-1.txt* to make it the active window.

2. From the **Select** menu, choose **All**. The text in the document appears highlighted.

3. From the **Edit** menu, choose **Copy**. The text is placed on the Clipboard.

4. Click anywhere in the *act6-2.wps* window. *Act6-2.wps* becomes the active window.

5. Press the **Right Arrow** key to move the cursor to the right side of the flag. Press **Enter** three times to create two blank lines.

6. From the **Edit** menu, choose **Paste**. The text you copied from *act6-1.txt* is placed in *act6-2.wps*.

7. Click anywhere in the *act6-1.txt* window.

8. From the **File** menu, choose **Close**. *Act6-1.txt* closes, leaving *act6-2.wps* on the screen.

9. Click the **Maximize** button to maximize the *act6-2.wps* window.

Activity 6-4 continued

10. Drag the mouse pointer over the flag graphic and the title of the document.

11. Center the flag and the title of the document.

12. Change the style of the two headings (*Respect for the Flag* and *Time and Occasions for Display*) to bold style.

13. Save the document to your data disk as *flagdoc*. Leave the file open for the next activity.

## WORKING WITH MULTIPAGE DOCUMENTS

When a document is only one page long, it isn't hard to edit or format the text. These tasks become more challenging in multipage documents because you cannot see the whole document on your screen at once. Works provides several tools that will help you to get around in a long document and control how the pages of your document display on the screen.

### Splitting Windows

Works lets you view two parts of your document at once by using the Split command from the Window menu. Suppose you want to edit text and accompanying footnotes at the same time. By splitting your document, you can see both parts of the document. Each area of the document, called a *pane*, contains separate scroll bars to allow you to move through that part of the document.

**ACTIVITY
6-5**

### Splitting Windows

In this activity, you will split the document window. *Flagdoc.wps* should be on your screen.

1. Press **Ctrl+Home** to return to the beginning of the document.

2. From the **Window** menu, choose **Split**. A horizontal bar appears with the mouse pointer as a positioning marker.

Activity 6-5 continued

3. Position the bar so that the document window is divided into two equal parts.

**FIGURE 6-5**
The Split command divides the document window into two panes, each with an independent set of scroll bars and rulers.

4. Click the mouse button. The document window is split into two separate panes, each with independent scroll bars and rulers, as shown in Figure 6-5.

5. Press the **down scroll** arrow in the bottom pane of the split window. Notice that the document scrolls downward while the flag in the upper pane remains stationary.

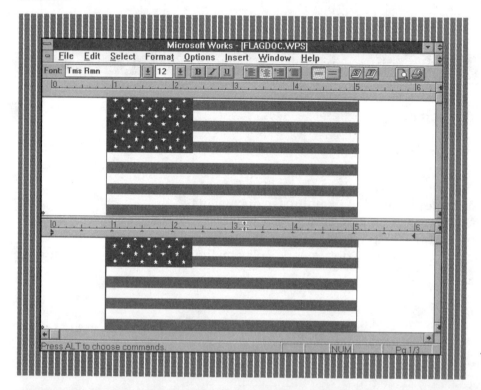

6. Place the mouse pointer on the horizontal bar until the pointer again turns into a positioning marker. Double-click on the split bar. The upper pane disappears.

7. Leave the file open for the next activity.

## Draft View

A multipage document might contain a variety of fonts, font styles, sizes, and typefaces. Choosing the Draft View command changes the different font options in a document to one font and size. In large documents, *Draft View* makes it easier to scroll from one place to another quickly because the computer does not have to draw fonts and graphics in the correct size and shape.

**ACTIVITY 6-6**

## Using Draft View

In this activity, you will use Draft View in a document. *Flagdoc.wps* should be on your screen.

Activity 6-6 continued

1. Press **Ctrl+Home** to return to the beginning of the document.

2. From the **Options** menu, choose **Draft View**. The text in the document appears in one font in one size, as shown in Figure 6-6.

3. Scroll through the document to observe the text in Draft View.

4. Again, choose **Draft View** from the **Options** menu. The normal text reappears.

5. Leave the file open for the next activity.

**FIGURE 6-6**
Choosing Draft View allows you to scroll through a document faster.

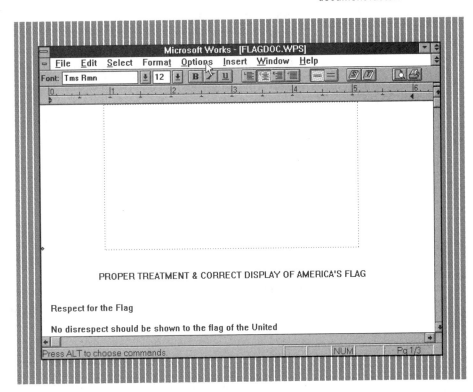

## The Go To Command

One of the quickest ways to move through a document is to use the Go To command. Go To allows you to skip to a specific page in a document. To skip to a page, choose Go To from the Select menu. Then key the page number you want to move to in the Go To box. Click OK. Works will move the cursor to the page number you specified.

## Paginate Now Command

Works automatically breaks long documents into pages by inserting page breaks. This process is called *pagination*. To keep from interrupting your work, Works paginates as you enter and edit text. Because Works is spending only part of its time paginating, it may need a few moments to repaginate your document completely. There may be times, however, when you need to see the result of pagination before you can continue your work. You can have Works stop everything it is doing and devote all its time to repaginating your document by choosing Paginate Now from the Options menu.

## Paragraph Breaks

Sometimes you may not want page breaks to split a paragraph or separate a paragraph from text following the paragraph. For example, you would not want a table to be split across two pages or a paragraph heading to be separated from the text following it. The Indents & Spacing command on the Format menu allows you to control how paragraphs break during pagination. If the Don't break paragraph option is checked in the Indents & Spacing dialog box, the paragraph will not be split by an automatic page break. If the Keep paragraph with next option is checked, the current paragraph and the one following it will appear on the same page. To use these options, place the cursor in the paragraph you want to affect and choose Indents & Spacing from the Format menu.

# FIND AND REPLACE

Using the Find and Replace commands, you can quickly search a document for every occurrence of a specific word or phrase. Find moves the cursor from its present position to the next occurrence of the word or phrase for which you are searching. Replace finds the text and then prompts you to replace it with new text.

Works allows you to find and replace words using the following options. By default, these commands will search the entire document. You can also find and replace words in a specific block of text by highlighting the text before you choose Find or Replace. You can find whole or partial words. For example, Works can find the word *all* or any word with *all* in it, such as *fall*, *horizontally*, or *alloy*. Works looks for words that match a specific capitalization that you type. For example, if you wanted to search for the word *page* in lower-case letters, Works would find *page* but not *Page* or *PAGE*. It is also possible to search for words using a question mark along with a word in the Find or Replace dialog box. Each question mark, called a *wildcard*, represents a single character in the same position in a word. See Table 6-1 for an example.

**TABLE 6-1**
Using Wildcards in the Word Processor

| To Find and Replace | Key |
|---|---|
| Both Caleb and Kaleb | ?aleb |
| Any five-letter word beginning with *a* and ending with *n* | a???n |
| June and July | Ju?? |

**ACTIVITY 6-7**

## Find and Replace Text

In this activity, you will use the Find and Replace commands to replace text in a document. *Flagdoc.wps* should be on your screen.

**FIGURE 6-7**
Key the word you are looking for in the Find dialog box.

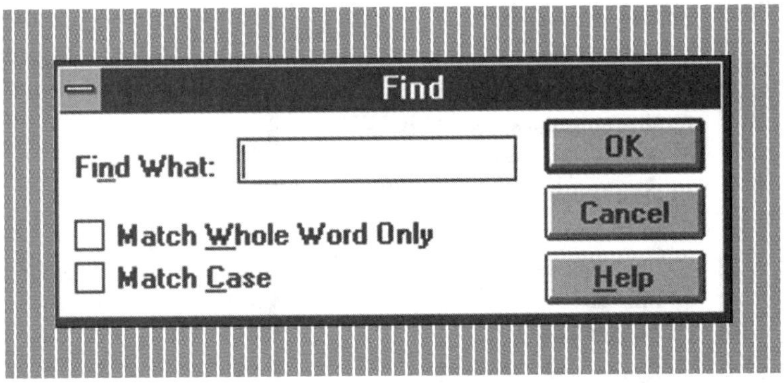

1. From the **Select** menu, choose **Find**. The Find dialog box appears, as shown in Figure 6-7.

2. In the **Find What** box, key **Lincoln?**

3. Click **OK**.

4. Works finds *Lincoln's* and highlights the word. Click the left mouse button to turn off highlighting.

5. Press **Ctrl+Home** to move the cursor to the beginning of the document.

**FIGURE 6-8**
The Replace dialog box contains different options to find and replace words.

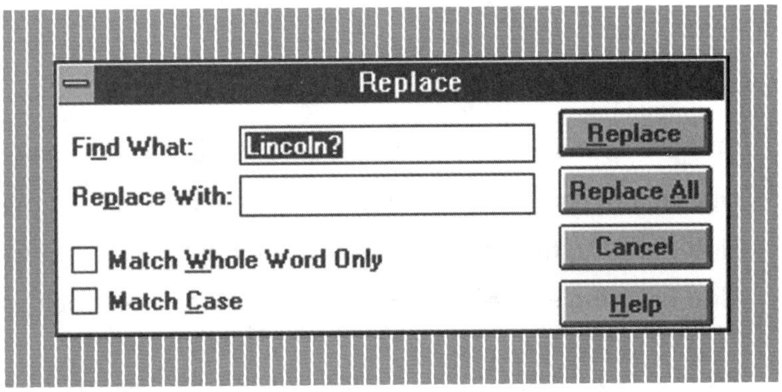

6. From the **Select** menu, choose **Replace**. The Replace dialog box appears, as shown in Figure 6-8.

7. In the **Find What** box, key **copy**. *Lincoln?* disappears after you press the first key.

8. Place the cursor in the Replace With box. Key **replica**.

9. Click **Replace All**. A message appears indicating the number of times that Works replaced the word *copy*. Click **OK**.

10. Save the document. Leave the file open for the next activity.

## SPECIAL CHARACTERS

Works has a number of special characters that can help you to format your document. You insert these characters using the Special Character

**FIGURE 6-9**
The Special Character dialog box contains several special character choices you can add to a document.

command. For example, you can insert characters that control hyphenation and that automatically print the time or the date. Special characters are particularly useful in headers and footers, as you will see in the next section.

To insert a special character, move the cursor to the place you want the character to appear. Choose Special Character from the Insert menu. In the Special Character dialog box, shown in Figure 6-9, choose the desired special character and click OK. Table 6-2 gives a listing of the special characters you can add to a document.

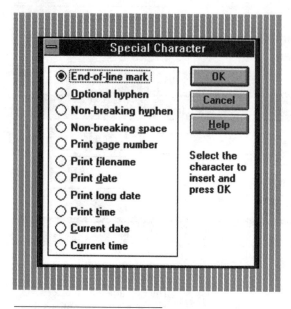

**TABLE 6-2**
Special Characters

| Character | Meaning |
| --- | --- |
| End-of-line mark | Starts a new line but not a new paragraph |
| Optional hyphen | Hyphenates a word if it is at the end of a line |
| Non-breaking hyphen | Prevents a hyphenated word from breaking at the end of a line |
| Non-breaking space | Prevents related words, such as first and last names, from breaking at the end of a line |
| Print page number | Inserts the current page number in a document and is displayed as *page* on the screen |
| Print filename | Inserts the filename in a document and is displayed as *filename* on the screen |
| Print date | Inserts the short form of the date on which a document was printed (for example, 5/01/9-) and is displayed as *date* on the screen |
| Print long date | Inserts the long form of the date on which a document was printed (for example, May 1, 199-) and is displayed as *longdate* on the screen |
| Print time | Inserts the time that a document was printed and is displayed as *time* on the screen |
| Current date | Inserts the current date in short form |
| Current time | Inserts the current time |

# HEADERS AND FOOTERS

**FIGURE 6-10**
Headers contain text that is printed at the top of a page, whereas footers are printed at the bottom of a page.

Headers and footers can be inserted by using the Headers and Footers command on the Edit menu. A *header* is text that is printed at the top of each page, whereas a *footer* is text that is printed at the bottom of each page, as shown in Figure 6-10. Standard headers and footers are centered horizontally on the page by default. Table 6-3 shows the codes that are inserted, beginning with an ampersand (Shift+7), to change the alignment and to add options, such as a page number or date.

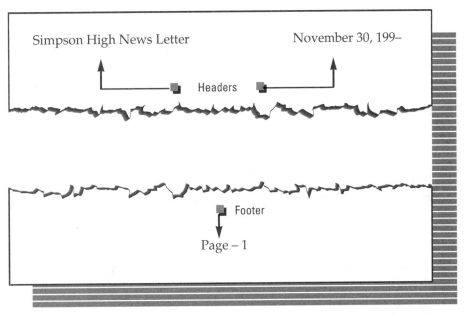

An alignment code, such as &L, &R, or &C, must precede the information that you want to align. For example, &L&D&RPage &P will print a header or footer with the short date left-aligned and the word *Page* and the page number right-aligned. The code &L&T&C&P&R&F will print the time left-aligned, the page number centered on the page, and the filename right-aligned.

Paragraph headers and footers may contain more than one line of text. The advantage of using this type of header or footer is that the ruler and Toolbar can be used to format the text. To create a multiline header choose Headers & Footers from the Edit menu. Click the check box next to Use header and footer paragraphs in the Headers & Footers dialog box. Click OK.

Works displays two special paragraphs, marked *H* and *F*, at the top of the document. If necessary, move the insertion point to the header paragraph by clicking in front of its paragraph mark. Key your header. To start a new line, press Shift+Enter.

**TABLE 6-3**
Header and Footer Codes

| To | Key |
|---|---|
| Align left | &L |
| Align right | &R |
| Center | &C |
| Print the page number | &P |
| Print the short date (1/01/9-) | &D |
| Print the long date (January 1, 199-) | &N |
| Print the time | &T |
| Print the filename | &F |
| Print an ampersand | && |

**ACTIVITY
6-8**

## Working with Headers and Footers

In this activity, you will add headers and footers to a document. *Flagdoc.wps* should be on your screen.

**FIGURE 6-11**

The Headers & Footers dialog box contains text boxes to key headers and footers.

1. From the **Edit** menu, choose **Headers & Footers**. The Headers & Footers dialog box appears with the cursor blinking in the Header box, as shown in Figure 6-11.

2. Key **&LYour Name&R&P**. Click the box next to the *No header on 1st page* option. Usually headers and footers are omitted on the first page of a document.

3. Place the cursor in the Footer box.

4. Key **U.S. Code TITLE 36**. Click the box next to the *No footer on 1st page* option.

**FIGURE 6-12**

Headers repeat at the top of the page; footers repeat at the bottom of the page.

5. Click **OK**. The headers and footers are inserted but you won't be able to see the changes on your screen. Use the Print Preview command to view the headers and footers, as shown in Figure 6-12. You should see a header with your name left-aligned and page number right-aligned. *U.S. Code TITLE 36* should be the centered footer.

6. Now you will insert the same information using paragraph headers and footers. From the **Edit** menu, choose **Headers & Footers**. The Headers & Footers dialog box appears.

7. Click the check box next to the *Use header and footer paragraphs* option.

Activity 6-8 continued

8.    Click **OK**. The document window appears with paragraph header and footer marks, as in Figure 6-13.

9.    Place the cursor after the paragraph header mark, *H.* Key your name.

10.    Press **Tab** twice to move the cursor to the right-aligned tab stop.

11.    From the **Insert** menu, choose **Special Character**. The Special Character dialog box appears. Choose the **Print page number** option. Click **OK**. The symbol *\*page\** is inserted into the document indicating that the page number will appear when the document is printed.

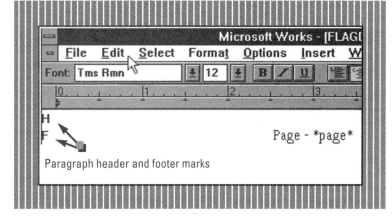

12.    Place the cursor after the paragraph footer mark, *F.* Press the **Delete** key until the default *Page - \*page\** code is deleted.

13.    Press **Tab** once to move the cursor to the centered tab stop.

14.    Key **U.S. Code TITLE 36**.

15.    Highlight the paragraph headers and footers. Change the headers and footers to a sans serif font. Review Chapter 4 if you need to refresh your memory on fonts. Change the font size to 8 point. If your computer does not have 8 point, change the headers and footers to a size smaller than the default font. Use Print Preview to view your changes.

16.    Press the left mouse button to turn off the highlight. Save the document. Leave the file open for the next activity.

## FOOTNOTES

A *footnote* is used to document quotations, figures, summaries, or other text that you do not want to include in the body of your document. Footnotes can be edited, deleted, moved, or copied like other text. After you create a footnote, a number or the symbol you specified in the Footnote dialog box will appear in the document and the corresponding footnotes will appear printed at the end of the document.

# ACTIVITY 6-9

**FIGURE 6-14**

You can represent footnotes in the text with numbers or symbols.

**FIGURE 6-15**

Footnotes can be edited, deleted, moved, or copied in the footnote pane.

## Working with Footnotes

In this activity, you will add footnotes to your document. *Flagdoc.wps* should be on your screen.

1. Place the cursor after the period following the word *honor* in the first paragraph of the document.

2. From the **Insert** menu, choose **Footnote**. The Footnote dialog box appears, as shown in Figure 6-14. The Numbered option appears highlighted in the Footnote Type box. This indicates that your footnotes will be numbered.

3. Click **OK**. The Footnote pane appears at the bottom of the document window with the cursor blinking after the number *1*, as in Figure 6-15.

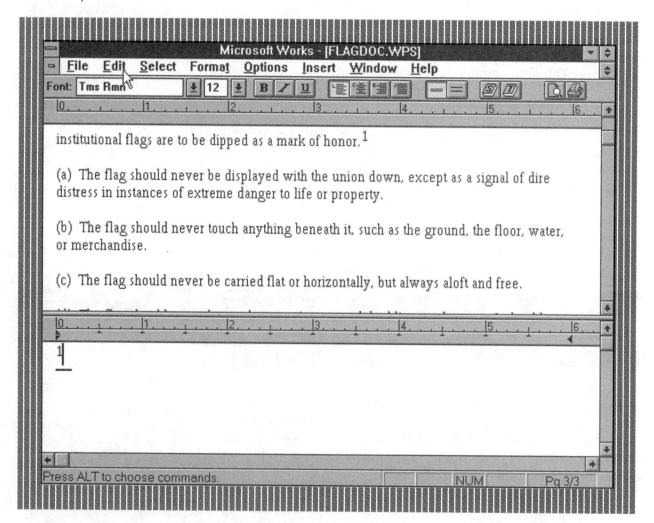

Activity 6-9 continued

4.   Key **Section 176. Respect for the Flag.**

5.   Scroll down in the document window until the heading *Time and Occasions for Display* appears. Place the cursor after the word *Display* in the heading.

6.   From the **Insert** menu, choose **Footnote**. After the Footnote dialog box appears, click **OK**.

7.   The cursor appears blinking after the number *2* in the footnote pane. Key **Section 174. Time and Occasions for Display.**

8.   Choose **Show Footnotes** from the **Options** menu to hide the Footnote pane.

9.   Use Print Preview to view the footnotes you added. They appear at the end of the document.

10.   Save the document. Leave the file open for the next activity.

# BOOKMARKS

A *bookmark* is a hidden code that is inserted into a document to mark a specific place. You might want to insert a bookmark, for example, to mark a date you need to check, a paragraph you want to edit later, or as mentioned earlier in the chapter, a specific page in the document. After you have inserted the bookmark code, Works will take you right to the bookmark so that you don't have to scroll through your document.

## Inserting a Bookmark

To insert a bookmark, first place the cursor at the point you want the bookmark to appear. Then choose Bookmark Name from the Insert menu. Key the name of the bookmark in the Name box and click OK. You can now use the Go To command to find the bookmark.

## Finding a Bookmark

Earlier, you learned that the Go To command will take you to a specific page. It will also take you to a bookmark. To find your bookmark, choose Go To from the Select menu. The Go To dialog box will appear. The Names box shows a list of the bookmark names in use. You can either key the name of your bookmark in the Go To box or highlight the name of your bookmark and then click OK. Works will almost instantly jump to the bookmark you have inserted into your document. If you later decide that you want to delete a bookmark, choose Bookmark Name from the Insert menu, select the name in the Names box, click Delete, and then click Close.

## ADDING BORDERS TO PARAGRAPHS

*Borders* are single, double, or bold lines that surround a paragraph and are used to emphasize the text. For example, you might want to place a bold border around the title of a document.

## ACTIVITY 6-10

### Adding Borders

In this activity, you will add borders to paragraphs in a document. *Flagdoc.wps* should be on your screen.

1.  Place the cursor in the title of the document.

2.  From the **Format** menu, choose **Border**. The Border dialog box appears, as shown in Figure 6-16.

3.  In the *Border* box, choose **Outline**. In the *Line Style* box, choose **Double**.  Click **OK**.

4.  A double-lined border is placed around the title of the document.

5.  Drag the left-indent marker to the right until the border is against the left side of the title. Drag the right-indent marker to the left until the border is against the right side of the title, as shown in Figure 6-17.

6.  Save the document. Leave the file open for the next activity.

**FIGURE 6-16**
The Border dialog box allows you to change the style of borders.

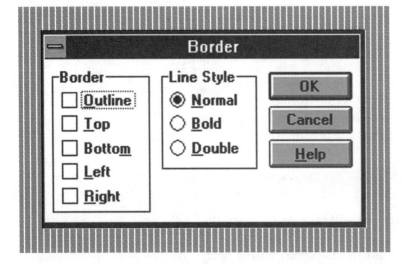

Activity 6-10 continued

**FIGURE 6-17**
Borders are useful when you
want to emphasize text.

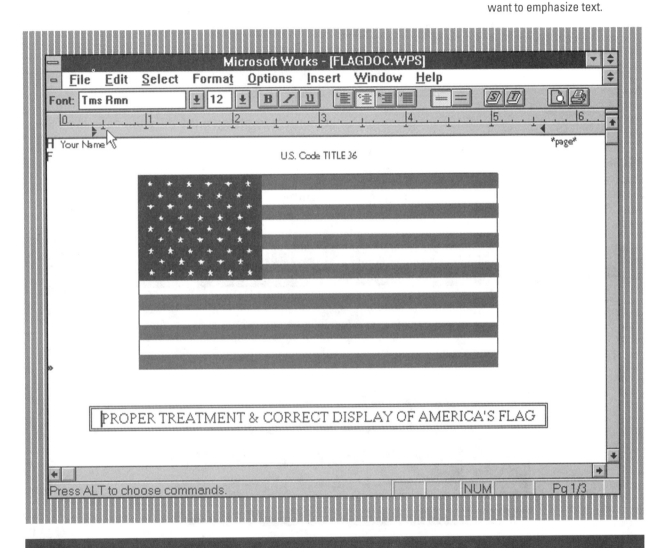

## SHOW ALL CHARACTERS

The Show All Characters command is used to view hidden special characters. You can view special characters from the keyboard, such as space bar marks or carriage return marks, or special characters from the Insert menu, such as an end-of-line mark. Being able to see these hidden characters can help you in editing your text.

**ACTIVITY
6-11**

### Showing Hidden Characters

In this activity, you will show hidden characters in a document. *Flagdoc.wps* should be on your screen.

1. From the **Options** menu, choose **Show All Characters**. Works makes the hard carriage return characters and space bar characters visible, as shown in Figure 6-18.

2. Scroll through the document to observe the different characters.

3. Again, choose **Show All Characters** from the **Options** menu. The characters are hidden.

4. Save and print the document.

5. Close the document.

**FIGURE 6-18**
Choosing the Show All Characters command makes hidden formatting characters appear.

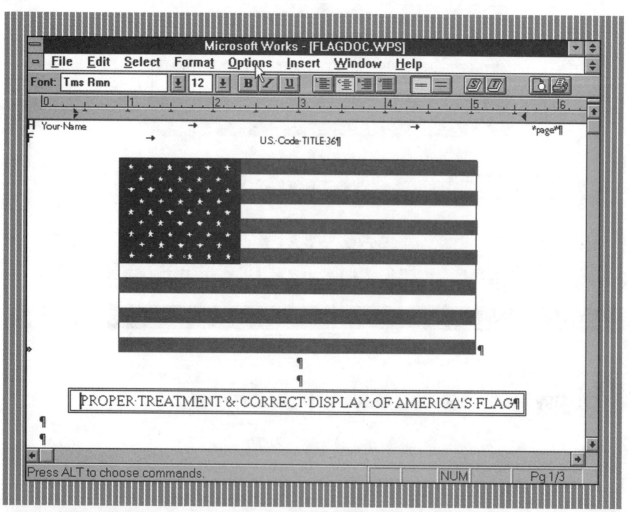

# PRINTING IN PORTRAIT AND LANDSCAPE ORIENTATION

**FIGURE 6-19**
Documents printed in portrait orientation are longer than they are wide.

Documents printed in *portrait orientation*, as seen in Figure 6-19, print pages longer than they are wide. The default in Works is set to print pages in portrait orientation. In contrast, documents printed in *landscape orientation*, as seen in Figure 6-20, print pages wider than they are long. Most documents are printed in portrait orientation. Some documents, however, such as documents with graphics or numerical information, look better when printed in landscape orientation.

## MOUNTAIN CABIN OPEN HOUSE

This beautiful mountain cabin features three bedrooms, two bathrooms, a wood burning fireplace, and a hot tub.

Located five miles south of Manytree, Colorado, on Old Elm Road, this cabin is just 20 miles from Slippery Slope Ski Resort.

Come see for yourself on November 19.

R.S.V.P. (845) 555-0097

**FIGURE 6-20**
Documents printed in landscape orientation are wider than they are long.

# Announcing

The Choir and Drama Students Present:

Ned Ermal's

## THE HARMONIOUS JANGLE OF SOUND

Friday, October 25, Saturday, October 26, 19--
8:00 p.m. at G.H. Snyder Auditorium

**ACTIVITY 6-12**

## Printing in Portrait and Landscape Orientation

In this activity, you will change the printing orientation of a document.

**FIGURE 6-21**

The Printer Setup dialog box contains options to change the way you want your document printed.

1.  Open *act6-12.wps* from your template disk. Use Print Preview to view the document before you make any changes.

2.  From the **File** menu, choose **Page Setup & Margins**. The Page Setup & Margins dialog box appears.

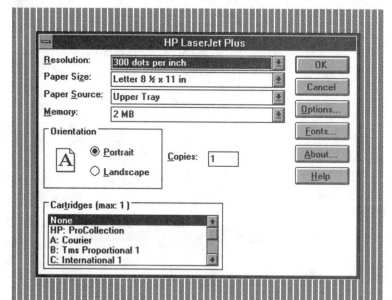

3.  Delete the *11"* measurement in the Page length box. Key **8.5**.

4.  Delete the *8.5"* measurement in the Page width box. Key **11**. Click **OK**.

5.  From the **File** menu, choose **Printer Setup**. The Printer Setup dialog box appears, as shown in Figure 6-21.

6.  In the **Orientation** box, choose the **Landscape** option. Click **OK**. Use Print Preview to view the changes you have made.

7.  Save the document to your data disk as *landscap*.

8.  Print and close the document.

## WORD COUNT

After you have completed a document, you may want to know how many words it contains. The Word Count command can count words in your document quickly. The cursor can be located anywhere in the document when you use Word Count. You can count the words in a specific section of text by first highlighting the text and then using Word Count. To use Word Count, choose Word Count from the Options menu. A message will appear with the number of words in the document. Click OK.

# SUMMARY

A text file does not contain any codes, such as those used to control fonts, margins, and paragraph formatting. Working with multiple documents is made easier by the Cascade and Tile commands. These commands allow you to position windows on the screen. Multipage documents are sometimes difficult to edit. The Split command, Draft View command, paragraph breaks, and the Paginate Now command allow you to work with multipage documents more effectively.

The Find and Replace commands are useful for quickly searching a document for a specific word. Works allows you to add headers, footers, special characters, footnotes, and bookmarks to a document. Borders can be added to emphasize text. The Show All Characters command reveals hidden characters.

In portrait orientation a printed page is longer than it is wide. In landscape orientation a printed page is wider than it is long.

# CHALLENGES

## TRUE/FALSE

Circle **T** or **F** to show whether the statement is true or false.

T    F    1.    A text file contains codes that control fonts, margins, and paragraph formatting.

T    F    2.    The Cascade command overlaps open document windows.

T    F    3.    You can split a document into two panes by using the Split command.

T    F    4.    Each area of a split document that contains a separate set of scroll bars and rulers is called a pagination.

T    F    5.    The Draft View command is found on the Options menu.

T    F    6.    The Find command will find and replace a word.

T    F    7.    Headers and footers can be inserted by using the Headers & Footers command on the Edit menu.

T    F    8.    You can use only numbers for footnotes.

T    F    9.    The Show All Characters command is used to view hidden special characters.

T    F    10.    The default in Works is set to print pages in landscape orientation.

# COMPLETION

**Write the correct answer in the space provided.**

1. What type of filename extension does Works attach to the end of a text file?

2. What command places open document windows side by side?

3. Which command updates pagination in large documents quickly?

4. Which command finds text and then prompts you to replace the text?

5. Where are standard headers and footers placed on a page by default?

6. After you have inserted a bookmark, which command must you use to find it?

7. When might you want to use borders?

8. Name the three types of line styles for borders contained in the Border dialog box.

9. On which menu is the Show All Characters command found?

10. What is the difference between landscape orientation and portrait orientation?

# APPLICATIONS

## APPLICATION 6-1

In the blank after the header or footer code, write the header or footer that will be printed.

1. &R Page-21

_____

2. &LChapter II&R&P

_____

3. &L&P&CBIBLIOGRAPHY&R&N

_____

4. &RHeaders && Footers

_____

5. &C&T&R&F

_____

6. &LSenior Theme&R&D

_____

7. &L&T&C&N&RPg. &P

_____

8. &L&D

_____

9. &&F completed on &

_____

10. &L&N&R&T

---

# APPLICATION 6-2

In the blank space, write the letter from the right-hand column that matches the special character and its meaning.

_____  1. End-of-line mark

_____  2. Optional hyphen

_____  3. Non-breaking hyphen

_____  4. Non-breaking space

_____  5. Print page number

_____  6. Print date

_____  7. Print long date

_____  8. Print time

_____  9. Current date

_____  10. Current time

a. Inserts the date a document was printed (for example, 5/01/9-) and is displayed as *date* on the screen

b. Inserts the current time

c. Starts a new line but not a new paragraph

d. Inserts the current page number in a document and is displayed as *page* on the screene.

e. Hyphenates a word if it is at the end of a line

f. Inserts the time that a document was printed and is displayed as *time* on the screen

g. Prevents related words, such as first and last names, from breaking at the end of a line

h. Inserts the date that a document was printed (for example, May 1, 199-) and is displayed as *longdate* on the screen

i. Prevents a hyphenated word from breaking at the end of a line

j. Inserts the current date in short form

---

# APPLICATION 6-3

1.   Open *update.wps* from your data disk.

2.   Find the name *Darrel* in the document and replace it with *Dwayne*.

3.   Create a centered footer that reads *Congratulations Debate Team!*

4.   Add a double-lined border to the title of the document. Use the left- and right-indent markers to adjust the size of the border to fit the title.

5.  Add a normal border to the line that begins with *Briarcliff High School*.

6.  Save the document as *flyer*. Close the document.

---

# APPLICATION 6-4

1.  Open *mountain.wps* from your data disk.

2.  Find the word *frequently* in the document and replace it with *usually*.

3.  Add a paragraph header with your name left-aligned and use a special character to insert the page number right-aligned. The header should not print on the first page.

4.  Use a special character in a paragraph footer to insert the centered long form of the date. The footer should not print on the first page.

5.  Change the font of the headers and footers to Times New Roman.

6.  Save the document as *headfoot*. Close the document.

# PART 3

# SPREADSHEET

# 7

# SPREADSHEET BASICS

## WHAT IS A SPREADSHEET?

A *spreadsheet* is a grid of rows and columns containing numbers and other information. The purpose of a spreadsheet is to solve problems that involve numbers. Before computers, spreadsheets were created with pencils on ruled paper. Calculators were used to solve complicated mathematical operations (see Figure 7-1). Computer spreadsheets also contain rows and columns, but they perform calculations much faster and more reliably than spreadsheets created with pencil, paper, and calculator.

Spreadsheets are used in many ways. For example, a spreadsheet can be used to calculate a grade in a class, prepare a budget for the next few months, or determine payments to be made on a loan. The primary advantage of the spreadsheet is the ability to complete complex and repetitive calculations accurately, quickly, and easily. For example, you might use a spreadsheet to calculate your grade in a class. However, your instructor may use a spreadsheet to calculate grades for the entire class.

Besides calculating rapidly and accurately, spreadsheets offer flexibility. Making changes to an existing spreadsheet is usually as easy

**FIGURE 7-1**

Spreadsheets automate
calculations and can make
paper, pencil, and calculator
unnecessary.

as pointing and clicking with the mouse. Suppose, for example, you
have prepared a budget on a spreadsheet and have overestimated the
amount of money you will need to spend on books. You may change a
single entry in your spreadsheet and watch the entire spreadsheet
recalculate the new budgeted amount. You can imagine the work this
change would require if you were calculating the budget with pencil
and paper.

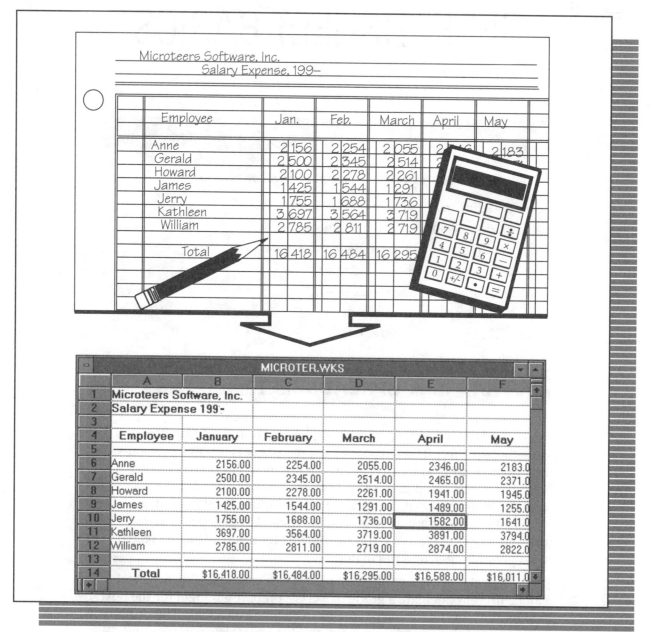

## PARTS OF A SPREADSHEET

You can open a new spreadsheet by starting Works and clicking the
Spreadsheet button in the Startup dialog box. When the spreadsheet

appears on the screen, you will see some of the basic features that you learned in the word processor: the title bar, the menu bar, and the Toolbar. However, other parts of the spreadsheet, such as the formula bar and the grid of cells created by columns and rows, do not appear in the word processor. Figure 7-2 shows the parts of the spreadsheet.

*Columns* appear vertically and are identified by letters at the top of the spreadsheet window. *Rows* appear horizontally and are identified by numbers on the left side of the spreadsheet window. A *cell* is the intersection of a row and column and is identified by a *cell reference*, the column letter and row number (for example, A1, B2, C4).

**FIGURE 7-2**

Some parts of the spreadsheet are similar to the word processor screen. The spreadsheet, however, has additional parts used with numerical data.

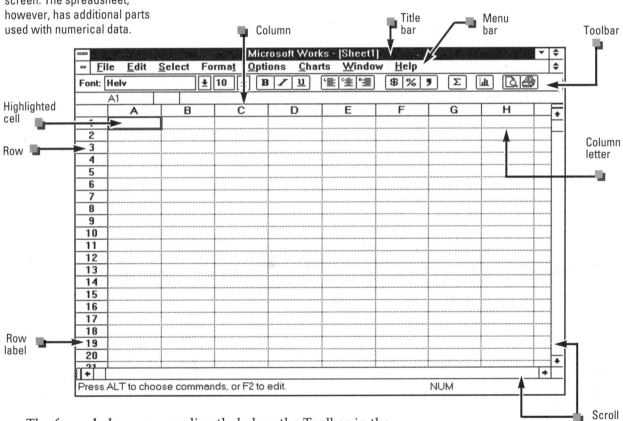

The *formula bar* appears directly below the Toolbar in the spreadsheet. On the far left side of the formula bar is the cell reference area that identifies the *active cell*. The active cell is the cell ready for data entry. On the grid of cells, the active cell is surrounded by a dark border. Your screen currently shows a border around the active cell on the spreadsheet, and the reference of the cell, A1, should appear in the cell reference area of the formula bar.

In the word processor, the point at which a character is keyed is indicated by the cursor. In the spreadsheet the entry point is called a *highlight*. You may change the active cell by moving the highlight from one cell to another.

# OPENING AN EXISTING SPREADSHEET

When you choose Spreadsheet, Works automatically opens a new, untitled spreadsheet, such as the one that currently appears on the screen. You may open an existing spreadsheet by using the File menu.

## ACTIVITY 7-1

### Opening an Existing Spreadsheet

In this activity, you will close the file on your screen and open an existing spreadsheet file.

1. From the **File** menu, choose the **Close** command. The spreadsheet on your screen will disappear from the screen.

2. From the **File** menu, choose the **Open Existing File** command. The Open dialog box will appear.

3. In the **Drives** selection box, click the down arrow to show your computer's drives.

**FIGURE 7-3**

The spreadsheet is ideal for solving numerical problems, such as constructing a summer budget.

4. Click the drive containing your template disk in the Drives list. The files on the disk will appear in the File Name list.

5. Double-click the filename **act7-1.wks** in the File Name list. The spreadsheet will appear on the screen and should be similar to the one shown in Figure 7-3.

6. Leave *act7-1.wks* on the screen for the next activity.

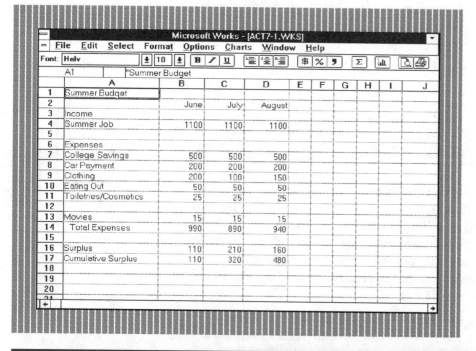

# MOVING THE HIGHLIGHT IN A SPREADSHEET

When working with a large spreadsheet, you may not be able to view the entire spreadsheet on the screen. You can scroll throughout the spreadsheet using the mouse by dragging the scroll box in the scroll bar to the desired position. You can also move the highlight to different parts of the spreadsheet using direction keys or the Go To command in the Select menu.

*Note: When the arrow keys are held down, the movement will repeat, allowing you to move quickly.*

## Using Keys to Move the Highlight

You can move the highlight by pressing certain keys or key combinations. Table 7-1 illustrates the use of these keys. You will see that many of these keys and key combinations are familiar to you from the word processor.

**TABLE 7-1**
You may move the highlight in the spreadsheet by pressing direction keys.

| HIGHLIGHT MOVEMENT | |
|---|---|
| **To Move** | **Press** |
| Left one column | Left Arrow |
| Right one column | Right Arrow |
| Up one row | Up Arrow |
| Down one row | Down Arrow |
| To the first cell of a row | Home |
| To the last cell of a row containing data | End |
| To Cell A1 | Ctrl+Home |
| To the last row or column containing data | Ctrl+End |
| Up one window | Page Up |
| Down one window | Page Down |
| Left one window | Ctrl+Page Up |
| Right one window | Ctrl+Page Down |

## Using the Go To Command to Move in the Spreadsheet

You may want to move the highlight to a cell that does not appear on the screen. The fastest way to move to the cell is by using the Go To command in the Select menu and then designating the cell reference of the cell in which you want the highlight to appear. The F5 key may be used as a shortcut to access the Go To command.

**ACTIVITY
7-2**

## Moving the Highlight in the Spreadsheet

In this activity, you will move the highlight in a spreadsheet. Your screen now shows the spreadsheet *act7-1.wks*.

1.  Move to the last cell in the spreadsheet by pressing **Ctrl+End**. The highlight will move to the lower right side of the spreadsheet.

2.  Move to the first cell of the row by pressing **Home**. The highlight will appear in a cell containing the words *Cumulative Surplus*.

3.  Move up one cell by pressing the **Up Arrow** key. The highlight will appear in a cell containing the word *Surplus*.

4.  Move to B4 by using the Go To command:

    a.  Press **F5**. The Go To dialog box will appear.

    b.  Key **B4**.

    c.  Click **OK**. The highlight should move to B4.

5.  Leave *act7-1.wks* on the screen for the next activity.

# SELECTING A GROUP OF CELLS

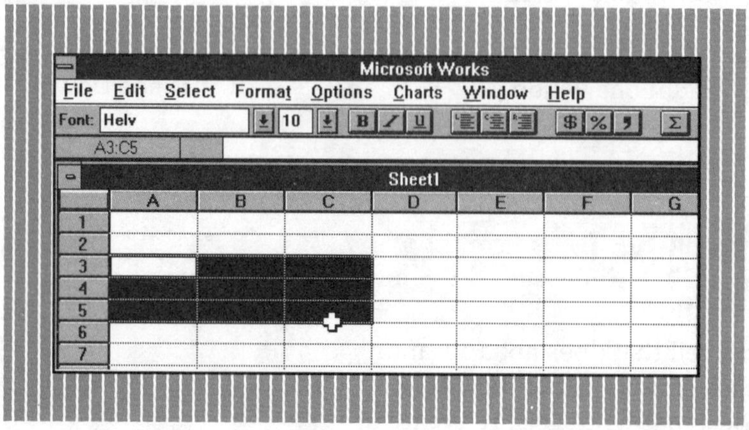

**FIGURE 7-4**

A range is selected by dragging the highlight from one corner of a range to the opposite corner.

In later chapters, you will perform operations on more than one cell at a time. A selected group of cells is referred to as a *range*. In a range, all cells touch each other and form a rectangle. The range is identified by the cell in the upper left corner and the cell in the lower right corner, separated by a colon (for example, A3:C5). To select a range of cells, place the highlight in one corner of the range of cells and drag the highlight to the cell in the opposite corner. As you drag the highlight, the range of selected cells will become shaded (except for the cell you originally selected), as in Figure 7-4.

# ENTERING DATA INTO A CELL

Spreadsheet cells may contain data in the form of text, numbers, or formulas. Text consists of alphabetical characters and is usually in the form of headings, labels, or explanatory notes. In the formula bar, textual data is preceded by a quotation mark, which indicates that the data in the cell will not be used in calculations performed by the spreadsheet. Numbers can be in the form of values, dates, or times. Formulas are equations that calculate a value stored in a cell. (Formulas will be discussed in Chapter 9.)

Data is entered by keying the data and then either clicking the Enter button or pressing the Enter key. If you choose not to enter data, you may simply click the Cancel button in the formula bar (indicated by an *X*) and the keyed data will be deleted.

**ACTIVITY
7-3**

## Entering Text and Numbers in Cells

In this activity, you will enter text and numbers into cells of the spreadsheet *act7-1.wks*. Notice that Row 12 does not contain data. Suppose you would like to change the budget to include expenses of $25 a month for compact discs.

1. Move the highlight to A12 and key **Compact Discs**. As you key, the letters will appear both in the cell and in the formula bar.

2. Click the **Enter** button (indicated by a check mark) in the formula bar or press the **Enter** key. Notice that the words in the formula bar are preceded by a quotation mark to indicate that they are textual data that will not be used in calculations.

3. Move to B12 and key **25**. Before entering the data by clicking the Enter button, notice the total expenses for June are 990.

4. Click the **Enter** button. The amount of total expenses for June changes from 990 to 1015. You can now appreciate the value of the spreadsheet in making quick calculations when data in the budget problem change. Also, notice the data, 25, is not preceded by a quotation mark. This is because the data is numerical and may be used in calculations in the spreadsheet.

5. Enter **25** into C12 and D12. Notice how the spreadsheet recalculates the amounts each time you make a change. Your screen should appear similar to Figure 7-5.

6. Leave *act7-1.wks* on the screen for the next activity.

Activity 7-3 continued

---

**FIGURE 7-5**

Both text and numbers may be
entered into spreadsheet cells.

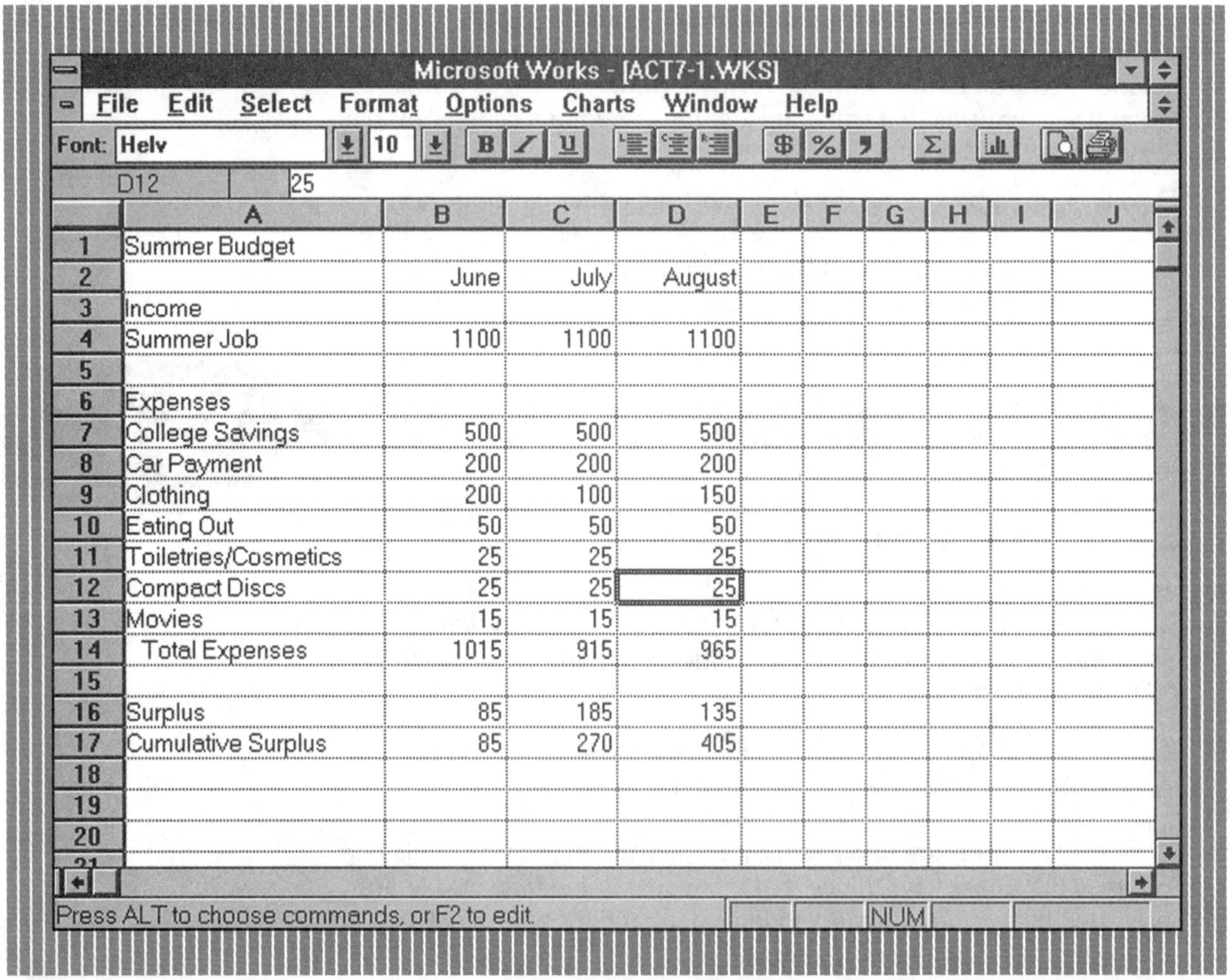

| | A | B | C | D | E | F | G | H | I | J |
|---|---|---|---|---|---|---|---|---|---|---|
| 1 | Summer Budget | | | | | | | | | |
| 2 | | June | July | August | | | | | | |
| 3 | Income | | | | | | | | | |
| 4 | Summer Job | 1100 | 1100 | 1100 | | | | | | |
| 5 | | | | | | | | | | |
| 6 | Expenses | | | | | | | | | |
| 7 | College Savings | 500 | 500 | 500 | | | | | | |
| 8 | Car Payment | 200 | 200 | 200 | | | | | | |
| 9 | Clothing | 200 | 100 | 150 | | | | | | |
| 10 | Eating Out | 50 | 50 | 50 | | | | | | |
| 11 | Toiletries/Cosmetics | 25 | 25 | 25 | | | | | | |
| 12 | Compact Discs | 25 | 25 | 25 | | | | | | |
| 13 | Movies | 15 | 15 | 15 | | | | | | |
| 14 | Total Expenses | 1015 | 915 | 965 | | | | | | |
| 15 | | | | | | | | | | |
| 16 | Surplus | 85 | 185 | 135 | | | | | | |
| 17 | Cumulative Surplus | 85 | 270 | 405 | | | | | | |
| 18 | | | | | | | | | | |
| 19 | | | | | | | | | | |
| 20 | | | | | | | | | | |

Microsoft Works - [ACT7-1.WKS]

File   Edit   Select   Format   Options   Charts   Window   Help

Font: Helv     10   B / U         $ % ,  Σ

D12          25

Press ALT to choose commands, or F2 to edit.          NUM

---

Sometimes the data you key will not fit in the column. When the
data is wider than the column, Works will respond by displaying a
series of number signs (######) in the cell. This problem is easily
remedied by placing the mouse pointer on the boundary of the right
edge of the column heading. The pointer will then turn into a vertical
bar with a double-headed arrow in the middle. (See Figure 7-6.) To
widen the column, drag the double-headed arrow to the right until the
column is the desired size.

**FIGURE 7-6**
To widen a column, drag the
vertical bar with the double-
headed arrow to the right.

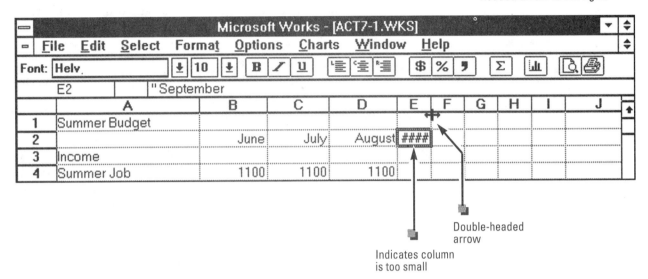

**ACTIVITY
7-4**

## Widening a Column

In this activity, you will widen a column on the spreadsheet *act7-1.wks*.
Add a column heading for September and widen the column by
following these steps:

1.  Key **September** into E2 and press **Enter**. Because the word is too
    large for the column, a series of number signs (#) will appear in the
    cell.

2.  Place the mouse pointer to the right of the heading for Column E.
    The pointer should turn into a double-headed arrow.

3.  Drag the double-headed arrow to the right and release. The word
    *September* should appear in E2. If it does not, you may need to drag
    the double-headed arrow farther.

4.  Leave *act7-1.wks* on the screen for the next activity.

# CHANGING DATA IN A CELL

As you work with the spreadsheet, you may change your mind about data or make a mistake. If so, you may edit, replace, or clear existing data in cells of the spreadsheet.

## Editing Data

Editing is performed when only minor changes to cell data are necessary. Data in a cell may be edited in the formula bar by using the Edit key, or F2 on your keyboard. To edit data in a cell, select the cell by placing the highlight in the cell and pressing F2. A cursor similar to the one in the word processor will appear in the formula bar. You may use the cursor to change the data shown in the formula bar and then reenter the data.

You may prefer to use the mouse to edit a cell. First, click the cell you want to edit; then click in the formula bar at the place you want to change the data. After you have made the changes you need, click the Enter button.

## Replacing Data

Cell contents are usually replaced when you must make significant changes to cell data. To replace cell contents, select the cell, key the new data, and enter the data by clicking the Enter button or by pressing the Enter key.

## Clearing Data

Clearing a cell will empty the cell of all its contents. To clear an active cell, you may either press the Delete key or choose the Clear command in the Edit menu.

## ACTIVITY 7-5

### Changing Data in a Cell

In this activity, you will change data in a cell by editing, replacing, and clearing. The file *act7-1.wks* should be on your screen. Make the following changes to cells in the spreadsheet:

1.  Cell A16 contains the word *Surplus*. Edit the cell so that it will contain the words *Cash Surplus*.

    a.  Move the highlight to **A16**.

    b.  Press **F2**. A cursor should appear in the formula bar.

Activity 7-5 continued

    c.   Move the cursor between the *quotation mark* and the the *S* by pressing the Left Arrow.

    d.   Key **Cash** and a space.

    e.   Click the **Enter** button on the formula bar. The edited contents should appear in the cell.

2.   A3 now contains the word *Income*. Replace this word with the word *Revenue*.

    a.   Move the highlight to **A3**.

    b.   Key **Revenue**.

    c.   Click the **Enter** button on the formula bar.

3.   In the previous activity, you entered the word *September* into E3. Suppose you change your mind and now want to delete that entry.

    a.   Move the highlight to **E2**.

    b.   Press the **Delete** key. The contents should be cleared from the cell. Your screen should appear similar to Figure 7-7.

4.   Leave *act.7-1.wks* on the screen for the next activity.

**FIGURE 7-7**

Changes may be made to a cell in a spreadsheet by editing or replacing data.

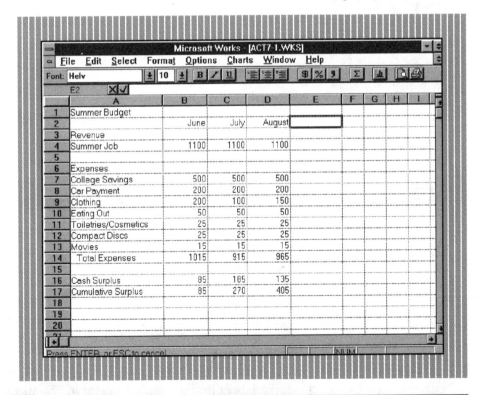

# CHANGING CELL APPEARANCES

**FIGURE 7-8**

The appearance of cell contents may be changed in style, alignment, and format.

You can change the appearance of a cell's contents to make them easier to read. In this section, you will learn to alter the appearance of cell contents by changing the font, font size, style, alignment, format, and borders. Examples of alternative appearances are shown in Figure 7-8. Most of the changes use the Toolbar, shown in Figure 7-9, which provides shortcuts to many spreadsheet commands.

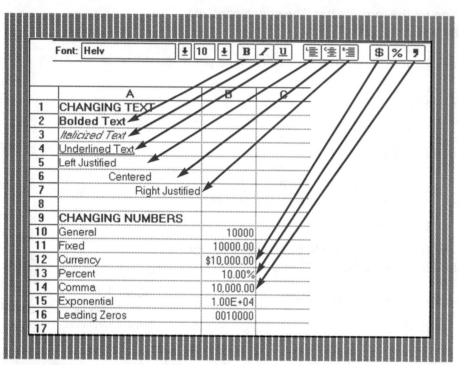

**FIGURE 7-9**

Spreadsheet cells can be formatted quickly using the Toolbar.

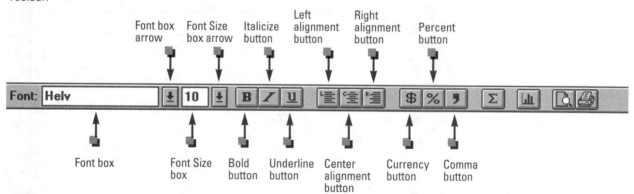

## Fonts and Font Sizes

The font and font size may significantly affect the readability of the spreadsheet if you decide to print it. The number and types of fonts available are determined by the printer you are using. The font and font size you specify will apply to the entire spreadsheet. Works does not permit more than one font or font size in a single spreadsheet.

To change the font of the spreadsheet, click the Font box arrow in the Toolbar and choose the name of the font you desire. Use the same procedure to specify the font size by clicking the Font Size box arrow. The Font box arrow and Font Size box arrow are illustrated in the margin.

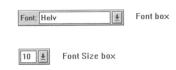

## Style

Bolding, italicizing, or underlining can add emphasis to the contents of a cell. Highlight the cell or cells you want to change and click the appropriate style button in the Toolbar. To return the contents of the cell to a normal style, simply click the button again.

## Cell Alignment

You may align the contents of a cell or cells in three ways: against the left margin of the cell, in the center of the cell, or against the right margin of the cell. Works will automatically align all text entries (those preceded by a quotation mark when viewed in the formula bar) with the left side of the cell. All numbers are aligned on the right side of the cell unless a different alignment is specified. To change the alignment of the cell, place the highlight in the cell and click the alignment button you prefer.

## Formats

Several cell formats are available for the spreadsheet. The default format is called *general format,* which accommodates both text and numerical data. However, you can use several other formats (see Table 7-2). Works includes the most frequently used formats on the Toolbar: currency, percent, and comma. You may format a cell in this way by highlighting the cell and clicking the appropriate tool button. However, you may want to use some of the other available formats. These formats are accessed in the Format menu.

## Borders

Emphasis may be added to a cell by placing a border around its edges. You may place the border around the entire cell or only on certain sides of the cell.

**TABLE 7-2**
Cells of a spreadsheet may be
formatted in several ways.

| Format | Display |
|---|---|
| General | The default format; displays both text and numerical data as keyed |
| Fixed | Displays numerical data with a fixed amount of places to the right of the decimal point |
| Currency | Displays numerical data preceded by a dollar sign |
| Comma | Displays numerical data with commas every third decimal place |
| Percent | Displays numerical data followed by a percent sign |
| Exponential | Displays numerical data in scientific notation |
| Leading Zeros | Displays numerical data with a specified number of decimal places to the left of the decimal point |
| True/False | Displays the word *True* for all nonzero number values and *False* for zero |
| Time/Date | Displays text and numerical data as times or dates |

## ACTIVITY 7-6

## Changing the Appearance of Cells in the Spreadsheet

In this activity, you will change the appearance of the cells in a spreadsheet. The spreadsheet file *act7-1.wks* now appears on your screen. Change the appearance of some of the cells in the spreadsheet by following these steps:

1.  Bold the following cells for emphasis:

    a.  Move the highlight to **A1**.

    b.  Click the **Bold** button in the Toolbar. The words *Summer Budget* should become bold.

    c.  Move the highlight to **B2**.

    d.  Drag the mouse pointer from B2 and release in D2 to define the range. The group of cells will become shaded. (B2 will not be shaded.)

    e.  Click the **Bold** button in the Toolbar. All of the month names in the cells should become bold.

    f.  Bold the following cells using the same procedure: **A3, A6, A14, A16,** and **A17**.

Activity 7-6 continued

2.  Underline the names of the months to show they are column headings:

    a.  Select **B2** through **D2**.

    b.  Click the **Underline** button on the Toolbar.

3.  Align the names of the months in the centers of the columns:

    a.  Make sure **B2** through **D2** are still selected.

    b.  Click the **Center Alignment** button on the Toolbar.

4.  Format the following cells in currency format by selecting with the highlight and clicking the Currency button on the Toolbar: **B4, C4, D4, B17, C17,** and **D17**.

5.  Format the cell range from B7 through D16 in Comma format:

    a.  Select the group of cells, **B7** through **D16**, by dragging from B7 and releasing at D16.

    b.  Click the **Comma** button in the Toolbar. The selected group should change to a comma format with two decimals to the right of the decimal point.

6.  Italicize the account names:

    a.  Click **A4**.

    b.  Click the **Italic** button.

    c.  Select **A7** through **A13**.

    d.  Click the **Italic** button.

7.  Place a border around the spreadsheet title, Summer Budget:

    a.  Highlight **A1**.

    b.  From the **Format** menu, choose **Border**. The Border dialog box will appear.

    c.  Click the **Outline** box. An *X* should appear in the box. If any of the other boxes in the Border dialog box contain an *X*, click the boxes so that the additional *X*'s are removed.

    d.  Click **OK**. A1 should appear with a border on all sides of the cell.

    Your screen should appear similar to Figure 7-10.

8.  Leave *act7-1.wks* on the screen for the next activity.

Activity 7-6 continued

**FIGURE 7-10**
The appearance of cell contents may be changed by bolding, underlining, and centering.

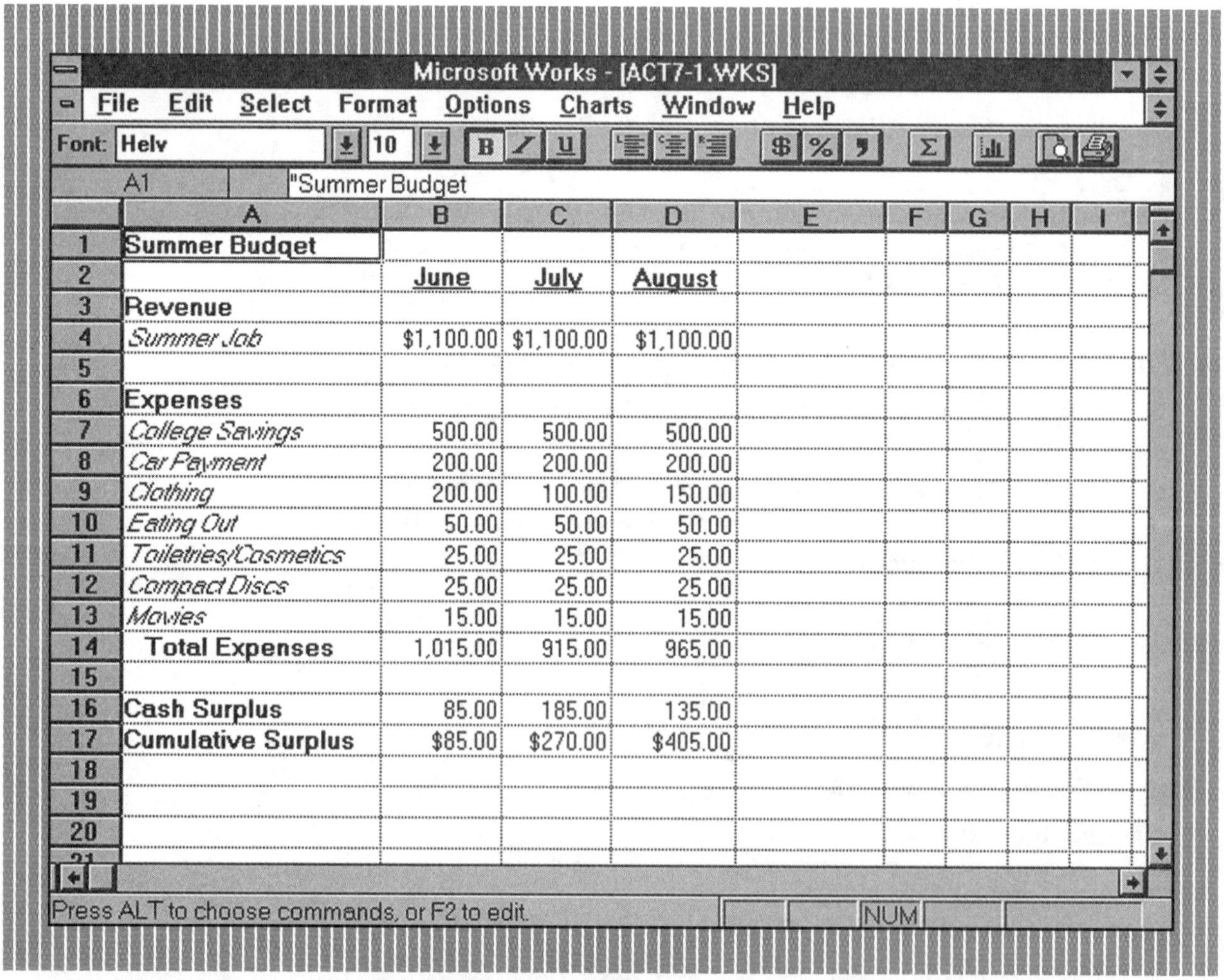

| | A | B | C | D | E | F | G | H | I |
|---|---|---|---|---|---|---|---|---|---|
| 1 | Summer Budget | | | | | | | | |
| 2 | | June | July | August | | | | | |
| 3 | Revenue | | | | | | | | |
| 4 | Summer Job | $1,100.00 | $1,100.00 | $1,100.00 | | | | | |
| 5 | | | | | | | | | |
| 6 | Expenses | | | | | | | | |
| 7 | College Savings | 500.00 | 500.00 | 500.00 | | | | | |
| 8 | Car Payment | 200.00 | 200.00 | 200.00 | | | | | |
| 9 | Clothing | 200.00 | 100.00 | 150.00 | | | | | |
| 10 | Eating Out | 50.00 | 50.00 | 50.00 | | | | | |
| 11 | Toiletries/Cosmetics | 25.00 | 25.00 | 25.00 | | | | | |
| 12 | Compact Discs | 25.00 | 25.00 | 25.00 | | | | | |
| 13 | Movies | 15.00 | 15.00 | 15.00 | | | | | |
| 14 | Total Expenses | 1,015.00 | 915.00 | 965.00 | | | | | |
| 15 | | | | | | | | | |
| 16 | Cash Surplus | 85.00 | 185.00 | 135.00 | | | | | |
| 17 | Cumulative Surplus | $85.00 | $270.00 | $405.00 | | | | | |
| 18 | | | | | | | | | |
| 19 | | | | | | | | | |
| 20 | | | | | | | | | |
| 21 | | | | | | | | | |

Microsoft Works - [ACT7-1.WKS]

File   Edit   Select   Format   Options   Charts   Window   Help

Font: Helv   10   B   I   U   $ % ,   Σ

A1    "Summer Budget

Press ALT to choose commands, or F2 to edit.    NUM

# SAVING AND EXITING A SPREADSHEET

Saving and exiting are the same operations you learned for word processor documents. The first time you save a spreadsheet, you will see the Save As dialog box asking you to name the spreadsheet. Once a spreadsheet has been saved, the Save command will update the latest version on disk. To exit a spreadsheet, choose the Close command from the File menu.

**ACTIVITY
7-7**

## Saving and Exiting a Spreadsheet

In this activity, you will save the file *act7-1.wks* to a new name and exit the document.

1. Insert your data disk in drive A.

2. From the **File** menu, choose **Save As**. The Save As dialog box will appear.

3. In the **File Name** box, key **a:\sumbudg** to rename your spreadsheet. Click **OK**.

4. From the **File** menu, choose **Close**.

5. From the **File** menu, choose **Exit Works**. You will be returned to the Program Manager of Windows.

# SUMMARY

The purpose of a spreadsheet is to solve problems involving numbers. The primary advantage of the spreadsheet is to complete complex and repetitious calculations quickly and easily.

The spreadsheet consists of columns and rows intersecting to form cells. Each cell is identified by a cell reference, which is the letter of the column and number of the row. You may move to different cells of the spreadsheet by using a series of keystrokes or by scrolling with the mouse. Both text and numerical data may be entered into the spreadsheet. Data may be altered by editing, replacing, or deleting.

The appearance of cell data may be changed to make the spreadsheet easier to understand. Font and font size may be changed for the entire spreadsheet. Style (bolding, italicizing, and underlining) and alignment (left, center, and right justification) of individual cells may be changed and borders may be added. In addition, the appearance of the cell may be changed to accommodate data in currency, comma, or percent format.

# CHALLENGES

## TRUE/FALSE

Circle **T** or **F** to show whether the statement is true or false.

| | | | |
|---|---|---|---|
| T | F | 1. | The primary advantage of the spreadsheet is to summarize text documents. |
| T | F | 2. | A cell is the intersection of a row and column. |
| T | F | 3. | The active cell reference will appear in the Toolbar. |
| T | F | 4. | To select a group of cells, click each cell individually until all cells in the range have been selected. |
| T | F | 5. | The Go To command saves a file and exits Works. |
| T | F | 6. | The Clear command removes the contents of a cell. |
| T | F | 7. | The best way to make minor changes to existing data in a cell is to key new data and press the Enter key. |
| T | F | 8. | To change the cell to exponential format, select the Exponential command from the Format menu. |
| T | F | 9. | Border formats define the portion of the spreadsheet that will be saved when the Save command is selected. |
| T | F | 10. | Saving a spreadsheet file differs significantly from saving a word processing file. |

# COMPLETION

**Write the correct answer in the space provided.**

1. What term describes a cell that is ready for data entry?

   _____

2. How are columns identified in a spreadsheet?

   _____

3. What indicates that a cell is ready to accept data?

   _____

4. What keys should be pressed to move the highlight to the last cell of the spreadsheet?

   _____

5. When text data appears in the formula bar, what punctuation mark precedes the text?

   _____

6. How does Works respond when the data is too wide for the column in which it has been entered?

   _____

7. What key is pressed to edit data in an active cell?

   _____

8. What key is pressed to clear data from an active cell?

   _____

9. What part of the spreadsheet provides shortcuts for the most frequently used commands?

   _____

10. What forms of cell alignment are available in the spreadsheet?

   _____

# APPLICATIONS

## APPLICATION 7-1

In the blank space, write the letter of the keystroke that matches the highlight movement.

| Highlight Movement | | Keystroke |
|---|---|---|
| ___ 1. Left one column | | a. Ctrl+Home |
| ___ 2. Right one column | | b. Page Up |
| ___ 3. Up one row | | c. End |
| ___ 4. Down one row | | d. Home |
| ___ 5. To the first cell of a row | | e. Ctrl+Page Up |
| ___ 6. To the last cell of a row containing data | | f. Left Arrow |
| ___ 7. To A1 | | g. Right Arrow |
| ___ 8. To the last row or column containing data | | h. Ctrl+End |
| ___ 9. Up one window | | i. Up Arrow |
| ___ 10. Down one window | | j. Ctrl+Page Down |
| ___ 11. Left one window | | k. Down Arrow |
| ___ 12. Right one window | | l. Page Down |

## APPLICATION 7-2

In the blank space, write the letter of the key or mouse procedure that matches the spreadsheet operation. You may use the items in the right-hand column more than once if necessary. For some questions, more than one answer may be correct; however, you are required to identify only one of the correct answers.

| Spreadsheet Operation | Key or Mouse Procedure |
|---|---|
| ___ 1. Open an existing spreadsheet file | a. Choose a command in the Format menu |
| ___ 2. Move to a specific cell | b. Press the Delete key |
| ___ 3. Edit data in a cell | c. Choose a command in the File menu |

| Spreadsheet Operation | Key or Mouse Procedure |
|---|---|
| ____ 4. Widen a spreadsheet column | d. Click a button on the Toolbar |
| ____ 5. Clear data in a cell | e. Drag a double-headed arrow |
| ____ 6. Change the style of a cell to italics | f. Press the F5 key |
| ____ 7. Change the format of a cell to exponential | g. Press the F2 key |
| ____ 8. Change the alignment of a cell | |
| ____ 9. Add borders to a cell | |
| ____ 10. Save a spreadsheet file | |
| ____ 11. Exit Works | |

# APPLICATION 7-3

As a volunteer for a local environmental awareness group, you have agreed to collect and survey the type of trash discarded on a one-mile stretch of highway in your community. To help with your survey calculations, you have prepared the spreadsheet *app7-3.wks* to account for trash items you have collected. Complete the spreadsheet by performing the following steps:

1. Open the file *app7-3.wks* from the template disk.
2. Enter the following number of trash items collected for Week 4. The totals for each category should change as you enter the data.

   | | |
   |---|---|
   | Beer Cans | 15 |
   | Soda Cans | 5 |
   | Fast Food Items | 20 |
   | Newspaper Pages | 3 |
   | Other Paper Items | 10 |
   | Cigarette Butts | 17 |

3. In addition to the items above, you picked up a tennis shoe. Enter a new category in Cell A11 called *Clothing*. Then enter the number **1** in Cell E11.
4. You made a mistake when entering data for Week 3. Edit the cell for cigarette butts to show 18 rather than 16.
5. Save the file as *litter* to your data disk and close the file after you have completed entering the new data.

# APPLICATION 7-4

In Application 7-3, you updated a spreadsheet by entering new data. In this application, you will improve the appearance of your spreadsheet so that you may present your results. Complete the following steps in the spreadsheet:

1.  Open the file *litter.wks* from your data disk.
2.  Change the appearance of the following cells and cell ranges in the style indicated:
    a.  Change Cell A1 to bold.
    b.  Change Range A3:F3 to bold.
    c.  Change Range B3:F3 to underline.
    d.  Change Range A13:F13 to bold.
    e.  Change Range F5:F11 to bold.
    f.  Change Range B11:F11 to have a border on the bottom.
3.  Save and close the file.

CHAPTER

# 8

# STRENGTHENING SPREADSHEET SKILLS

## LEARNING OBJECTIVES

**When you complete this chapter, you will be able to:**

1. Copy data to other cells.
2. Move data to other cells.
3. Insert and delete columns and rows.
4. Freeze headings.
5. Protect parts of a spreadsheet.
6. Print a spreadsheet.

In Chapter 7, you learned the basics of a spreadsheet. In this chapter, you will strengthen your skills by creating and refining a spreadsheet. Throughout this chapter, you will use a spreadsheet to calculate semester grades for several classes.

## COPYING DATA

When creating or enlarging a spreadsheet, you may want to use the same text or numbers in another portion of the spreadsheet. Rather than key the same data over again, the data may be copied. There are several ways to copy data in a spreadsheet. In this chapter, you will learn to copy and paste, fill down, and fill right. These operations can significantly decrease the amount of time you need to prepare a spreadsheet. All of these commands are in the Edit menu, as shown in Figure 8-1.

## FIGURE 8-1

The Copy, Paste, Fill Right, and Fill Down commands copy data from one part of a spreadsheet to another.

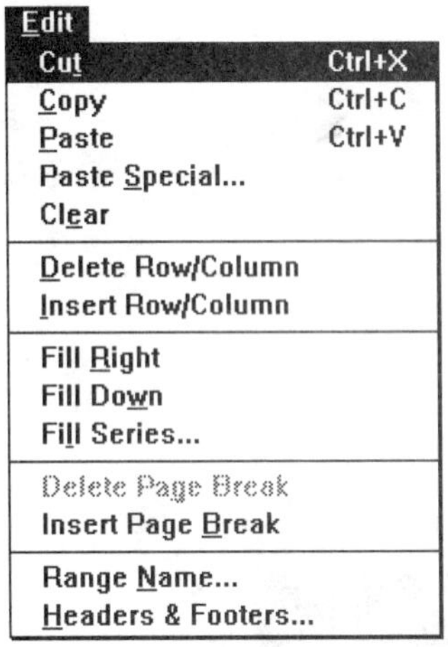

| Edit | |
|---|---|
| Cut | Ctrl+X |
| Copy | Ctrl+C |
| Paste | Ctrl+V |
| Paste Special... | |
| Clear | |
| Delete Row/Column | |
| Insert Row/Column | |
| Fill Right | |
| Fill Down | |
| Fill Series... | |
| Delete Page Break | |
| Insert Page Break | |
| Range Name... | |
| Headers & Footers... | |

*Note: Although copying data can increase the efficiency of creating a spreadsheet, there is one danger. Data copied into a cell will replace data already in that cell. Check your destination cells for existing data before copying.*

## Copy and Paste

The Copy command duplicates the contents of a cell or cells on the Clipboard so that you can enter the data in another part of the spreadsheet, as seen in Figure 8-2. The Copy command, however, will not affect the data in the original cell(s).

After placing the highlight in the part of the spreadsheet where the data is to be copied, use the Paste command to enter the stored data into the cell or cells. It is not necessary to select the entire range of cells; you need to only highlight the upper left corner of the range into which data will be copied.

The data stored on the Clipboard will remain until it is replaced with new data. If you would like to make multiple copies, you may simply choose the Paste command once more.

## FIGURE 8-2

Data in one part of the spreadsheet may be duplicated in another part of the spreadsheet by using the Copy and Paste commands.

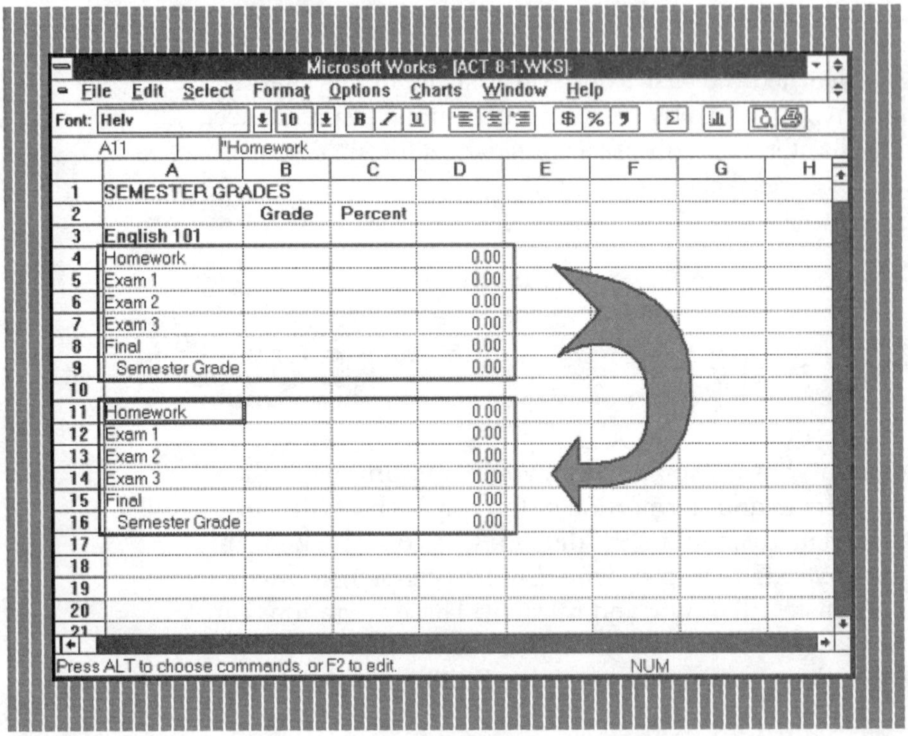

## Copying and Pasting

In this activity, you will practice copying and pasting. *Act8-1.wks* is a spreadsheet intended to calculate the semester grade of an English class. The spreadsheet will be expanded to calculate the grades of a history and biology class.

1. Open the file *act8-1.wks* from your template disk. The spreadsheet contains columns for grades and percentages of homework and examinations.

2. Expand the spreadsheet to calculate grades for a history class:

   a. Select **Range A4:D9**.

   b. From the **Edit** menu, choose **Copy**.

   c. Highlight **A11**.

   d. From the **Edit** menu, choose **Paste**. The range of cells should be copied from A4:D9 to A11:D16.

3. Key **History 101** into A10.

4. Expand the spreadsheet to calculate grades for a biology class.

   a. Highlight **A18**.

   b. From the **Edit** menu, choose **Paste**. The range of cells should be copied from A4:D9 to A18:D23.

5. Key **Biology 101** into A17.

6. Bold the contents of Cells A10 and A17.

7. Compare your screen to Figure 8-3.

8. Leave *act8-1.wks* on the screen for the next activity.

**FIGURE 8-3**

Copying and pasting speeds the process of creating a spreadsheet.

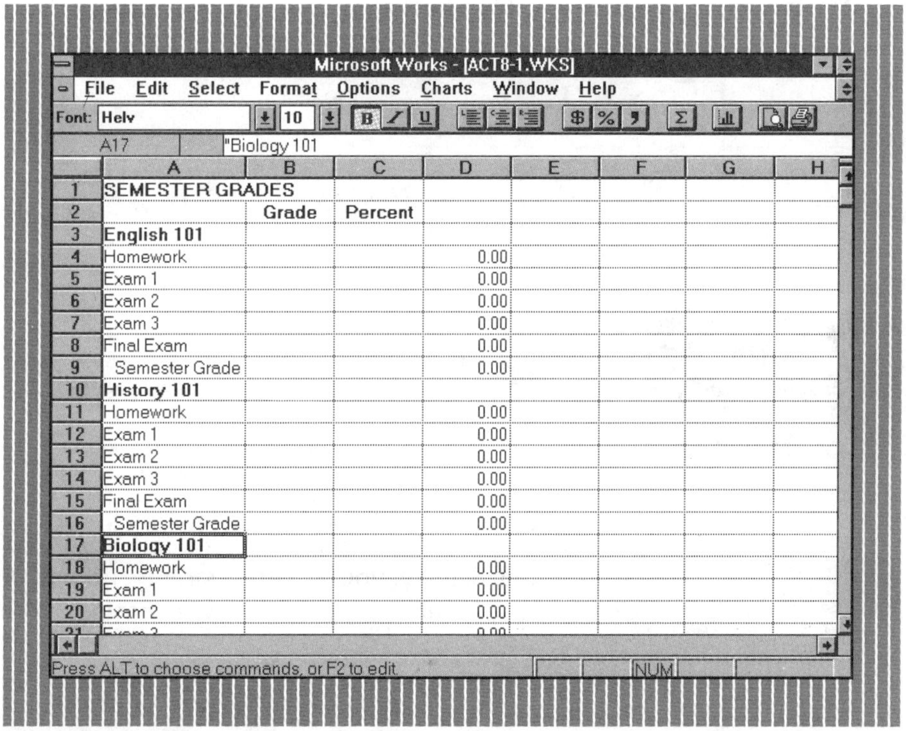

## Fill Down and Fill Right

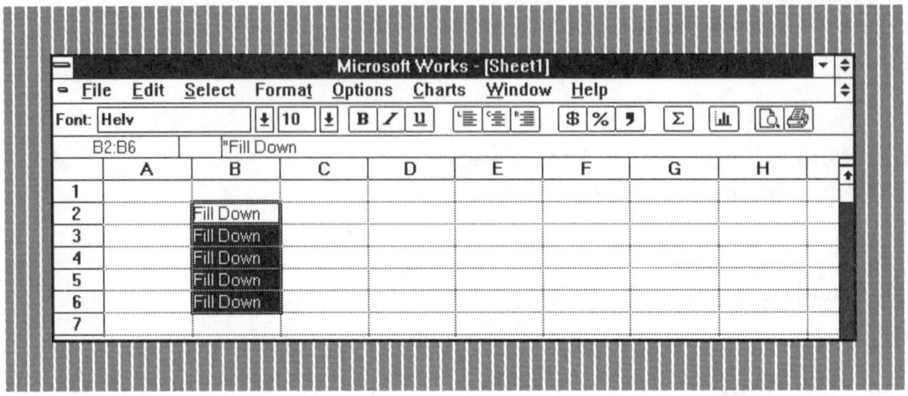

**FIGURE 8-4**

The Fill Down command copies data to adjacent cells below the original cell.

The Fill Down and Fill Right commands copy data into the cell(s) adjacent to the original. The Fill Down command will copy data into the cell(s) directly below the original cell, as shown in Figure 8-4. The Fill Right command will copy data into the cell(s) to the right of the original cell, as shown in Figure 8-5. Either command will make multiple copies if more than one destination cell is selected. For example, the Fill Down command can copy data into the next several cells below the original cell. The Fill commands are somewhat faster than copying and pasting because filling requires choosing only one command. However, filling can be used only when the destination cells are adjacent to the original cell.

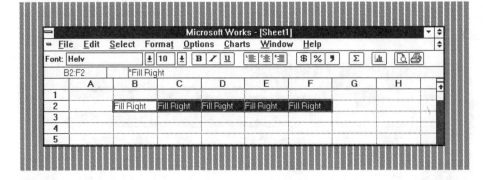

**FIGURE 8-5**

The Fill Right command copies data to adjacent cells to the right of the original cell.

## ACTIVITY 8-2

### Using the Fill Down Command

In this activity, you will enter grade and percentage data into a spreadsheet using the Fill Down command. Your screen should now

Activity 8-2 continued

show the file *act8-1.wks*. The table to the right shows the data for grades earned in classes. Follow the steps below to enter this data in the spreadsheet:

1. Each of the exams in English 101 is 20% of the semester grade. Enter the percent for the exams in English 101 by following these steps:

   a. Enter **.2** in C5. (.2 is the decimal equivalent of 20%.)

   b. Drag from C5 to C7 to select the range to be filled.

   c. From the **Edit** menu, choose **Fill Down**. The contents of C5, 20.00%, will be copied to cells C6 and C7.

2. Use the same procedure to enter percentages for the history and biology exams. Enter **.2** in C12 and **.15** in C19.

3. Use the Fill Down command to copy data from C12 to C13:C14 and C19 to C20:C21.

4. Enter the remaining data into the spreadsheet by inserting the percentages for homework and final exams; enter the grades for all items.

5. After completing the spreadsheet you may notice that the semester grades have been calculated based on the data entered. Compare your screen to the one shown in Figure 8-6.

6. Leave *act8-1.wks* on your screen for the next activity.

| Subject | Grade | Percent |
|---|---|---|
| **English 101** | | |
| Homework | 87 | 10.00% |
| Exam 1 | 82 | 20.00% |
| Exam 2 | 75 | 20.00% |
| Exam 3 | 78 | 20.00% |
| Final Exam | 81 | 30.00% |
| **History 101** | | |
| Homework | 76 | 5.00% |
| Exam 1 | 74 | 20.00% |
| Exam 2 | 80 | 20.00% |
| Exam 3 | 77 | 20.00% |
| Final Exam | 79 | 35.00% |
| **Biology 101** | | |
| Homework | 89 | 30.00% |
| Exam 1 | 92 | 15.00% |
| Exam 2 | 87 | 15.00% |
| Exam 3 | 95 | 15.00% |
| Final Exam | 93 | 25.00% |

**FIGURE 8-6**
In this spreadsheet, the Fill
Down command was used to
copy the percentages for the
exams from C5 to C6 and C7.

**FIGURE 8-6**
In this spreadsheet, the Fill
Down command was used to
copy the percentages for the
exams from C5 to C6 and C7.

| | A | B | C | D | E | F | G | H |
|---|---|---|---|---|---|---|---|---|
| 1 | SEMESTER GRADES | | | | | | | |
| 2 | | Grade | Percent | | | | | |
| 3 | English 101 | | | | | | | |
| 4 | Homework | 87 | 10.00% | 8.70 | | | | |
| 5 | Exam 1 | 82 | 20.00% | 16.40 | | | | |
| 6 | Exam 2 | 75 | 20.00% | 15.00 | | | | |
| 7 | Exam 3 | 78 | 20.00% | 15.60 | | | | |
| 8 | Final Exam | 81 | 30.00% | 24.30 | | | | |
| 9 | Semester Grade | | | 80.00 | | | | |
| 10 | | | | | | | | |
| 11 | History 101 | | | | | | | |
| 12 | Homework | 76 | 5.00% | 3.80 | | | | |
| 13 | Exam 1 | 74 | 20.00% | 14.80 | | | | |
| 14 | Exam 2 | 80 | 20.00% | 16.00 | | | | |
| 15 | Exam 3 | 77 | 20.00% | 15.40 | | | | |
| 16 | Final Exam | 79 | 35.00% | 27.65 | | | | |
| 17 | Semester Grade | | | 77.65 | | | | |
| 18 | | | | | | | | |
| 19 | Biology 101 | | | | | | | |
| 20 | Homework | 89 | 30.00% | 26.70 | | | | |
| 21 | Exam 1 | 92 | 15.00% | 13.80 | | | | |

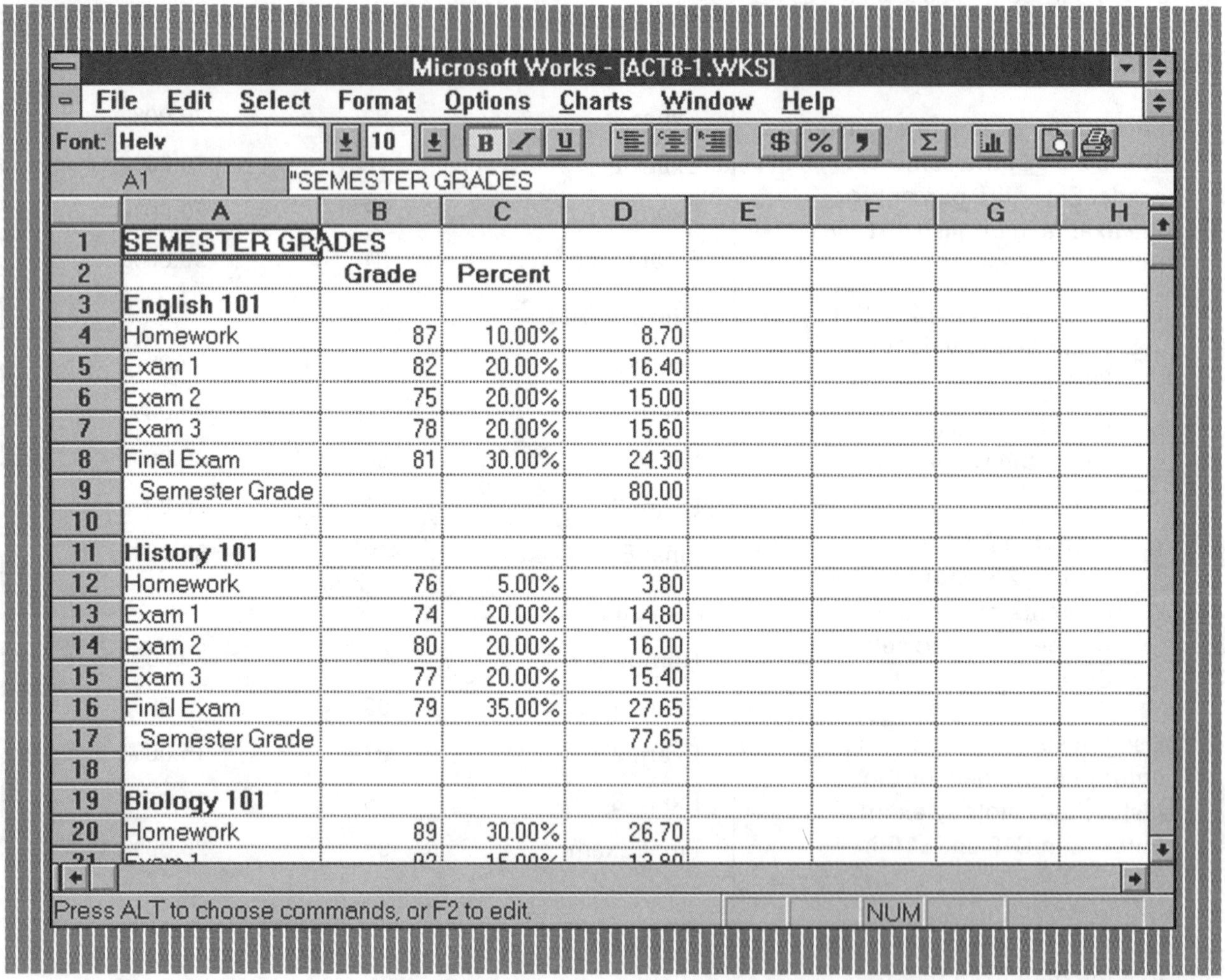

# MOVING DATA

Data is sometimes moved in the spreadsheet to improve the
appearance of the spreadsheet. Moving is referred to in Works as
"cutting and pasting."

Previously, you learned that the Copy command places data on the
Clipboard so that it may be copied into another area of the spreadsheet.
The Cut command also places selected data on the Clipboard; however,
it will remove data from its original position in the spreadsheet.
Because cut data is stored on the Clipboard, you may restore the data at

any time by simply choosing the Paste command. This procedure is particularly useful if you mistakenly cut data from the spreadsheet and would like to put it back.

**ACTIVITY
8-3**

## Moving Data in a Spreadsheet

In this activity, you will move data in the spreadsheet file *act8-1.wks*, now on your screen. You decide that the spreadsheet may be easier to read if there is a blank row between each class. Perform the following operations to move the data:

1.  Move the data for Biology 101 down two rows:

    a.  Select **A17:D23**.

    b.  From the **Edit** menu, choose **Cut**. The data in the range will disappear from the spreadsheet.

    c.  Highlight **A19**.

    d.  From the **Edit** menu, choose **Paste**. The data will appear in the range A19:D25.

2.  Perform similar operations to move the data for History 101 down one row. The data should appear in the range A11:D17. After completing the activity, your screen should be similar to Figure 8-7.

3.  Leave *act8-1.wks* on the screen for the next activity.

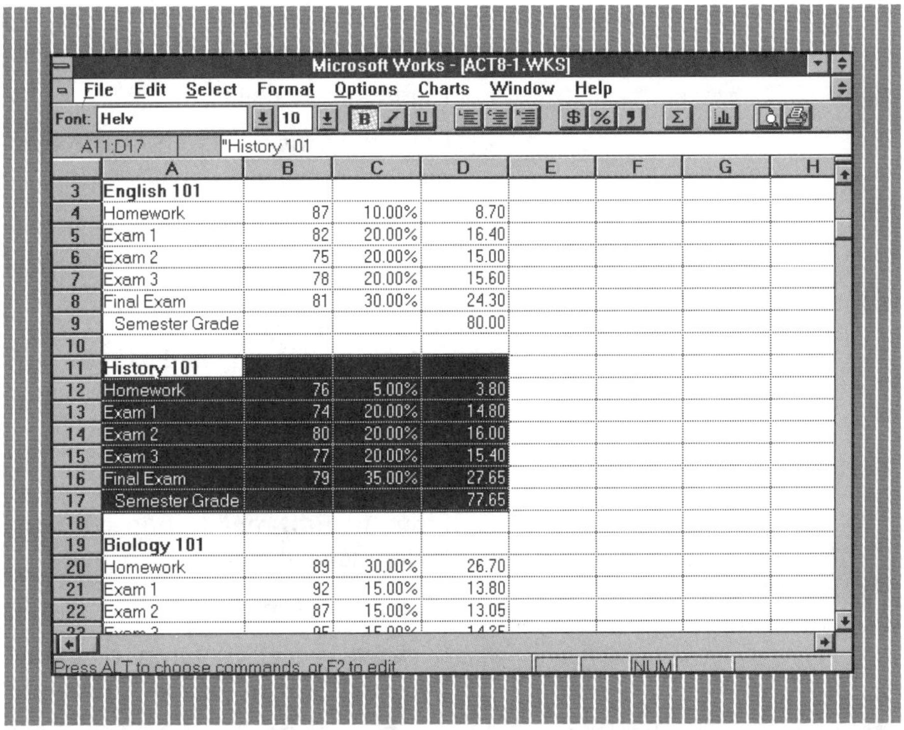

**FIGURE 8-7**
The Copy command duplicates data in a spreadsheet; the Cut command moves data to another part of the spreadsheet.

# INSERTING AND DELETING ROWS AND COLUMNS

The appearance of the spreadsheet may also be changed by adding and removing rows and columns of the spreadsheet. In fact, in the previous activity, you could have inserted rows between the classes rather than move existing data.

Inserting adds a row above the highlight or a column to the left of the highlight. Deleting removes the row or column in which the highlight appears. The Delete Row/Column command is potentially dangerous because it erases the data contained in the row or column. If you accidentally delete the wrong column or row, all the data contained in that row or column will be lost. The Undo command that is available in the word processor is not available in the spreadsheet.

## ACTIVITY 8-4

### Inserting and Deleting Rows and Columns

In this activity, you will insert a row and insert and delete a column in the file *act8-1.wks*, which now appears on your screen. Perform the following steps:

1. Insert a row near the top of the spreadsheet:

    a. Highlight any cell in Row 3.

    b. From the **Edit** menu, choose **Insert Row/Column**. The Insert dialog box will appear.

    c. The **Row** button should be selected. If it is not, click the **Row** button and then click **OK**. Row 3 will be blank. The original Row 3 will be moved to Row 4.

2. Suppose you want to include a column in the spreadsheet for the date the examination was taken. Insert a column between Columns A and B:

    a. Highlight any cell in Column B.

    b. From the **Edit** menu, choose **Insert Row/Column**. The Insert dialog box will appear.

    c. Click the **Column** button.

    d. Click **OK**. A blank column will appear as Column B. The original Column B will be moved to Column C.

    e. Key **Date** in B2.

    f. Press **Enter**.

Activity 8-4 continued

3.  Suppose you change your mind about the date column. Delete Column B.

    a.  Highlight any cell in Column B.

    b.  From the **Edit** menu, choose **Delete Row/Column**.

    c.  Click **Column**.

    d.  Click **OK**. The date column will disappear.

4.  Leave *act 8-1.wks* on the screen for the next activity.

# FREEZING TITLES

Often a spreadsheet can become so large that it is difficult to view the entire spreadsheet on the screen. As you scroll to lower parts of the spreadsheet column, titles may disappear from the screen, making it difficult to identify the contents of the column. For example, you may have noticed that the column titles (Grade and Percent) in previous activities scrolled off the screen when you were working in the lower part of the spreadsheet.

Freezing will keep the row or column titles on the screen no matter where you scroll in the spreadsheet. To freeze titles, select the Freeze Titles command in the Options menu. All rows above the highlight and columns to the left of the highlight will be frozen. Frozen titles are indicated by a check mark in the Options menu by the Freeze Titles command. (See Figure 8-8.) To unfreeze a row or column title, choose the Freeze Titles command again; the check mark will disappear and the titles will be unfrozen.

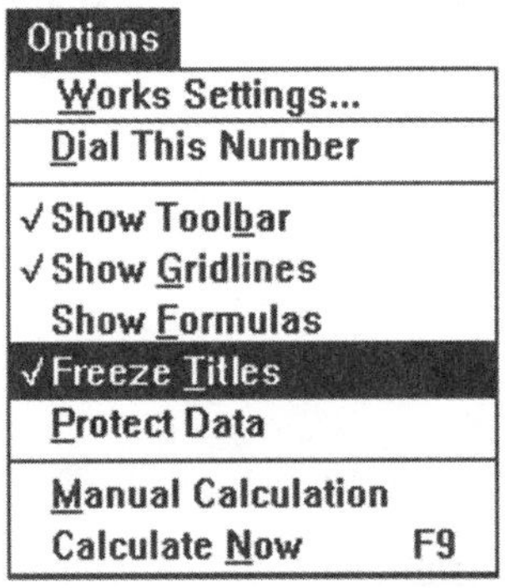

**FIGURE 8-8**
The check mark by the Freeze Titles command indicates that headings in the spreadsheet will remain on the screen no matter where the highlight is moved.

| Options |  |
| --- | --- |
| Works Settings... | |
| Dial This Number | |
| √ Show Toolbar | |
| √ Show Gridlines | |
| Show Formulas | |
| √ Freeze Titles | |
| Protect Data | |
| Manual Calculation | |
| Calculate Now | F9 |

ACTIVITY
8-5

## Freezing Titles

In this activity, you will freeze the column headings in the spreadsheet file *act8-1.wks*, which is now on the screen.

1.  Highlight **A3**.

2.  From the **Options** menu, choose **Freeze Titles**. The column headings in Rows 1 and 2 are now frozen.

Activity 8-5 continued

3. Click **Options** again and notice the check mark beside the Freeze Titles command. This indicates titles are now frozen.

4. Scroll to the lower part of the spreadsheet. You will notice that the column headings remain at the top of the screen no matter where you move.

5. Leave *act8-1.wks* on the screen for the next activity.

When titles are frozen, you cannot scroll into the frozen cells. If you need to change the data in a frozen cell, you should either use the Go To command from the Select menu, click the frozen cell, or unfreeze the title. Also, as you move back to the uppermost screen of the spreadsheet, you will notice that the frozen titles will double on your screen. This doubling indicates that the titles are frozen and does not interfere with operations of the spreadsheet.

## PROTECTING CELLS

Protecting data in a cell prevents anyone from making changes to the cell inadvertently. In other words, the cell becomes "locked" until someone removes the protection.

To use the Protect Data command, you must first select the cells you want to protect, then choose the Style command from the Format menu. When the Style dialog box appears, as shown in Figure 8-9, click the Locked check box. After the Locked option is on, you may protect the cells by choosing the Protect Data command from the Options menu.

**FIGURE 8-9**

The Locked check box in the Style command must be turned on before you can protect data.

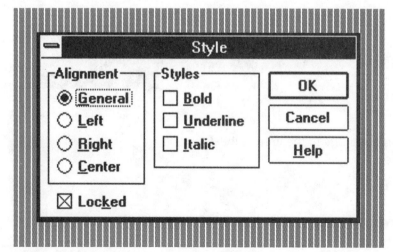

Works locks the entire spreadsheet as a default option. In other words, if you select the Protect Data command in a new spreadsheet, the entire spreadsheet will be protected. Therefore, you need to "unlock" all contents of the spreadsheet before selecting the specific cells you want to lock.

If you attempt to change the data in cells after they have been protected, Works will display a dialog box telling you the cells cannot be changed. If you intend to change the cells, you must first unprotect them.

**ACTIVITY
8-6**

## Protecting Cells

In this activity, you will protect the cells in a portion of the spreadsheet. Suppose you plan to add future classes at the bottom of the spreadsheet and plan to use the original portion of the file *act8-1.wks* as a long-term record of your grades. Because your past grades cannot be changed, you desire to protect the data so that they are not changed by mistake.

1.  Unlock all data in the spreadsheet:

    a.   Select **A1:D26**.

    b.   From the **Format** menu, choose **Style**.

    c.   Click the **Locked** check box so that it becomes blank.

    d.   Click **OK**.

2.  Lock the data to be protected:

    a.   Select the range **A4:D26**, which contains the classes for which grades have already been recorded.

    b.   From the **Format** menu, choose **Style**. The Style dialog box will appear. The Locked check box at the bottom of the dialog box is filled with a gray square.

    c.   Click the **Locked** check box until an *X* appears.

    d.   Click **OK**. The selected range of cells is now available for protection.

3.  From the **Options** menu, choose **Protect Data**. The selected range is now protected.

4.  Check the protection of the cells.

    a.   Move the highlight to **B5**, a cell within the protected range.

    b.   Key **45**.

    c.   Click the **Enter** box. Works should display a dialog box telling you the cell cannot be changed.

    d.   Click **OK** to eliminate the dialog box.

5.  Leave *act8-1.wks* on the screen for the next activity.

If you desire to enter data into cells currently protected, choose the Protect Data command in the Options menu again. You may then enter data without the dialog box appearing. To protect the cells again, choose the Protect Data command once more.

# PRINTING A SPREADSHEET

Printing a spreadsheet is similar to printing a word processor document. The File menu contains three commands to help you prepare the spreadsheet for printing: Set Print Area, Page Setup & Margins, and Print Preview.

## Setting the Print Area

You may print the entire spreadsheet or a portion of the spreadsheet. The Set Print Area command tells Works the part of the spreadsheet you want to print. To designate the area you want to print, select the range and then, in the File menu, choose Set Print Area.

## Setting the Margins and Page Size

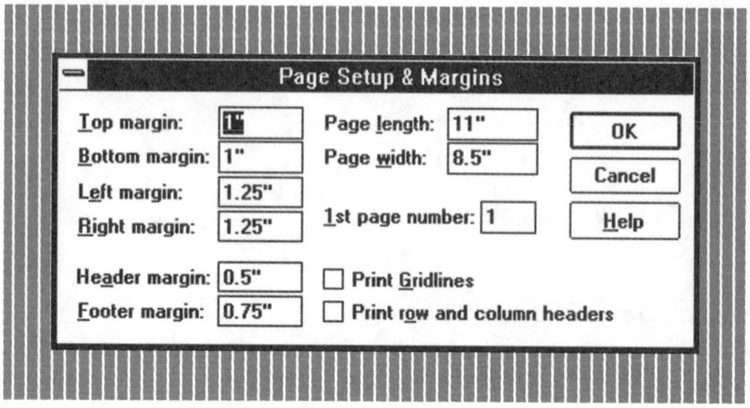

**FIGURE 8-10**
The margins and page size are determined in the Page Setup & Margins command in the File menu.

The Page Setup & Margins command in the File menu will produce a dialog box that allows you to set page margins, set page lengths and widths, designate page numbers, and determine whether column letters, row numbers, and gridlines should be printed. Figure 8-10 shows the settings available in the Page Setup & Margins dialog box. These settings are described below.

▶ *Margin settings* can be in inches (the default), centimeters (cm), picas (pi), or points (pts). To adjust the settings, click the box and enter the margin size with the appropriate abbreviation.

▶ *Page dimensions* are in inches. To adjust the page size, click the box and enter the new page dimensions.

▶ *1st page number* designates the page number of the first page of the spreadsheet. To change the number of the first page, click the box and enter a new page number.

▶ When the *Print Gridlines* check box contains an X, Works will print the gridlines appearing between the cells. If the check box is not checked, the gridlines will not be printed.

▶ When the *Print row and column headers* check box contains an X, Works will print the row number and column letter.

## Previewing a Spreadsheet before Printing

Print Preview button

The Print Preview command of the spreadsheet is exactly the same as in the word processor. The Print Preview command shows how your

printed pages will
appear before you
actually print them. To
access the Print Preview
screen (see Figure 8-11),
choose the Print
Preview command from
the File menu or click
the Print Preview button
on the Toolbar. When
you have finished
previewing the printed
pages, you may either
return to the
spreadsheet by clicking
Cancel or print the
spreadsheet by clicking
Print.

**FIGURE 8-11**
Use the Print Preview screen
to check the spreadsheet
before printing.

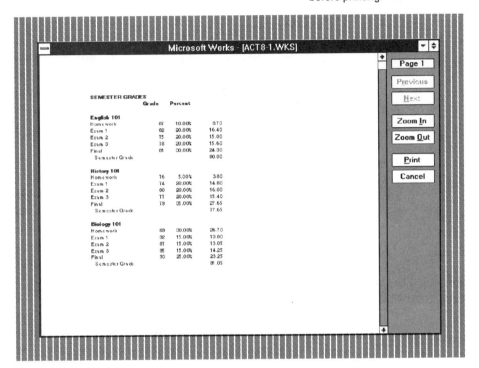

## Printing the Spreadsheet

When you are ready to print, click the Print button on the Toolbar or
choose the Print command from the File menu. A Print button also
appears in the Print Preview screen. The Print dialog box (see Figure 8-
12) will request the number of copies and the specific pages to print.

Print button

**FIGURE 8-12**
The Print dialog box requests the number of copies and the specific pages
you want to print.

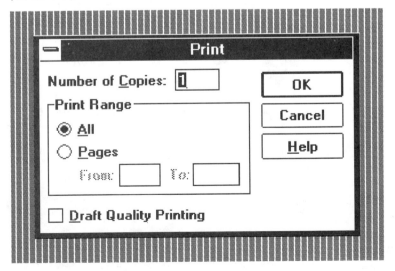

## ACTIVITY 8-7

### Printing a Spreadsheet

In this activity, you will print the spreadsheet in file *act8-1.wks*.

1. Set the area of the spreadsheet to be printed:

   a. Select **A1:D26**.

   b. From the **File** menu, choose **Set Print Area**.

2. Change the margin of the printed document:

   a. From the **File** menu, choose **Page Setup & Margins**. The Page Setup & Margins dialog box will appear. The dialog box contains the default settings for the margins and page size.

   b. Change the **Left margin** setting from **1.25"** to **1"**.

   c. Click **OK**.

3. Preview the spreadsheet to be printed:

   a. Click the **Print Preview** button on the Toolbar.

   b. Click the **Zoom In** button twice. A portion of the previewed page will become larger so that it can be examined in more detail.

4. Print the spreadsheet:

   a. Click the **Print** button. The Print dialog box will appear. This spreadsheet has only one page and you want only one copy, so you will not need to make any changes in the default settings.

   b. Click **OK**. The spreadsheet should begin printing.

5. Compare your printed page to Figure 8-13.

6. Save the file to your data disk as *semgrade* and close the file.

**FIGURE 8-13**

You may print a spreadsheet by specifying the area to be printed and clicking the Print button.

| SEMESTER GRADES | Grade | Percent | |
|---|---|---|---|
| **English 101** | | | |
| Homework | 87 | 10.00% | 8.70 |
| Exam 1 | 82 | 20.00% | 16.40 |
| Exam 2 | 75 | 20.00% | 15.00 |
| Exam 3 | 78 | 20.00% | 15.60 |
| Final Exam | 81 | 30.00% | 24.30 |
| Semester Grade | | 80.00 | |
| **History 101** | | | |
| Homework | 76 | 5.00% | 3.80 |
| Exam 1 | 74 | 20.00% | 14.80 |
| Exam 2 | 80 | 20.00% | 16.00 |
| Exam 3 | 77 | 20.00% | 15.40 |
| Final Exam | 79 | 35.00% | 27.65 |
| Semester Grade | | 77.65 | |
| **Biology 101** | | | |
| Homework | 89 | 30.00% | 26.70 |
| Exam 1 | 92 | 15.00% | 13.80 |
| Exam 2 | 87 | 15.00% | 13.05 |
| Exam 3 | 95 | 15.00% | 14.25 |
| Final Exam | 93 | 25.00% | 23.25 |
| Semester Grade | | 91.05 | |

# SUMMARY

The data in a spreadsheet can be moved or copied to another location in the spreadsheet by using the Cut, Copy, Paste, Fill Right, and Fill Down commands from the Edit menu. These commands can save time by eliminating the need to rekey large quantities of data.

The appearance of the spreadsheet can be changed by inserting or deleting rows and columns. Be careful when deleting because the data in the rows and columns can be lost.

When a spreadsheet becomes large, the column or row titles will disappear from the screen as you scroll to distant parts of the spreadsheet. You may keep the titles on the screen at all times by freezing them.

The cells of a spreadsheet may be protected from accidental change by choosing the Protect Data command in the Options menu. The protection can be applied to the entire spreadsheet or to a portion of the spreadsheet. Cells may be unprotected if changes are necessary.

Printing a spreadsheet is similar to printing a word processing document. The Set Print Area command designates the portion of the spreadsheet you want to print. The Page Setup & Margins command controls the page size and the margins that will be printed. To view the spreadsheet as it will appear before actually printing it, use the Print Preview command.

# CHALLENGES

## TRUE/FALSE

Circle **T** or **F** to show whether the statement is true or false.

T  F  1. If you copy into cells already containing data, the data will be replaced by the copied data.

T  F  2. The Fill Down and Fill Right commands are available only if you plan to copy to cells adjacent to the original cell.

T  F  3. The Paste command is used for both copying and moving.

T  F  4. Deleting a row or column will erase the data contained in the row or column.

T  F  5. The Insert Row/Column command is in the Insert menu.

T  F  6. When using the Delete Row/Column command, the row above the highlight will be deleted.

T  F  7. The Freeze Titles command will freeze rows above and columns to the right of the highlight.

T  F  8. A dialog box will appear if you attempt to edit a cell that has been protected.

T     F     9.   The Page Setup & Margins command is used to designate the part of the spreadsheet that will be printed.

T     F     10.  A spreadsheet may be previewed before printing by clicking the Print Preview button on the Toolbar or by choosing the Print Preview command in the File menu.

---

# COMPLETION

Write the correct answer in the space provided.

1. What command is always used in conjunction with the Copy command and the Cut command?

2. Identify the three methods of copying data in the spreadsheet.

3. In what menu are the commands used for copying data located?

4. *Cutting and pasting* is a term used in Works that refers to what process?

5. When the Insert Row/Column command is chosen, how does Works know whether to insert a row or a column?

6. What command keeps the titles of a spreadsheet on the screen no matter where the highlight is moved?

7. The Protect Data command is contained in which menu?

8. Which command shows the Locked check box on screen?

9. Which command designates the margins of a printed spreadsheet?

_____

10. Which menu contains the commands that control printing?

_____

_____

# APPLICATIONS

## APPLICATION 8-1

In the blank space, write the letter of the spreadsheet command that will solve the spreadsheet problem.

### Spreadsheet Problem

_____ 1. You are tired of keying repetitive data.

_____ 2. A portion of the spreadsheet would be more useful in another area of the spreadsheet.

_____ 3. You forgot to key a row of data in the middle of the spreadsheet.

_____ 4. You no longer need a certain column in the spreadsheet.

_____ 5. Column headings cannot be viewed on the screen when you are working in the lower part of the spreadsheet.

_____ 6. You would like to avoid entering data in cells that should not be altered.

_____ 7. Your boss would rather not view your spreadsheet on the screen and has requested a copy on paper.

_____ 8. You would like to print only a portion of the spreadsheet.

### Spreadsheet Commands

a. Print command or Print button in the Toolbar

b. Fill Right, Fill Down, or Copy command

c. Insert Row/Column command

d. Protect Data command

e. Cut command, Paste command

f. Set Print Area command

g. Delete Row/Column command

h. Freeze Titles command

# APPLICATION 8-2

File *app8-2.wks* is a spreadsheet for the Bates family, which is preparing to purchase furniture for a new home. The spreadsheet is not currently organized by rooms in the house. In addition, the family wants to purchase more than one piece of certain items.

| FURNITURE PURCHASES | |
|---|---|
| **Item** | **Purchase Price** |
| **Utility Room** | |
| Washer | $340.00 |
| Dryer | $299.00 |
| **Living Room** | |
| Couch | $500.00 |
| Arm Chair | $260.00 |
| End Table | $250.00 |
| End Table | $250.00 |
| **Bedroom** | |
| Bed | $550.00 |
| Dresser | $400.00 |
| Drawers | $250.00 |
| **Dining Room** | |
| Table | $400.00 |
| Dining Chair | $120.00 |
| Dining Chair | $120.00 |
| Dining Chair | $120.00 |
| Dining Chair | $120.00 |

1.  Open *app8-2.wks*. Organize the spreadsheet following the format given in the table. The new spreadsheet should have furniture items organized by rooms, with proper headings. Remember to use the Fill Down command to copy repetitive items and the Insert Row/Column command to provide headings. Use the Cut and Paste commands to move some of the data.

2.  Print the spreadsheet.

3.  Save the spreadsheet to your data disk as *furn* and close the file.

# APPLICATION 8-3

You are a member of a club that participates in school athletic activities. You have been allocated $1,210 to purchase sports equipment for the club. You decide to prepare a spreadsheet to help you calculate the cost of various purchases.

Open the file *app8-3.wks* from your template disk and make the following adjustments to the spreadsheet:

1.  Bold and center the column headings appearing in Row 2.

2.  Insert a row above Row 3.

3.  Freeze the column headings in Row 2. (*Hint:* The highlight should be placed in A3.)

4.  Insert a row above Row 8 and key **Bats** into Column A of the new row.

5.  Use the Fill Down command to copy the formula in E4 to E5:E12.

6.  Format the Cost (D4:D11) and Total (E4:E12) columns for currency.

7.  Key the data for Sport and Cost, as given in the table that follows. Use the Fill Down command as needed to copy repetitive data. Widen the columns if necessary.

8.  The organization has requested you to purchase the items listed below. Any remaining cash should be used to purchase as many basketballs as possible.

    Basketballs    5

    Hoops          2

    Backboards     2

    Softballs      20

    Bats           5

    Masks          1

    Volleyballs    7

    Nets           1

    (*Hint:* You should use $1,203.00 and have $7.00 left over.)

9.  The costs of these items are not expected to change any time soon. Protect the data in the Cost column (D4:D11) so that the data cannot be accidentally changed. Remember to unlock all the contents of the spreadsheet before locking the portion you want to protect.

| SPORTS EQUIPMENT PURCHASES | | |
|---|---|---|
| **Item** | **Sport** | **Cost** |
| Basketballs | Basketball | $28.00 |
| Hoops | Basketball | $40.00 |
| Backboards | Basketball | $115.00 |
| Softballs | Softball | $5.00 |
| Bats | Softball | $30.00 |
| Masks | Softball | $35.00 |
| Volleyballs | Volleyball | $25.00 |
| Nets | Volleyball | $125.00 |

10. Set the print area and print the spreadsheet.

11. Save the spreadsheet to your data disk as *sports* and close the file.

# ADVANCED SPREADSHEET OPERATIONS

## LEARNING OBJECTIVES

**When you complete this chapter, you will be able to:**

1. Define a spreadsheet formula.
2. Create spreadsheet formulas.
3. Enter and edit formulas.
4. Distinguish between relative and absolute cell references.
5. Use the Autosum[1] button.
6. Display formulas in the spreadsheet.
7. Perform immediate and delayed calculations.
8. Use function formulas.

In previous chapters, you learned to enter text and numbers in a spreadsheet. Spreadsheets can use numbers entered in certain cells to calculate values in other cells. The equations used to calculate values in a cell are known as *formulas*. Formulas are visible in the formula bar of the spreadsheet. In this chapter, you will learn to create, enter, and use formulas in a spreadsheet.

A primary advantage of the spreadsheet is the power of rapid calculation. In fact, the spreadsheet will perform the same functions as a hand or desk calculator.

---

[1] Autosum is a trademark of Microsoft Corporation.

## Using the Spreadsheet as a Calculator

In this activity, you will observe the computing power of the spreadsheet.

1.  Open the file *act9-1.wks* from your template disk. This spreadsheet contains headings for the four primary mathematical functions of addition, subtraction, multiplication, and division.

2.  Key **10** in A5 and **24** in C5. The value in E5 should display 34, which is the sum of 10 and 24.

3.  Highlight **E5**. Notice that the formula bar at the top of the screen displays the formula =A5+C5. The formula indicates that E5 contains the sum of the values in A5 and C5.

4.  Key **48** in A14 and **8** in C14. The value in E14 should display 6, which is the result of 48 divided by 8.

5.  Highlight **E14**. Notice that the formula bar at the top of the screen displays the formula =A14/C14. The formula indicates that E14 contains the result of the value in A14 divided by the value in C14.

6.  Experiment by entering numbers into other cells of the spreadsheet. Calculations will take place as soon as you press the Enter key or click the Enter box.

7.  Leave *act9-1.wks* on your screen for the next activity.

## WHAT ARE FORMULAS?

A *formula* is an equation that calculates a new value from existing values. Works recognizes the contents of a cell as a formula when an equal sign (=) is the first character in the cell. For example, if the formula =8+6 were entered into cell B3, the value of 14 would be displayed in the spreadsheet. The formula bar displays the formula =8+6, as shown in Figure 9-1.

### Structure of a Formula

A spreadsheet formula is composed of two types of characters: operands and operators. An *operand* is a number or cell reference used

**FIGURE 9-1**

Works recognizes an entry as a formula when an equal sign is the first character in the cell. In Cell B3, the formula =8+6, displayed in the formula bar, produces produced the value of 14 in the cell.

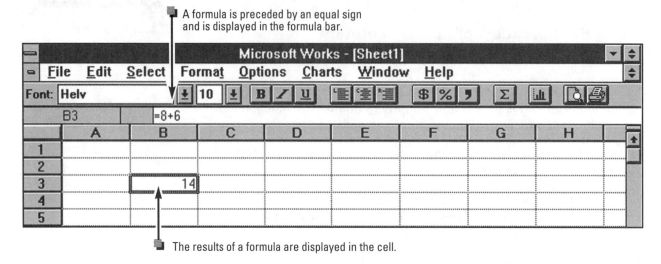

A formula is preceded by an equal sign and is displayed in the formula bar.

The results of a formula are displayed in the cell.

in formulas. An *operator* tells Works what to do with the operands. For example, in the formula =B3+5, B3 and 5 are operands. The plus sign (+) is an operator that tells Works to add the value contained in Cell B3 to the number 5. The operators used in formulas are shown in Table 9-1. You may observe the formulas for the spreadsheet now on your screen by highlighting Cells E5, E8, E11, or E14.

**TABLE 9-1**

Operators tell Works what to do with operands.

| Operator | Operation | Example | Meaning |
|---|---|---|---|
| + | Addition | B5+C5 | Adds the values in B5 and C5 |
| - | Subtraction | C8-232 | Subtracts 232 from the value in C8 |
| * | Multiplication | D4*D5 | Multiplies the value in D4 by the value in D5 |
| / | Division | E6/4 | Divides the value in E6 by 4 |
| ^ | Exponentiation | B3^3 | Raises the value in B3 to the third power |

## Order of Evaluation

Formulas containing more than one operator are called *complex formulas*. For example, the formula =C3*C4+5 will perform both multiplication and addition to calculate the value in the cell. The sequence used to calculate the value of a formula is called the ***order of evaluation***. Formulas are evaluated in the following order:

1. Contents within parentheses are evaluated first. You may use as many sets of parentheses as you desire. Works will evaluate the innermost set of parentheses first.

2. Mathematical operators are evaluated in order of priority, as shown in Table 9-2.

3. Equations are evaluated from left to right if two or more operators have the same order of evaluation. For example, in the formula =20-15-2, 15 would be subtracted from 20; then 2 would be subtracted from the difference (5).

**TABLE 9-2**
The sequence of calculations in a formula is determined by the order of evaluation.

| Order of Evaluation | Operator | Symbol |
|---|---|---|
| First | Exponentiation | ^ |
| Second | Positive or negative | + or - |
| Third | Multiplication or division | * or / |
| Fourth | Addition or subtraction | + or - |

## EDITING FORMULAS

If you key a formula incorrectly, Works will not let you enter the formula. When you try to enter the formula, an Error dialog box will appear and the incorrect area of the formula will be shaded in the formula bar. You may then edit the formula in the same way you edited number and text data in previous chapters.

You may also edit formulas already entered in the spreadsheet. After highlighting the cell, press the Edit key (F2) or click in the formula bar and add or delete data as necessary.

## ACTIVITY 9-2

### Entering Formulas into a Spreadsheet

In this activity, you will create formulas that perform calculations using the numbers in spreadsheet file *act9-2.wks*.

1. Close the file *act9-1.wks* currently on your screen.

2. Open the file *act9-2.wks* from your template disk.

3. Enter the formulas given at right in the cells. Remember to precede each formula with an equal sign. After you enter a formula, the formula result will appear in the cell. You may check your results by comparing them to the screen shown in Figure 9-2.

4. Enter a complex formula in D3 that will add the values in cells A3 and B3, then multiply the result by 20.

| Cell | Formula |
|---|---|
| C3 | =A3+B3 |
| C4 | =A4-B4 |
| C5 | =A5*B5 |
| C6 | =A6/B6 |

Activity 9-2 continued

---

**FIGURE 9-2**

Formulas may be used to
determine values in the cells of
a spreadsheet.

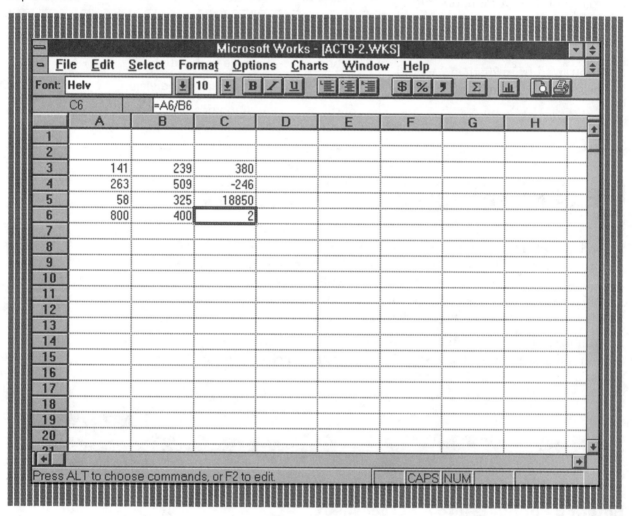

a.   Move the highlight to **D3**.

b.   Key **=(A3+B3)*20**.

c.   Press **Enter**. The resulting value should be 7600.

5.   You can see the importance of the parentheses in the order of
     evaluation by creating an identical formula without the parentheses.

a.   Move the highlight to **E3**.

b.   Key **=A3+B3*20**, the same formula as in D3 but without the
     parentheses.

c.   Press **Enter**. The resulting value in E3 should be 4921. This
     value differs from the value in D3 because Works multiplied the

Activity 9-2 continued

> value in B3 by 20 before adding A3. In D3, the values in A3 and
> B3 were added together and the sum multiplied by 20.

6.  Save the file to your data disk as *calc* and leave the file on the screen
    for the next activity.

## RELATIVE, ABSOLUTE, AND MIXED CELL REFERENCES

Three types of cell references are used to create formulas: relative, absolute, and mixed. A *relative cell reference* adjusts to its new location when copied or moved. For example, in Figure 9-3, if the formula =B2+A3 is copied or moved from B3 to C4, the formula will be changed to =C3+B4. In other words, this particular formula is instructing Works to add the cell directly above to the cell directly to the right. When the formula is copied or moved, the cell references change, but the instructions remain the same.

*Absolute cell references* contain row numbers and column letters preceded by a dollar sign ($). They do not adjust to the new cell location when copied or moved. For example, in Figure 9-3, if the formula =$A$8+$B$7 is copied from B8 to C9, the formula will remain the same in the new location.

Cell references containing both relative and absolute references are called *mixed cell*

**FIGURE 9-3**
When Cell B3 is copied to Cell C4, the relative cell reference will change. When Cell B8 is copied to Cell C9, the absolute cell reference will not change.

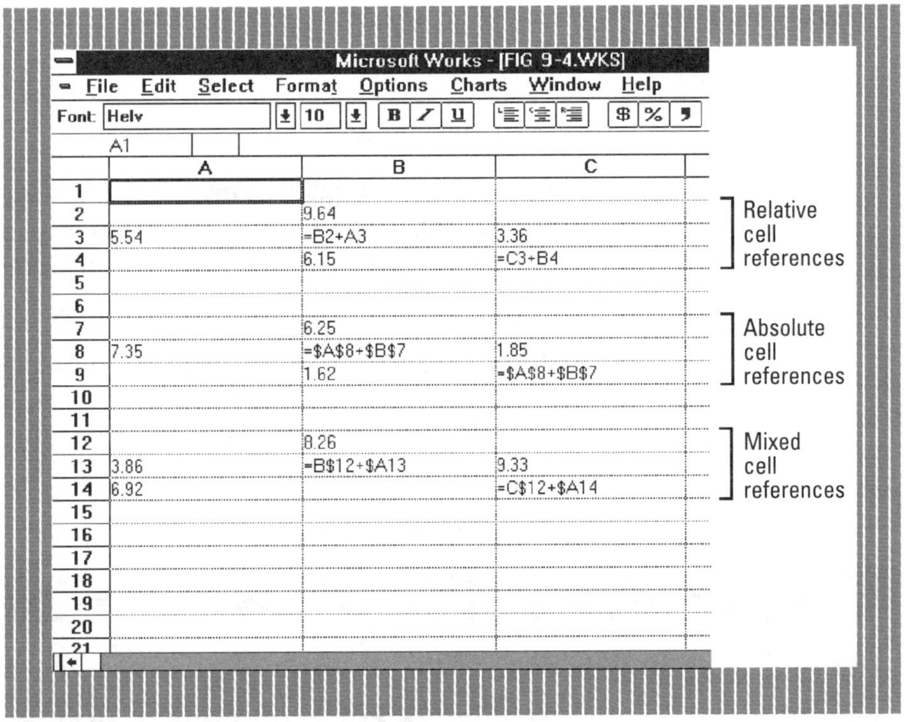

*references*. When formulas with mixed cell references are copied or moved, the row or column references preceded by a dollar sign will not change; the row or column references not preceded by a dollar sign will adjust relative to the cell to which they are moved. For example, if the formula =B$12+$A13 is copied from B13 to C14, the formula will change to =C$12+$A14.

The use of relative and absolute cell references is important only when you are copying and moving data in a spreadsheet. If you want a moved or copied cell formula to use values in a specific part of the spreadsheet, you should use absolute cell references. If you want a moved or copied cell formula to use values that correspond to the new location of the data, you should use relative cell references.

**ACTIVITY 9-3**

### Relative and Absolute Cell References

In this activity, you will enter formulas with relative and absolute cell references into the spreadsheet *calc.wks*, which is now on your screen.

1.  Place the highlight in **D3**. All cell references in the formula =(A3+B3)*20 (shown in the formula bar) are relative because neither the row nor the columns are preceded by a dollar sign.

2.  Copy the formula in **D3** to **D4**. The value in D4 should be 15440, and the formula in the formula bar should be =(A4+B4)*20. The operators in the formula remain the same as the formula in D3. However, because the cell references are relative, the row references in the operands changed down one row to reflect a change in the location of the formula.

3.  Key **=$A$3*($B$3-200)** in D5. The value in D5 should be 5499. The formula in the formula bar contains absolute cell references, which are indicated by the dollar signs that precede row and column references.

4.  Copy the formula in **D5** to **D6**. The value in D6 should be 5499, the same as in D5. Because the formula in D5 contains absolute cell references, the formula appearing in the formula bar should also be exactly the same as the formula for D5.

5.  Save and close the file.

## CREATING FORMULAS QUICKLY

You have already learned how to create formulas by keying the formula or editing existing formulas. In this section, you will learn ways to create formulas quickly by using the Point and Click method and clicking the Autosum button.

## Point and Click Method

Previously you constructed formulas by keying the entire formula in the cell of the spreadsheet. You may include cell references in a formula more quickly by clicking on the cell you want to reference rather than keying the reference. This is known as the *Point and Click method*. The Point and Click method is particularly helpful when you have to enter long formulas that contain several cell references.

To enter the formula =A3+B3 in a cell, you would:

1.  Highlight the cell that will contain the formula.
2.  Press =.
3.  Click **A3**.
4.  Press +.
5.  Click **B3**.

### ACTIVITY 9-4

### Pointing and Clicking to Create Formulas

In this activity, you will create formulas using the Point and Click method. The file *act9-4.wks* is a spreadsheet that records the portions of meat and cheese sold in a sandwich shop during a month. Portions are allocated as in the table given at right.

Create formulas to calculate the total ounces of meat and cheese sold during the month by completing the following steps:

|  | Large | Small |
|---|---|---|
| Meat | 6 ounces | 3 ounces |
| Cheese | 4 ounces | 2.5 ounces |

1.  Open the spreadsheet file *act9-4.wks* from your template disk.

2.  Enter a formula in D4 to calculate the total ounces of meat sold:
    a.  Highlight **D4**.
    b.  Key **=(6\***.
    c.  Click **B4**.
    d.  Key **)+(3\***.
    e.  Click **C4**.
    f.  Key **)**.
    g.  Press **Enter**.

3.  Use the Fill Down Command to copy the formula in D4 to D5:D7.

4.  Enter a formula in D8 to calculate the total ounces of cheese sold.

Activity 9-4 continued

   a.   Highlight **D8**.

   b.   Key **=(4\***.

   c.   Click **B8**.

   d.   Key **)+(2.5\***.

   e.   Click **C8**.

   f.   Key **)**.

   g.   Press **Enter**.

5.   Use the Fill Down command to copy the formula in D8 to D9.

6.   Compare your screen to the one in Figure 9-4.

**FIGURE 9-4**
Spreadsheet formulas may be created quickly using the mouse.

7.   Leave *act9-4.wks* on your screen for the next activity.

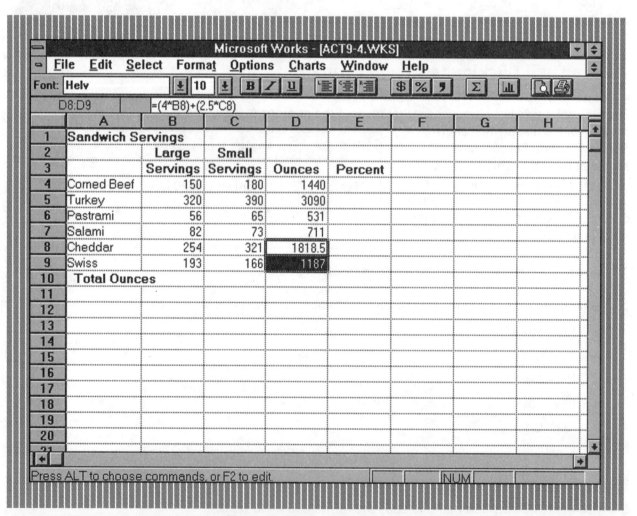

## The Autosum Button

Σ
Autosum button

Spreadsheet users frequently need to sum long columns of numbers. Works has a button on the Toolbar, the Autosum button, that makes the process of summing a simple operation. The Autosum button has the Greek letter *sigma* on it. When you click the Autosum button, Works scans the spreadsheet to determine the most logical column of numbers to sum in the cell and highlights the range of cells to be summed. This range is displayed in the cell where you want the sum to appear. If you prefer a range other than the one Works selects, choose an alternate range by dragging those cells. When you click the Autosum button a second time, the sum will appear in the cell.

The sum of a range is indicated by a special formula in the formula bar called a *function formula*. For example, if the sum of the range D5:D17 is entered in a cell, the function formula in the formula bar will be =SUM(D5:D17). The SUM function is the most frequent type of function formula. Function formulas will be discussed in detail later in this chapter.

**ACTIVITY
9-5**

## Creating Formulas Quickly

In this activity, you will change cell references in the spreadsheet file *act9-4.wks*, using the F4 key, and will perform Autosum operations. Suppose the manager of a sandwich shop would like to determine the total ounces of meat and cheese sold during the month. The manager also wants to know what percentage each meat and cheese item is of total food items sold.

1. Determine the total ounces of meat and cheese sold this month by summing D4:D9.

   a. Highlight **D10**.

   b. Click the **Autosum** button. The range D4:D9 should be highlighted. Works has correctly selected the range of cells you would like to sum.

   c. Click the **Autosum** button. The formula =SUM(D4:D9) should appear in the formula bar. Cell D10 should display 8777.5.

2. Format **E4:E10** for percent.

3. Determine the percent of total ounces sold for each type of meat and cheese.

   a. Highlight **E4**.

   b. Press **=**.

Activity 9-5 continued

c. Click **D4**.

d. Press **/**.

e. Key **$D$10**.

f. Press **Enter**. The cell should display 16.41%.

4. Copy the formula in **E4** to **E5:E10** using the Fill Down command. All of the food items should be expressed as a percentage of the total food items. E10 should show 100%.

5. Compare your screen to the one shown in Figure 9-5.

6. Leave *act9-4.wks* on your screen for the next activity.

**FIGURE 9-5**
The Autosum button will add a column of numbers quickly.

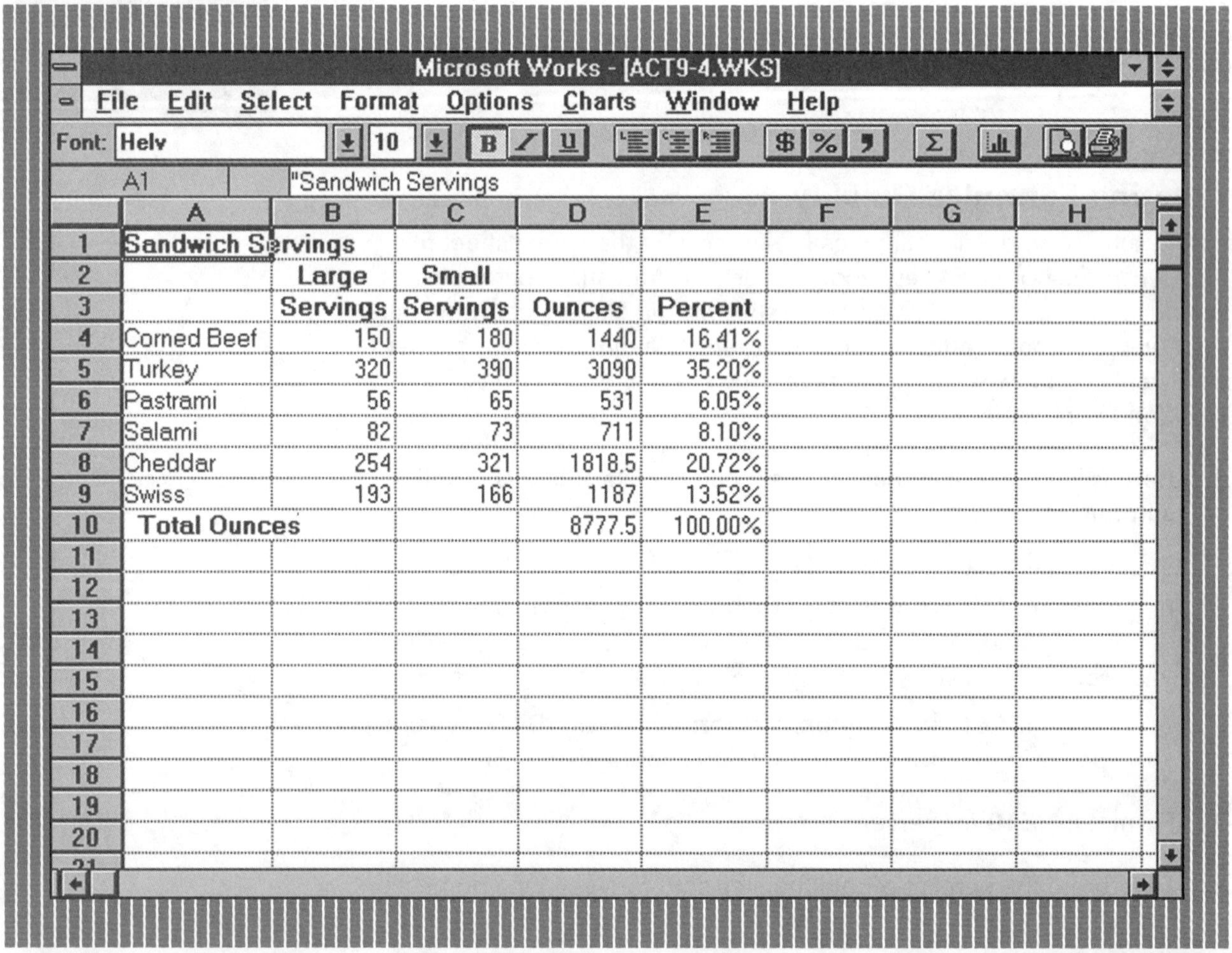


| | A | B | C | D | E |
|---|---|---|---|---|---|
| 1 | Sandwich Servings | | | | |
| 2 | | Large | Small | | |
| 3 | | Servings | Servings | Ounces | Percent |
| 4 | Corned Beef | 150 | 180 | 1440 | 16.41% |
| 5 | Turkey | 320 | 390 | 3090 | 35.20% |
| 6 | Pastrami | 56 | 65 | 531 | 6.05% |
| 7 | Salami | 82 | 73 | 711 | 8.10% |
| 8 | Cheddar | 254 | 321 | 1818.5 | 20.72% |
| 9 | Swiss | 193 | 166 | 1187 | 13.52% |
| 10 | Total Ounces | | | 8777.5 | 100.00% |

# FORMULA HELPERS

Two commands, Show Formulas and Manual Calculation, can help you to use formulas in the spreadsheet. The Show Formulas command will replace the values in the cells of the spreadsheet with the formulas that created them. The Manual Calculation command will prevent spreadsheet formulas from calculating until you press the F9 key. Both commands are located in the Options menu.

## Showing Formulas on the Spreadsheet

In previous activities, you were able to view formulas only in the formula bar. Cells of the spreadsheet contained the values created by formulas rather than the formulas themselves. When creating a spreadsheet containing many formulas, you may find it easier to organize formulas and detect formula errors when you can view all formulas simultaneously.

Selecting the Show Formulas command from the Options menu (see Figure 9-6) will display formulas rather than values in the cells of the spreadsheet. When the Show Formulas command is selected, a cell that does not contain a formula will display the content entered in the cell. A check mark will appear by the Show Formulas command in the Options menu when the command is turned on. To display values determined by the formulas again, select the Show Formulas command once more.

**FIGURE 9-6**
The Show Formulas command displays formulas in the spreadsheet. The Manual Calculation command delays spreadsheet calculation until F9 is pressed.

| Options |
| --- |
| <u>W</u>orks Settings... |
| <u>D</u>ial This Number |
| ✓ Show Tool<u>b</u>ar |
| ✓ Show <u>G</u>ridlines |
| Show <u>F</u>ormulas |
| Freeze <u>T</u>itles |
| <u>P</u>rotect Data |
| Manual Calculation |
| Calculate <u>N</u>ow    F9 |

## Delayed Calculations

The calculation of values in the spreadsheet will usually occur as a new value is entered in the spreadsheet, but you can also calculate in the spreadsheet at a specific moment. Delayed calculation can be useful when you are working with a large spreadsheet that will take longer than usual to calculate; or you may want to view the difference in a particular cell after you have made changes throughout the spreadsheet.

To delay calculation, select the Manual Calculation command from the Options menu, as shown in Figure 9-6. No calculation will occur until you press the F9 key. To return to automatic calculation, select the Manual Calculation command again.

## ACTIVITY 9-6

### Showing Formulas and Delaying Calculation

In this activity, you will view simultaneously the formulas used to create spreadsheet *act9-4.wks*. You will also delay calculation of changes to the spreadsheet using the Manual Calculation command.

Activity 9-6 continued

1. From the **Options** menu, choose **Show Formulas**.

2. Scroll to the right so that Columns D and E appear on the screen. Each value in the spreadsheet created by a formula has now been replaced by the formula creating the value.

3. From the **Options** menu, choose **Show Formulas**. The values determined by the formulas will reappear on the screen.

4. From the **Options** menu, choose **Manual Calculation**.

5. Change the following values in the spreadsheet.

   a. Key **190** in B4.

   b. Key **410** in C5.

   c. Key **96** in B7.

6. Press **F9** while watching the screen. Calculations will be made as you press the key.

7. Save the file to your data disk as *deli* and close the file.

# FUNCTION FORMULAS

*Function formulas* are special formulas that do not use operators to calculate a result. They perform complex calculations in specialized areas of mathematics, statistics, logic, trigonometry, accounting, and finance. Function formulas are also used to convert spreadsheet values to dates and times. There are 57 function formulas in Works. In this section, you will learn the more frequently used function formulas.

## Parts of Function Formulas

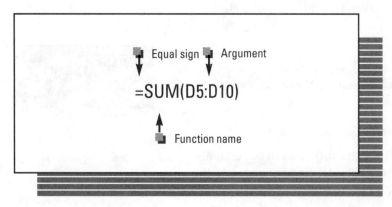

Equal sign   Argument

=SUM(D5:D10)

Function name

A function formula contains three components: the equal sign, a function name, and an argument.

▶ The *equal sign* tells Works a formula will be entered into the cell.

▶ The *function name* identifies the operation to be performed. A function name is usually two to seven characters long.

▶ The *argument* is a value, cell reference, range, or text that acts as an operand in a function formula. The argument is enclosed in parentheses after the function name. If a function formula contains more than one argument, the arguments are separated by commas. The range of cells that make up the argument is separated by a colon.

You have already created a function formula in a previous activity by using the Autosum button. When pressed, the Autosum button inserted an equal sign followed by the word *SUM*. The range of cells to be summed was designated within parentheses; for example, =SUM(D5:D10). In this function formula, the word SUM is the function name that identifies the operation. The argument is the range of cells that are to be operated upon.

## Mathematical Functions

*Mathematical functions* manipulate quantitative data in the spreadsheet. You have already learned mathematical operations, such as addition, subtraction, multiplication, and division, that do not require function formulas. You have also used the Autosum button to create SUM functions. Two other mathematical functions, the square root and rounding functions, are described in Table 9-3. Notice that two arguments are required to perform the rounding operation.

**TABLE 9-3**

Mathematical functions manipulate quantitative data in the spreadsheet.

| Function | Operation |
|---|---|
| SUM(Range) | Displays the sum of the range identified in the argument. |
| SQRT(X) | Displays the square root of the value *X* identified in the argument. For example, =SQRT(C4) will display the square root of the value in C4. |
| ROUND(X,Places) | Displays the rounded value of *X* to the number of places designated by the second argument. For example, =ROUND(14.23433,2) will display 14.23. If the second argument is a negative number, the first argument will be rounded to the left of the decimal point. |

**ACTIVITY 9-7**

## Mathematical Functions

In this activity, you will perform mathematical functions on numbers contained in the file *act9-7.wks*. You may compare your results to the screen shown in Figure 9-7.

1.   Open the file *act9-7.wks* from your template disk.

Activity 9-7 continued

2.  Determine the sum of the numbers in Column B using the SUM function.

    a.   Highlight **B9**.

    b.   Enter **=SUM(B4:B8)**. (The same operation could have been performed using the Autosum button on the Toolbar.)

3.  Determine the square root of the sum determined in B9 using the SQRT function.

    a.   Highlight **B10**.

    b.   Enter **=SQRT(B9)**.

**FIGURE 9-7**

Mathematical functions perform calculations, such as summing, determining square roots, and rounding, on spreadsheet data.

4.  Round the square root determined in B10 to the tenths place using the ROUND function.

    a.   Highlight **B11**.

    b.   Enter **=ROUND(B10,2)**.

5.  Leave *act9-7.wks* on your screen for the next activity.

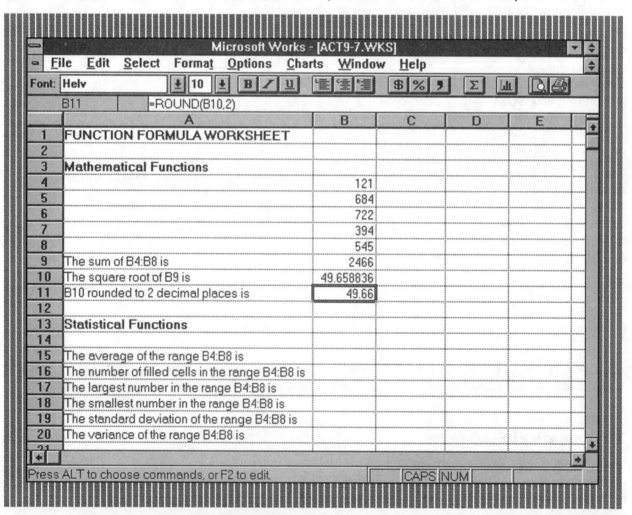

## Statistical Functions

*Statistical functions* are used to describe large quantities of data. For example, function formulas can be used to determine the average, standard deviation, or variance of a range of data. Statistical functions can also be used to determine the number of values in a range, the largest value in a range, and the smallest value in a range. Table 9-4 shows some of the statistical functions available in Works. Notice that all the statistical functions contain a range for the argument. The range is the body of numbers the statistics will describe.

**TABLE 9-4**
Statistical functions are used to analyze large amounts of numbers.

| Function | Operation |
|---|---|
| AVG(Range) | Displays the average of the range identified in the argument. For example, =AVG(E4:E9) will display the average of the numbers contained in the range E4:E9. |
| COUNT(Range) | Displays the number of filled cells in the range identified in the argument. For example, =COUNT(D6:D21) will display 16 if all the cells in the range are filled. |
| MAX(Range) | Displays the largest number contained in the range identified in the argument. |
| MIN(Range) | Displays the smallest number contained in the range identified in the argument. |
| STD(Range) | Displays the standard deviation of the values contained in the range of the argument. |
| VAR(Range) | Displays the variance for the values contained in the range of the argument. |

**ACTIVITY
9-8**

## Statistical Functions

In this activity, you will use function formulas to calculate statistics on a range of values in the file *act9-7.wks*. You may compare your results to the screen shown in Figure 9-8.

1.  Determine the average of the values in the range B4:B8.

    a.  Highlight **B15**.

    b.  Enter **=AVG(B4:B8)**.

2.  Determine the number of filled cells in the range B4:B8.

    a.  Highlight **B16**.

    b.  Enter **=COUNT(B4:B8)**.

3.  Determine the largest number in the range B4:B8.

    a.  Highlight **B17**.

    b.  Enter **=MAX(B4:B8)**.

Activity 9-8 continued

4. Determine the smallest number in the range B4:B8.

    a. Highlight **B18**.

    b. Enter **=MIN(B4:B8)**.

5. Determine the standard deviation of the range B4:B8.

    a. Highlight **B19**.

    b. Enter **=STD(B4:B8)**. (Your rounded amount may vary depending on your column width.)

6. Determine the variance of the range B4:B8.

    a. Highlight **B20**.

    b. Enter **=VAR(B4:B8)**. The value 47962.16 should appear in the cell.

7. Leave *act9-7.wks* on the screen for the next activity.

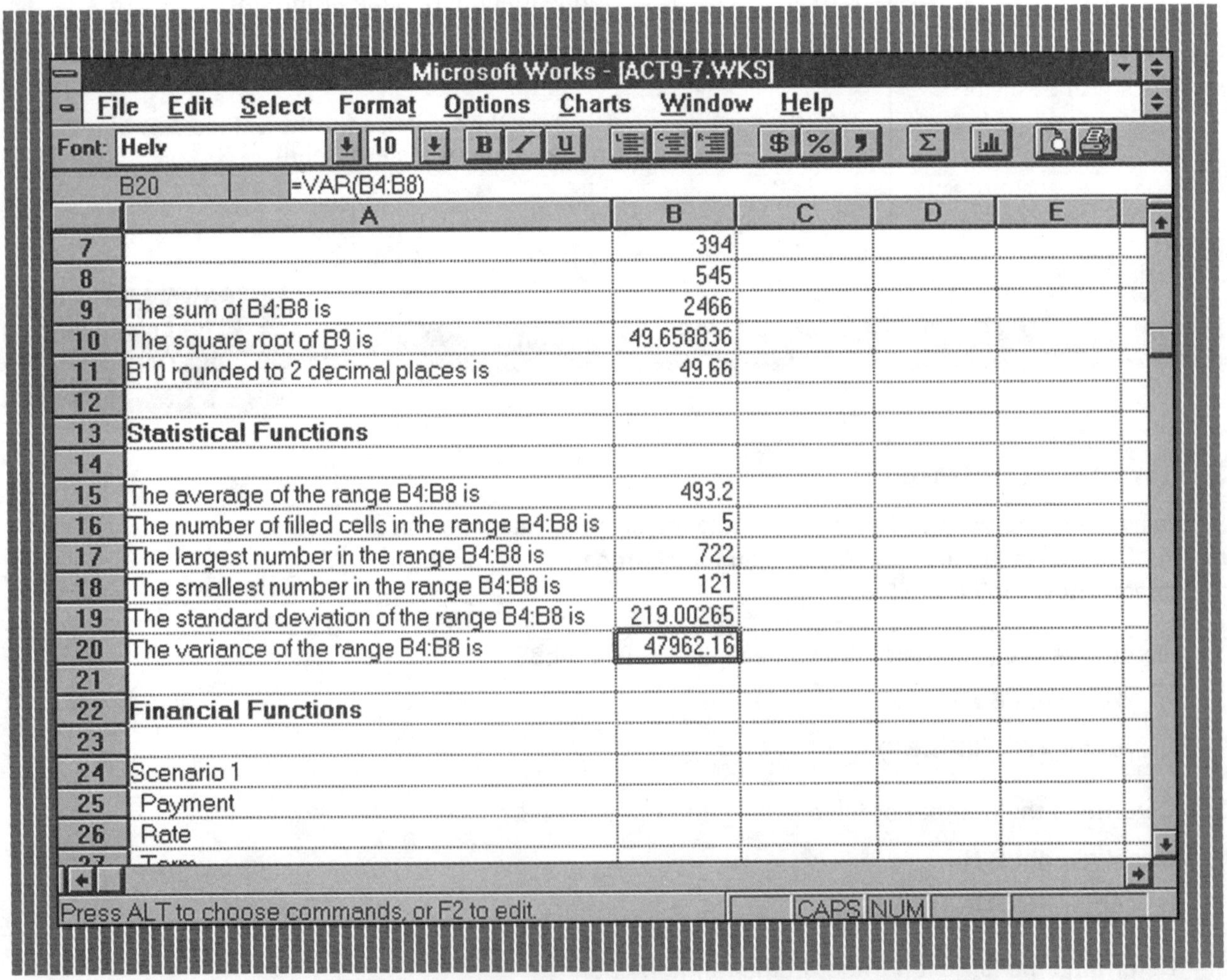

**FIGURE 9-8**

Statistical functions perform various operations, such as finding the average, maximum, minimum, standard deviation, and variance.

Microsoft Works - [ACT9-7.WKS]

File   Edit   Select   Format   Options   Charts   Window   Help

Font: Helv    10   B   I   U    $   %   ,    Σ

B20     =VAR(B4:B8)

| | A | B | C | D | E |
|---|---|---|---|---|---|
| 7 | | 394 | | | |
| 8 | | 545 | | | |
| 9 | The sum of B4:B8 is | 2466 | | | |
| 10 | The square root of B9 is | 49.658836 | | | |
| 11 | B10 rounded to 2 decimal places is | 49.66 | | | |
| 12 | | | | | |
| 13 | Statistical Functions | | | | |
| 14 | | | | | |
| 15 | The average of the range B4:B8 is | 493.2 | | | |
| 16 | The number of filled cells in the range B4:B8 is | 5 | | | |
| 17 | The largest number in the range B4:B8 is | 722 | | | |
| 18 | The smallest number in the range B4:B8 is | 121 | | | |
| 19 | The standard deviation of the range B4:B8 is | 219.00265 | | | |
| 20 | The variance of the range B4:B8 is | 47962.16 | | | |
| 21 | | | | | |
| 22 | Financial Functions | | | | |
| 23 | | | | | |
| 24 | Scenario 1 | | | | |
| 25 | Payment | | | | |
| 26 | Rate | | | | |
| 27 | Term | | | | |

Press ALT to choose commands, or F2 to edit.     CAPS NUM

# Financial Functions

*Financial functions* are used to analyze loans and investments. The primary financial functions are future value, present value, and payment, which are described in Table 9-5.

TABLE 9-5
Financial functions are used to analyze loans and investments.

| Function | Operation |
|---|---|
| FV(Payment,Rate,Term) | Displays the future value of a series of equal payments (first argument), at a fixed rate (second argument), over a specified period of time (third argument). For example, =FV($100,.08,5) will determine the future value of five $100 payments at the end of five years if you can earn a rate of 8%. |
| PV(Payment,Rate,Term) | Displays the present value of a series of equal payments (first argument), at a fixed rate (second argument), over a specified period of time (third argument). For example, =PV($500,.1,5) will display current value of five payments of $500 at a 10% rate. |
| PMT(Principal,Rate,Term) | Displays the payment per period needed to repay a loan (first argument), at a specified interest (second argument), for a specified period of time (third argument). For example, =PMT(10,000,.01,36) will display the monthly payment needed to repay a $10,000 loan at a 12% annual rate (.01 times 12 months), for three years (36 months divided by 12*). |

*Rate and term functions should be compatible. In other words, if payments are monthly rather than annual, the annual rate should be divided by 12 to determine the monthly rate.

## ACTIVITY 9-9

## Financial Functions

In this activity, you will calculate answers to three scenarios. Use the lower part of the spreadsheet in the file *act9-7.wks* for your calculations. You may compare your results to the screen shown in Figure 9-9.

1. You plan to make six yearly payments of $150 into a savings account that earns 9.5% annually. Use the FV function to determine the value of the account at the end of six years.

   a. Enter **150** in B25.

   b. Enter **.095** in B26.

   c. Enter **6** in B27.

   d. Enter **=FV(B25,B26,B27)** in B28. The savings account will have grown to the amount shown in B28 after six years.

2. You have a choice of receiving $1,200 now or eight annual payments of $210. A typical rate for a savings account in your local bank is 6%.

Activity 9-9 continued

Use the PV function to determine which is the most profitable alternative.

a. Enter **210** in B30.

b. Enter = **.06** in B31.

**FIGURE 9-9**

Financial functions perform various operations, such as finding present and future values.

c. Enter **8** in B32.

d. Enter **=PV(B30,B31,B32)** in B33. The best decision is to take the delayed payments because the present value, $1,304.06, is greater than $1,200.

```
┌──────────────────────────────────────────────────────────────┐
│            Microsoft Works - [ACT9-7.WKS]                      │
│  File  Edit  Select  Format  Options  Charts  Window  Help     │
│  Font: Helv      ±10  ±  B / U  ≡≡≡  $ % ,  Σ  ⅢⅠ  ▣🖨         │
│      B38          =PMT(B35,B36,B37)                             │
│            A              B       C       D       E            │
│  22  Financial Functions                                       │
│  23                                                            │
│  24  Scenario 1                                                │
│  25   Payment           $150.00                                │
│  26   Rate               9.50%                                 │
│  27   Term                   6                                 │
│  28    Future Value    $1,142.83                               │
│  29  Scenario 2                                                │
│  30   Payment           $210.00                                │
│  31   Rate               6.00%                                 │
│  32   Term                   8                                 │
│  33    Present Value   $1,304.06                               │
│  34  Scenario 3                                                │
│  35   Principal        $5,000.00                               │
│  36   Rate               1.00%                                 │
│  37   Term                  60                                 │
│  38   Payment           $111.22                                │
│  39                                                            │
│  40                                                            │
│  41                                                            │
│  Press ALT to choose commands, or F2 to edit.     CA S NUM     │
└──────────────────────────────────────────────────────────────┘
```

3. You need to borrow $5,000. Your banker has offered you an annual rate of 12% interest for a five-year loan. Use the PMT function to determine what your *monthly* payments on the loan would be.

a. Enter **5000** in B35.

b. Enter **.01** in B36. [A 1% monthly rate (12% divided by 12 months) is used because the problem requests monthly, rather than annual, payments.]

c. Enter **60** in B37. [A period of 60 months (5 years times 12 months) is used because the problem requests monthly, rather than annual, payments.]

d. Enter **=PMT(B35,B36,B37)** in B38. The value $111.22 will be in the cell. You will have to pay a total of $1,673.20 [($111.22 * 60 months) −$5,000 principal] in interest over the life of the loan.

4. Save the file to your data disk as *funct* and close the file.

Works has many more function formulas available to help you with number problems. You may consult the appendix in a Works manual for a complete list.

# SUMMARY

The spreadsheet has the power to perform rapid calculations. Spreadsheet formulas perform calculations on values referenced in other cells of the spreadsheet.

Cell references in formulas may be relative or absolute. Relative cell references adjust to a different location when copied or moved. Absolute cell references describe the same cell location in the spreadsheet regardless of where it is copied or moved. Mixed cell references contain both relative and absolute cell references.

Formulas may be created quickly by using the Point and Click method. This method inserts cell references by clicking the cell with the mouse rather than keying its column letter and row number.

A group of cells may be summed quickly by using the Autosum button on the Toolbar. Works will insert the SUM formula function and determine the most likely range to be summed.

Function formulas are special formulas that do not require operators. Works has 57 function formulas that may be used to perform mathematical, statistical, financial, and other operations.

# CHALLENGES

## TRUE/FALSE

Circle **T** or **F** to show whether the statement is true or false.

T    F    1. Works recognizes an entry as a formula when it is preceded by an equal sign (=).

T    F    2. An operator is a number or cell reference used in formulas.

T    F    3. In a complex formula, subtraction will be performed before multiplication.

T    F    4. Operations within parentheses will be performed before operations outside parentheses in a formula.

T    F    5. An absolute cell reference will change if the formula is copied or moved.

T    F    6. The Autosum button creates the function formula =SUM in the highlighted cell.

T    F    7. The Show Formulas command will display formulas rather than values in the spreadsheet.

T    F    8. Manual calculation is performed by pressing the F2 key.

T    F    9. Statistical function formulas are used to analyze loans and investments.

T    F    10. Function formulas do not have operators.

# COMPLETION

1. Which operator has the highest priority in the order of evaluation in a spreadsheet formula?

_____

2. What type of cell reference adjusts to its new location when it is copied or moved?

_____

3. What type of cell reference will remain the same when it is copied or moved?

_____

4. What technique inserts cell references in a formula by clicking the mouse?

_____

5. Which function formula is inserted in a cell by clicking the Autosum button?

_____

6. What Toolbar button is used to create a function formula that adds a column of numbers?

_____

7. Which command will display formulas in the spreadsheet?

_____

8. Which command delays calculation until the F9 key is pressed?

_____

9. What is the name of the item enclosed in parentheses in a function formula?

_____

10. What type of function formula describes the characteristics of large quantities of data?

_____

## APPLICATION 9-1

Match the letter of the spreadsheet formula to the description of the spreadsheet operation performed by the formula.

**Spreadsheet Operation**

**Spreadsheet Formula**

____ 1. Adds the values in A3 and A4

a. =A3/(27+A4)

____ 2. Subtracts the value in A4 from the value in A3

b. =A3^27

c. =A3^27/A4

____ 3. Multiplies the value in A3 times 27

d. =A3+A4

____ 4. Divides the value in A3 by 27

e. =A3/27

____ 5. Raises the value in A3 to the 27th power

f. =A3/27+A4

____ 6. Divides the value in A3 by 27, then adds the value in A4

g. =(A3*27)/A4

____ 7. Divides the value in A3 by the result of 27 plus the value in A4

h. =A3-A4

i. =A3*(27/A4)

____ 8. Multiplies the value in A3 times 27, then divides the product by the value in A4

j. =A3*27

____ 9. Divides 27 by the value in A4, then multiplies the result by the value in A3

____ 10. Raises the value in A3 to the 27th power, then divides the result by the value in A4

## APPLICATION 9-2

The file *app9-2.wks* is a spreadsheet containing several values. Enter formulas in the specified cells that will perform the requested operations. After you enter each formula, write the resulting value in the space provided. When you have completed the application, save the file to your data disk and close it.

**Resulting Value      Cell    Operation**

_____  1.   C3      Add the values in A3 and B3

| Resulting Value | Cell | Operation |
|---|---|---|
| _____ 2. | C4 | Subtract the value in B4 from the value in A4 |
| _____ 3. | C5 | Multiply the value in A5 by the value in B5 |
| _____ 4. | C6 | Divide the value in A6 by the value in B6 |
| _____ 5. | B7 | Sum the values in the range B3:B6 |
| _____ 6. | D3 | Add the values in A3 and A4, then multiply the sum by 3 |
| _____ 7. | D4 | Add the values in A3 and A4, then multiply the sum by B3 |
| _____ 8. | D5 | Raise the value in A5 to the 3rd power |
| _____ 9. | D6 | Subtract the value in B6 from the value in A6, then divide by 2 |
| _____10. | D7 | Divide the value in A6 by 2, then subtract the value in B6 |

# APPLICATION 9-3

Your organization, the Entrepreneurs Club, has decided to have a holiday sale in which bags of oranges and grapefruit and tins of fruitcake and hard candy will be sold at a profit. You have been asked to create a spreadsheet that will calculate the bills of individuals who purchase holiday gifts from your organization. Because your organization is not a nonprofit organization, you will be required to charge a sales tax of 4% on each sale. The file *app9-3.wks* is a spreadsheet lacking the formulas required to calculate the bills. Complete the spreadsheet following these steps:

1.  Open the file *app9-3.wks*.
2.  Enter formulas in D7, D8, D9, and D10 to calculate the cost of each food item when quantities are entered in Column C.
3.  Enter a formula in D11 to sum the totals in D7:D10.
4.  Enter a formula in D12 to calculate a sales tax equal to 4% of the subtotal in D11.
5.  Enter a formula in D13 to add the subtotal and sales tax.
6.  Change the spreadsheet for manual calculation.
7.  Format D7:D13 for currency.
8.  Save the file. The saved data applies to all customers. The spreadsheet is now ready to accept data unique to the individual customer.
9.  Suppose a customer purchases three bags of oranges, four bags of grapefruit, two fruitcakes, and one tin of hard candy. Enter the quantities in Column C and press **F9** to calculate.
10. Check the calculations made by the formulas by hand to make sure that you have entered the formulas correctly. If any of the formulas are incorrect, edit them and recalculate the spreadsheet.
11. When you are confident that the spreadsheet is calculating as you intended, print the customer's bill.
12. Close the file without saving the most recent changes.

# APPLICATION 9-4

Write the appropriate function formula to perform each of the described operations. You may refer to Tables 9-3 through 9-5 to help you prepare the function formulas.

_____ 1.   Determine the smallest value in A4:A90

_____ 2.   Determine the standard deviation of the values in K6:K35

_____ 3.   Determine the average of the values in B9:B45

_____ 4.   Determine the yearly payments on a $5,000 loan at 8% for 10 years

_____ 5.   Determine the value of a savings account at the end of 5 years after making $400 yearly payments; the account earns 8%

_____ 6.   Round the value in C3 to the tenths place

_____ 7.   Determine the present value of a pension plan that will pay you 20 yearly payments of $4,000; the current rate of return is 7.5%

_____ 8.   Determine the square root of 225

_____ 9.   Determine the variance of the values in F9:F35

_____ 10.  Add all the values in D4:D19

_____ 11.  Determine how many cells in H7:H21 are filled with data

_____ 12.  Determine the largest value in E45:E92

---

# APPLICATION 9-5

The file *app9-5.wks* contains a spreadsheet of student grades for one examination. Calculate statistics on these grades by following these steps:

1.   Open the file *app9-5.wks* from your template disk.

2.   Determine the number of students taking the examination by entering a function formula in B26.

3.   Determine the average exam grade by entering a function formula in B27.

4.   Determine the highest exam grade by entering a function formula in B28.

5.   Determine the lowest exam grade by entering a function formula in B29.

6.   Determine the standard deviation of the exam grades by entering a function formula in B30.

7.   Save the file to your data disk and close it.

# APPLICATION 9-6

Generic National Bank makes a profit by taking money deposited by customers and lending it to others at a higher rate. In order to encourage depositing and borrowing, you have helped the bank develop a spreadsheet that will inform depositors about the future value of their investments. Another portion of the spreadsheet informs borrowers of the yearly payments they must make on their loans. The incomplete spreadsheet is in file *app9-6.wks*. Complete the spreadsheet by following these steps:

1.  Enter a function formula in B11 that will inform borrowers of the yearly payment. Assume that the loan principal will be entered in B5, the lending rate will be entered in B7, and the term of the loan will be entered in B9. (ERR, indicating an error, will appear in the cell because no data are in the argument cell references yet.)

2.  A potential borrower inquires about the payments on a $5,500 loan for four years. The current lending rate is 11%. Determine the yearly payment on the loan.

3.  Print the portion of the spreadsheet that pertains to the loan (A1:B12) so that it may be given to the potential borrower.

4.  Enter a function formula in B24 informing depositors of the future value of periodic payments. Assume the yearly payments will be entered in B18, the term of the payments will be entered in B20, and the interest rate will be entered in B22. ($0.00 will appear because no data are in the argument cell references yet.)

5.  A potential depositor is starting a college fund for her son. She inquires about the value of yearly deposits of $450 at the end of 15 years. The current interest rate is 7.5%. Determine the future value of the deposits.

6.  Print the portion of the spreadsheet that applies to the deposits (A14:B25) so that it may be given to the potential depositor.

7.  Save the file to your data disk and close it.

# SPREADSHEET CHARTS

## LEARNING OBJECTIVES

**When you complete this chapter, you will be able to:**

1. Identify the purpose of charting spreadsheet data.
2. Identify the types of spreadsheet charts.
3. Create a chart.
4. Save a chart.
5. Print a chart.

## WHAT IS A SPREADSHEET CHART?

A *chart* is a graphical representation of data contained in a spreadsheet. Charts make the data of a spreadsheet easier to understand. For example, the spreadsheet in Figure 10-1 shows the populations of four major American cities for three years. You may be able to detect the changes in the populations by carefully examining the spreadsheet. However, the increases and decreases in the populations of each city are more easily recognized when the contents of the spreadsheet are illustrated in a chart, such as the one shown in Figure 10-2.

## TYPES OF SPREADSHEET CHARTS

In this chapter, you will create four of the most commonly used spreadsheet charts: bar chart, line chart, pie chart, and scatter chart. Each of these types of charts is illustrated in Figure 10-3.

**FIGURE 10-1**
Spreadsheets contain numerical data but do not illustrate relationships between data.

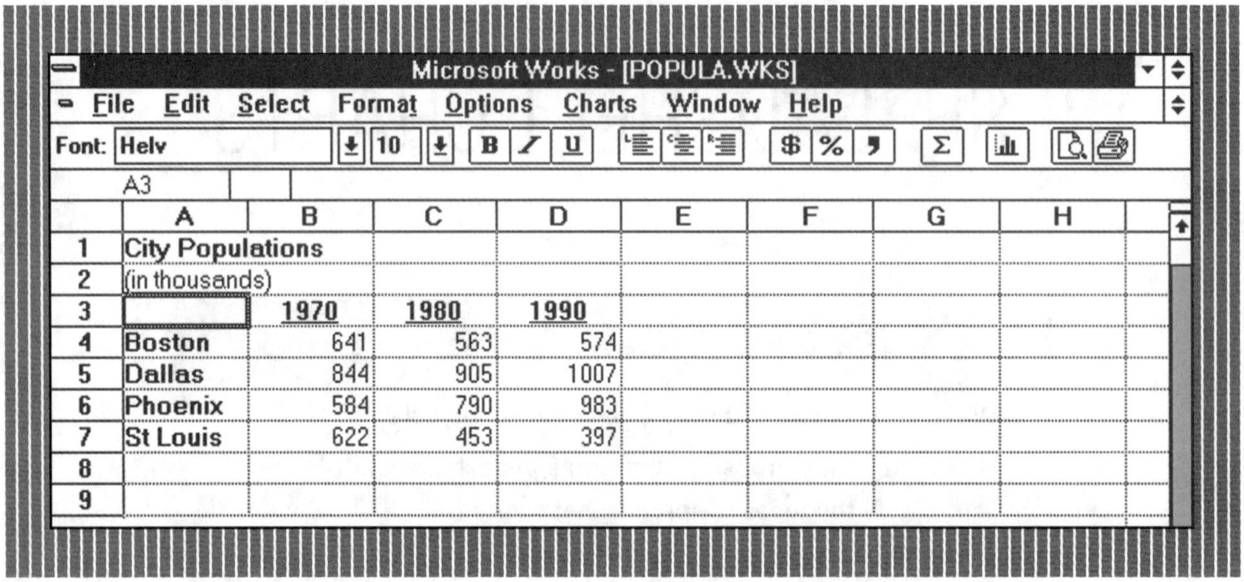
Microsoft Works - [POPULA.WKS]
File Edit Select Format Options Charts Window Help
Font: Helv 10 B / U $ % , Σ
A3
A B C D E F G H
1 City Populations
2 (in thousands)
3 1970 1980 1990
4 Boston 641 563 574
5 Dallas 844 905 1007
6 Phoenix 584 790 983
7 St Louis 622 453 397
8
9

*Data source*: U.S. Bureau of the Census, *Statistical Abstract of the United States*, 1990.

## Bar Chart

A ***bar chart*** uses rectangles of varying heights to illustrate values in a spreadsheet. For example, the bar chart in Figure 10-2 has one vertical bar to show the population of a city for each year. A bar chart is well suited for showing relationships among categories of data. The chart shows how the population of one city compares to populations of other cities.

## Line Chart

A ***line chart*** is similar to the bar chart except bars are replaced by points connected by a line. The line chart is ideal for illustrating trends of data over time. For example, Figure 10-4, a line chart printed in landscape orientation, shows the growth of the U. S. federal debt from 1980 to 1990. The vertical axis represents the level of the deficit, and the horizontal axis shows years in chronological order, from 1980 to 1990, representing the passage of time. The line chart makes it easy to see how the federal deficit has grown over time.

## Pie Chart

***Pie charts*** show the relationship of a part to a whole. Each part is presented as a "slice" of the pie. For example, a teacher could create a

**FIGURE 10-2**
Spreadsheet charts are ideal for illustrating the relationships among data contained in a spreadsheet.

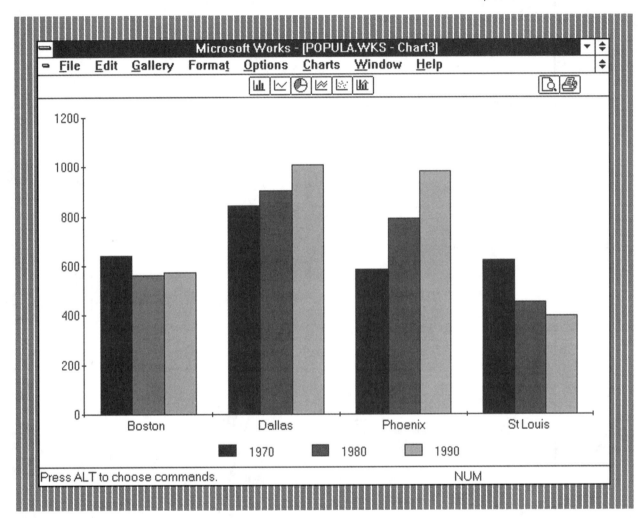

pie chart of the distribution of grades in a class, as shown in Figure 10-5. Each slice represents the portion of grades given for each letter grade.

## Scatter Chart

*Scatter charts*, sometimes called *XY charts*, show the relationship between two categories of data. One category is represented on the vertical (*Y*) axis, and the other category is

**FIGURE 10-3**
Several types of charts are available in Works. Four of the most commonly used charts are the bar, line, pie, and scatter charts.

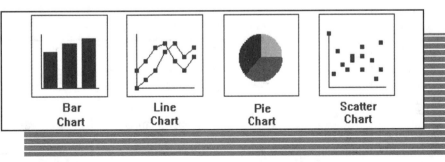

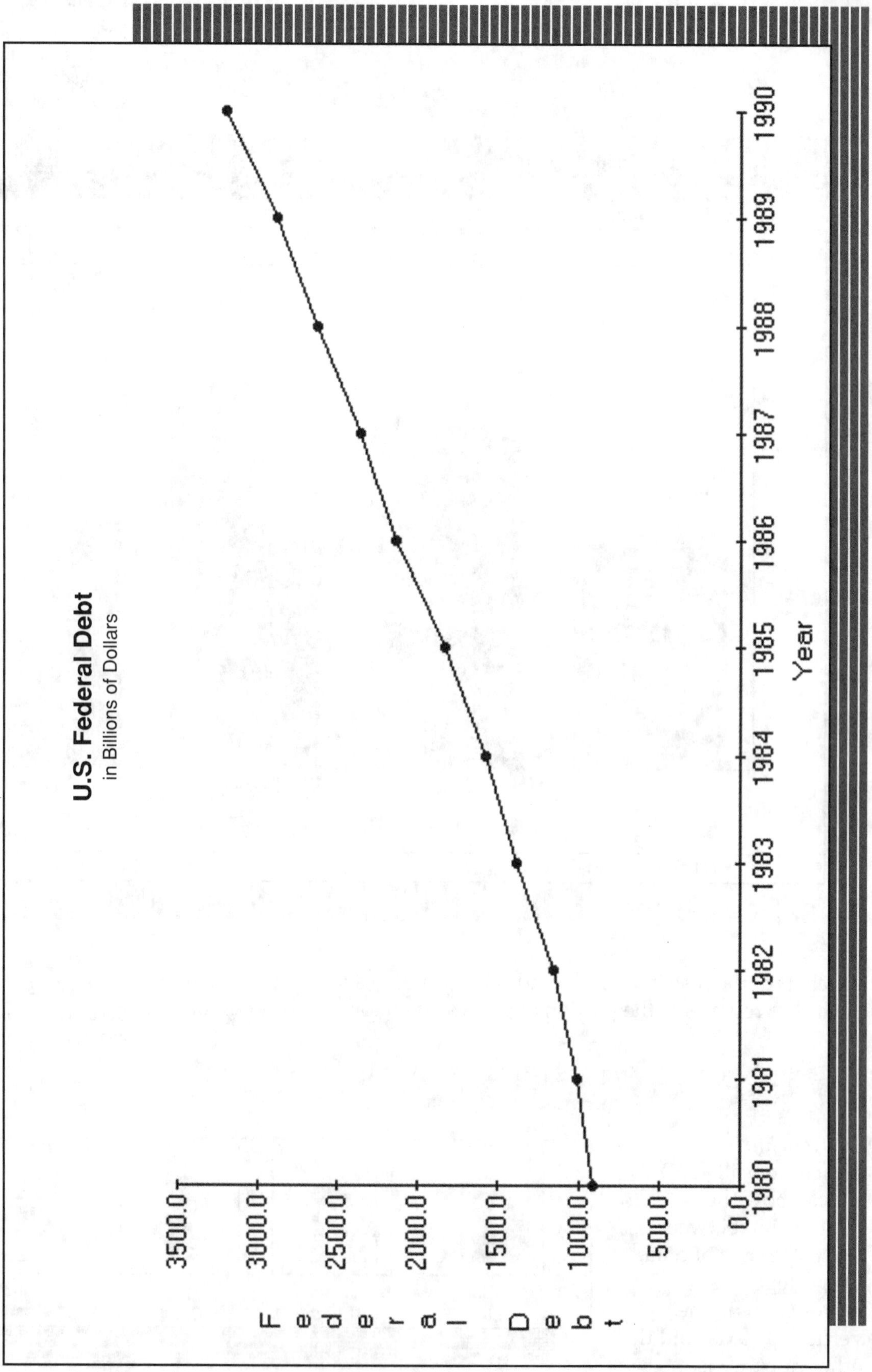

**FIGURE 10-4**

A line chart is ideal for illustrating trends of data over time.

## U.S. Federal Debt
in Billions of Dollars

Year

represented on the horizontal (X) axis. The result is a "cloud" of data points that may or may not have a recognizable shape. It is not practical to connect the data points with a line because points on a scatter chart usually do not relate to each other, as they do in a line chart. For example, the scatter chart in Figure 10-6 shows a data point for each of 12 individuals based on their height and weight. In most cases, a tall person tends to be heavier than a short person. However, because some people are tall and skinny, whereas others are short and stocky, the relationship between height and weight cannot be represented by a line.

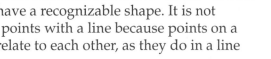
**FIGURE 10-5**
Each "slice" of a pie chart represents part of a larger group.

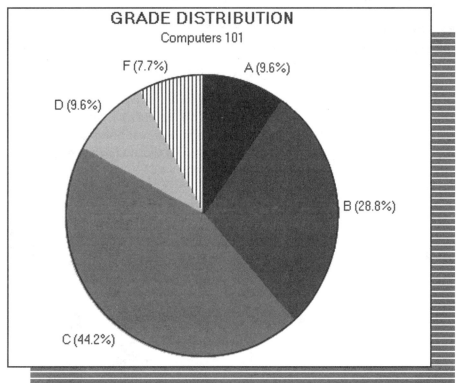

## CREATING A CHART FROM THE SPREADSHEET

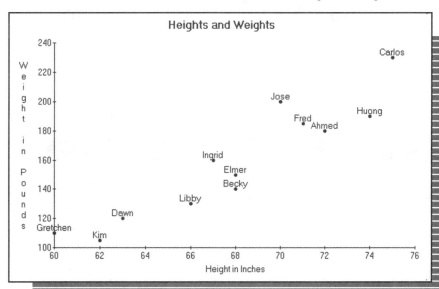
**FIGURE 10-6**
Scatter charts show the relationship between two categories of data, such as height and weight.

To create a chart, begin with a spreadsheet containing data you want to display in a chart. Then highlight the data you want to include in the chart. After you select the Create New Chart command, the Charts menu will appear and Works will create a bar chart with its best estimate of how the data in the spreadsheet should appear. In some cases, you will be satisfied with the chart Works has created. You may, however, alter the chart to fit your specific requirements.

## ACTIVITY 10-1

### Creating a Spreadsheet Chart

**FIGURE 10-7**
When the Create New Chart command is selected, Works automatically creates a bar chart from data highlighted in the spreadsheet.

In this activity, you will create a bar chart illustrating the contents of a spreadsheet.The file *act10-1.wks* is a spreadsheet containing the median income of heads of households according to the educational level they have achieved. The words *high school* have been abbreviated as *HS* and the word *College* as *C*.

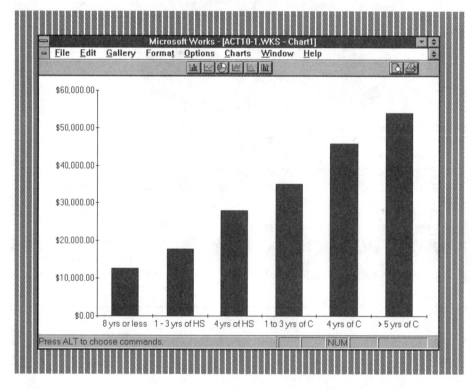

1. Open the file *act10-1.wks* from the template disk. Column A contains educational levels and Column B contains the median incomes of those with that level of education.

2. Highlight **A5:B10**. The highlighted items are the data to be included in the chart that you will create.

3. From the **Charts** menu, choose **Create New Chart**. A bar chart similar to the chart in Figure 10-7 will appear.

4. Save the file to your data disk.

The chart illustrates the value of education in attaining higher income. Notice that the bars get higher on the right side of the chart, indicating that those who stay in school will be rewarded with higher incomes.

You may also notice a slight change in the menus appearing at the top of the screen. Your screen is now showing the *chart window*. This window is used to create, refine, and print charts prepared from spreadsheet data.

## Switching between Chart and Spreadsheet Windows

A chart is closely related to the spreadsheet from which it is created. For example, if you change the data in a spreadsheet, these changes will automatically be made in the chart created from the spreadsheet.

The initial name of the chart is also related to the spreadsheet from which it is created. Works will name the chart the same name as the spreadsheet, followed by *Chart1*. If additional charts are created from the spreadsheet, they will become Chart2, Chart3, and so on. A maximum of eight charts may be created from one spreadsheet.

To return to the spreadsheet from which a chart was created, choose the spreadsheet from the Window menu. To access the chart again, select the chart name from the Window menu.

**ACTIVITY 10-2**

### Switching To and From the Chart Window

In this activity, you will edit *act10-1.wks - Chart1* by switching to the spreadsheet and editing a cell in the spreadsheet.

1.  From the **Window** menu, choose **act10-1.wks**. The spreadsheet will appear.

2.  Edit the contents of A5 from 8 yrs or less to < **8 yrs.**

3.  From the **Window** menu, choose **act10-1.wks - Chart1**. The chart window will appear. The name under the first bar will be changed to < 8 yrs.

4.  Leave *act10-1.wks - Chart1* on the screen for the next activity.

## Inserting Chart Titles

Chart titles and headings make the chart easier to understand. Chart titles are centered at the top of the chart. Vertical, or *Y*-axis, titles appear along the right side of the chart; and horizontal, or *X*-axis, titles appear along the bottom of the chart.

## ACTIVITY 10-3

### Inserting Chart Titles

In this activity, you will insert headings in the chart *act10-1.wks - Chart1* by following these steps:

1.  From the **Edit** menu, choose **Titles**. The Titles dialog box will appear.

2.  Enter **YOUR EDUCATION PAYS** in the Chart Title box.

3.  Enter **Incomes For Six Education Levels** in the Subtitle box. (Remember, you may use the Tab key to move to the next box.)

**FIGURE 10-8**

Chart titles may be inserted at the top of the chart and along the X- and Y-axes of the chart.

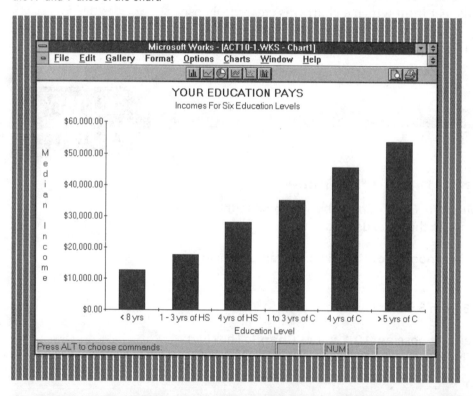

4.  Enter **Educational Level** in the Horizontal (X) Axis box.

5.  Enter **Median Income** in the Vertical (Y) Axis box.

6.  Click **OK**. The titles will appear in the chart. Compare your screen to the one shown in Figure 10-8.

7.  Leave *act10-1.wks - Chart1* on the screen for the next activity.

### Naming a Chart

Naming a chart is particularly useful after you have prepared several charts from one spreadsheet. These charts may become difficult to distinguish by their chart number and would be easier to recognize with more descriptive names. Change the name of the chart by choosing the Name command from the Charts menu of the chart window.

**ACTIVITY
10-4**

## Naming a Chart

In this activity, you will rename the chart from *Chart1* to *Education Pays* by following these steps.

1.  From the **Charts** menu, choose **Name**.

2.  Key **Education Pays** in the Name box.

3.  Click the **Rename** button. The name in the Charts box will change from *Chart1* to *Education Pays*.

4.  Click **OK**. You may confirm the name change by clicking the Window menu. The new name should appear in the menu.

# SAVING A CHART

A spreadsheet chart is considered part of a spreadsheet. When you save the spreadsheet, you will also save the charts you have created from the spreadsheet. Save the spreadsheet and its associated charts by choosing Save from the File menu. The File menu may be accessed from either the spreadsheet window or the chart window.

**ACTIVITY
10-5**

## Saving a Chart

In this activity, you will save the chart and the spreadsheet it was created from.

1.  From the **File** menu, choose the **Save**. You will be returned to the chart window.

2.  Leave *act10-1.wks - Education Pays* on the screen for the next activity.

# CHANGING THE TYPE OF CHART

When the Create New Chart command is chosen, Works will create a bar chart. If you prefer a different type of chart, you may select it by clicking a chart button on the Toolbar of the chart window (see Figure 10-9).

**FIGURE 10-9**
Select the chart type in the Toolbar of the chart window.

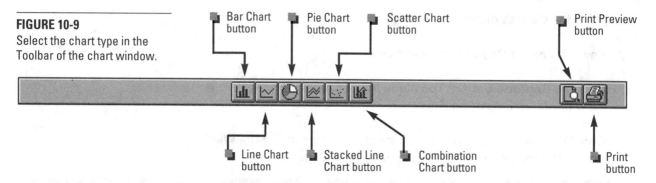

Bar Chart button    Pie Chart button    Scatter Chart button    Print Preview button

Line Chart button    Stacked Line Chart button    Combination Chart button    Print button

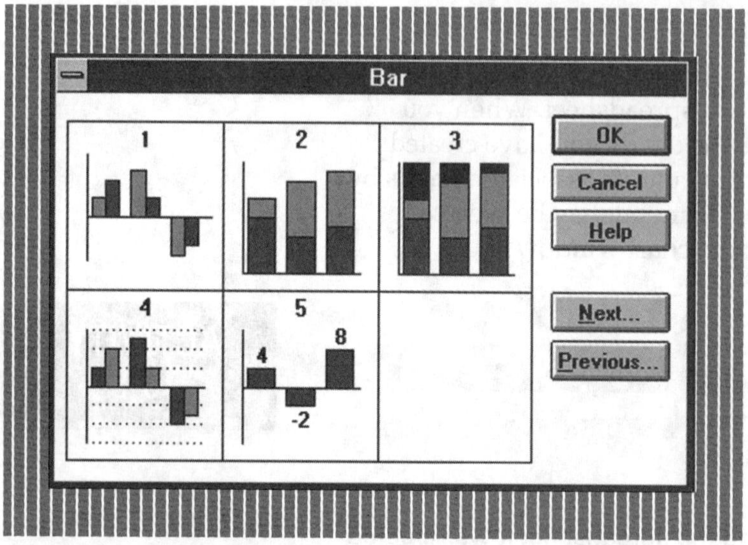

**FIGURE 10-10**
The Bar dialog box displays various bar charts available in Works.

After you click the type of chart in the Toolbar, Works will offer several variations of the chart. For example, when the Bar Chart button is clicked, the Bar dialog box shown in Figure 10-10 will appear. If you click the Bar Chart button, you can select a bar chart with gridlines by clicking Option 4 or a bar chart with values at the top of the bars by selecting Option 5.

## ACTIVITY 10-6

### Changing the Type of Chart

In this activity, you will create three new charts. The chart *act10-1.wks* -

Activity 10-6 continued

*Education Pays* is now on the screen.

1.  Create a bar chart with gridlines by following these steps:

    a.  Click the **Bar Chart** button. A dialog box will appear.

    b.  Click **Option 4**. The option box will be highlighted.

    c.  Click **OK**. A bar chart with gridlines will appear on your screen.

2.  Create a line chart with gridlines by following these steps:

    a.  Click the **Line Chart** button. A dialog box will appear.

    b.  Click **Option 5**. The option box will be highlighted.

    c.  Click **OK**. A line chart with gridlines similar to that in Figure 10-11 will appear on your screen.

**FIGURE 10-11**
Works will first create a basic line chart in the chart window.

3.  In the next activity, you will print this chart. Name and save the chart as a new chart by following these steps:

    a.  From the **Charts** menu, choose **Name**.

    b.  Key **Line Chart** in the Name box.

    c.  Click the **Rename** button.

    d.  Click **OK**.

    e.  From the **File** menu, choose **Save**.

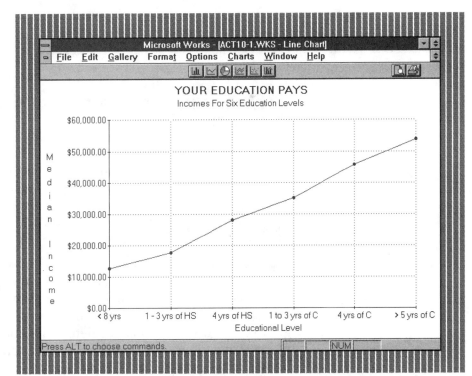

# PRINTING CHARTS

Charts are printed in the same way word processing documents and spreadsheets are printed. The Toolbar of the charts window has a Print and a Print Preview button that will print or preview the chart you plan to print.

## Printing a Spreadsheet Chart

In this activity, you will print *act10-1.wks - Line Chart*, which is now on the screen.

1. Click the **Print Preview** button. The chart, as it will be printed, will appear.

2. Click the **Print** button. The Print dialog box appears.

3. Click **OK**. Printing will begin.

4. After printing is complete, save and close the chart and spreadsheet files.

## CREATING OTHER TYPES OF CHARTS

You have already created a bar chart and a line chart. In the remainder of this chapter, you will learn to create a pie chart and a scatter chart.

### Pie Charts

A pie chart differs from a bar or line chart because it uses only one set of data. For example, in the bar chart you created, you compared the level of education to median incomes. Pie charts compare items within one group to other items within the same group. For example, of a total group of pet owners, it may be determined how many (or what percent) own dogs, cats, or fish. When you prepared a bar chart or a line chart, you selected two columns of data. To create a pie chart, you will select only one column of numerical data before choosing the Create New Chart command.

### Creating a Pie Chart

In this activity, you will create a pie chart of the sources of energy production in the United States during 1989.

Activity 10-8 continued

1. Open file *act10-8.wks*.

2. Create a pie chart by following these steps:

   a. Select **A6:B11**.

   b. From the **Charts** menu, choose **Create New Chart**. A bar chart will appear.

   c. Click the **Pie Chart** button. The Pie dialog box will appear.

   d. Click **Option 4**.

   e. Click **OK**. A labeled pie chart will appear.

3. Title the pie chart by following these steps:

   a. From the **Edit** menu, choose **Titles**.

   b. Key **ENERGY PRODUCTION IN THE U.S.** in the Chart Title box.

   c. Key **For the Year 1989** in the Subtitle box.

   d. Click **OK**.

4. Name the chart file by following these steps:

   a. From the **Charts** menu, choose **Name**.

   b. Key **Production** in the Name box.

   c. Click **Rename**.

   d. Click **OK**.

5. Compare your screen to the one shown in Figure 10-12. Save the file to your data disk as *energy* and close the file.

**FIGURE 10-12**
Pie charts can express parts as a percentage of a whole.

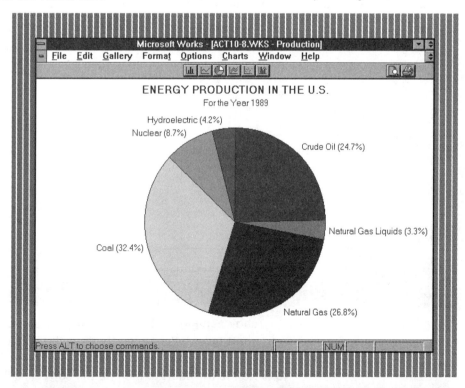

## Scatter Charts

Scatter charts are sometimes referred to as *XY charts* because they place data points between an *X*- and *Y*-axis. Scatter charts are usually more difficult to prepare because Works has difficulty identifying which data should be used as a scale on each axis of the chart. To overcome this, you should designate the *X*- and *Y*-axis scales in the Series command in the Edit menu of the chart window.

**ACTIVITY 10-9**

### Creating a Scatter Chart

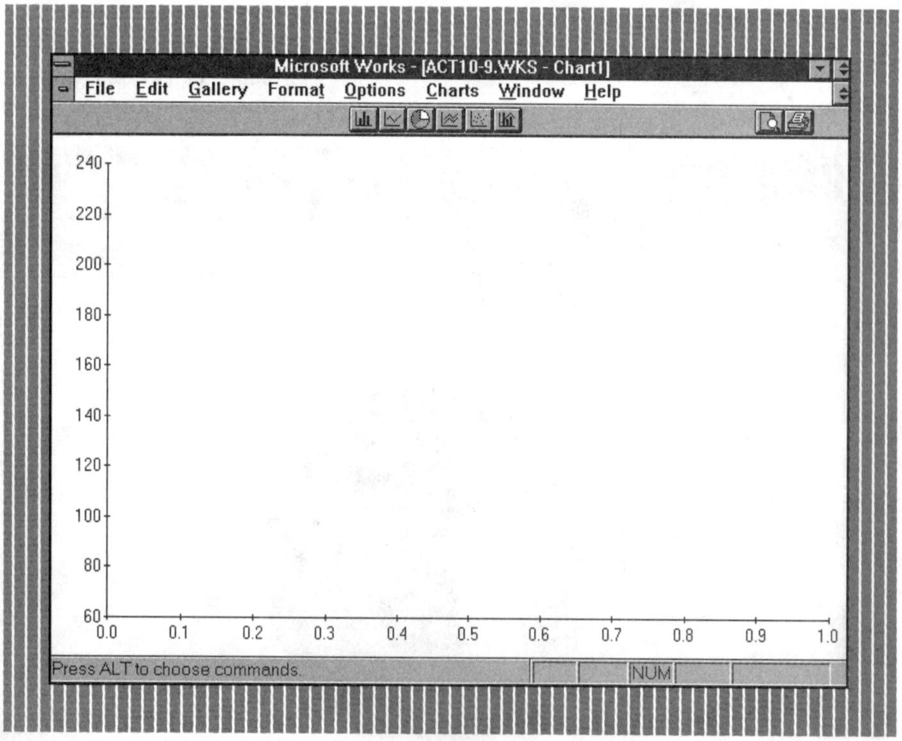

**FIGURE 10-13**

At times, the default options in Works will not select a logical axis for a chart. The correct axis is designated by using the Series command in the Edit menu.

In this activity, you will create a scatter chart. The file *act10-9.wks* is a spreadsheet containing the height and weight of 12 people.

1. Open the file *act10-9.wks*.

2. Prepare a scatter chart in which a data point appears at the intersection of a person's weight on the vertical (*Y*) axis and height on the horizontal (*X*) axis:

   a. Select **A4:C15**.

   b. From the **Charts** menu, choose **Create New Chart**. A bar chart will appear.

   c. Click the **Scatter Chart** button in the Toolbar. **Option 1** will be highlighted.

   d. Click **OK**.

The vertical (*Y*) axis scale appears to show the weights of the individuals; however, the horizontal (*X*) axis scale is not recognizable, as shown in Figure 10-13. Works has not created a logical chart. This chart must be changed to make the horizontal scale recognizable.

3. Refine the chart to include the correct scale on the horizontal axis:

   a. From the **Edit** menu, choose **Series**. The range A4:A15, which contains the people's names, appears in the Category (X) Series

**Activity 10-9 continued**

box. Because the names cannot produce a numerical scale, no data points were graphed. The contents of the Category (X) Series box should be changed to include the height data.

b.   Key **C4:C15** in Category (X) Series box.

c.   The Value (Y) Series boxes designate sets of data points appearing on the scatter chart. This chart should include only one set of data points. Delete the contents of the Value (Y) Series 2nd box.

d.   Click **OK**. Data points will appear on the scatter chart, and the horizontal axis will show a scale for the heights.

4.   Place labels on the data points of the scatter chart:

a.   From the **Edit** menu, choose **Data Labels**.

b.   Key **A4:A15** in the Value (Y) Series 1st box. This will designate the names of the people as the data labels.

c.   Click **OK**. The names will appear on each of the data points.

5.   Place titles in the chart:

a.   From the **Edit** menu, choose **Titles**.

b.   Key **HEIGHT AND WEIGHT** in the Title box.

c.   Key **Twelve Person Survey** in the Subtitle box.

d.   Key **Height in Inches** in the Horizontal (X) Axis box.

**FIGURE 10-14**
Scatter charts can show labeled points between two axes.

e.   Key **Weight in Pounds** in the Vertical (Y) Axis box.

f.   Click **OK**. The titles will appear in the chart.

Your screen should appear similar to the screen in Figure 10-14.

6.   Print the chart in landscape orientation.

7.   Save the file to your data disk as *survey* and close the file.

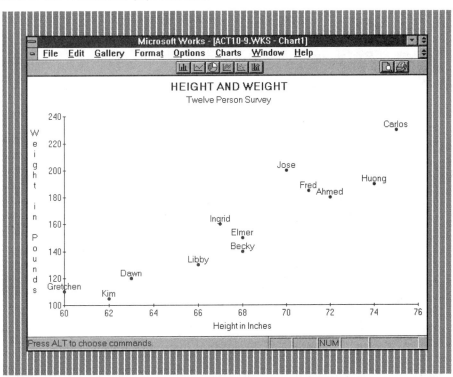

# SUMMARY

A chart is a graphical representation of spreadsheet data. You can create several types of spreadsheet charts, including bar charts, line charts, pie charts, and scatter charts. A maximum of eight charts may be created from one spreadsheet.

When the Create New Chart command is chosen, the chart window will appear. The chart window is used to create, refine, and print charts prepared from spreadsheet data.

Works will automatically create a bar chart when the Create New Chart command is chosen. If you prefer a different type of chart, you may select it by clicking chart buttons of the Toolbar of the chart window.

A chart created from a spreadsheet is considered part of that spreadsheet. When you save the spreadsheet, you will also save the charts you have created from the spreadsheet. You may save the spreadsheet and its associated charts by choosing Save from the File menu in either the spreadsheet window or the chart window.

# CHALLENGES

## TRUE/FALSE

Circle **T** or **F** to show whether the statement is true or false.

T    F    1.    Charts are a graphical representation of spreadsheet data.

T    F    2.    Bar charts are the best way to represent data groups that are part of a whole.

T    F    3.    Line charts are well suited for representing trends over a period of time.

T    F    4.    A scatter chart produces a "cloud" of data points not connected by lines.

T    F    5.    A bar chart represents values in the spreadsheet by varying heights of rectangles.

T    F    6.    Works automatically creates a line chart when the Create New Chart command is chosen.

T    F    7.    When the spreadsheet data changes, charts created from the spreadsheet will also change.

T    F    8.    To switch from a spreadsheet window to a chart window, choose Chart from the File menu.

T    F    9.    The charts of a spreadsheet file are erased when the spreadsheet file is closed.

T    F   10.    A chart may be printed from the chart window.

# COMPLETION

Write the correct answer in the space provided.

1. What type of chart represents values in a spreadsheet by points connected by a line?

_____

2. What type of chart uses rectangles to represent values in a spreadsheet?

_____

3. What type of chart is represented by a circle divided into portions?

_____

4. How many charts may be created from one spreadsheet?

_____

5. What command is chosen to title a chart?

_____

6. Unless you rename a chart, what will Works name the first chart prepared from a spreadsheet?

_____

7. Which menu contains the Name command, which is used to rename a spreadsheet chart?

_____

8. Where are the buttons that select the type of chart located?

_____

9. What characteristics may be added to a bar chart to help in identifying the spreadsheet value a bar represents?

_____

10. What Toolbar button in the chart window allows you to see a printed chart before it is printed?

_____

# APPLICATIONS

## APPLICATION 10-1

The file *app10-1.wks* contains the populations of the world's largest cities. Create a bar chart indicating larger populations with a higher bar.

1.  Open *app10-1.wks*.

2.  Create a bar chart from the data in A5:B11.

3.  Title the bar chart **Population of World's Largest Cities**.

4.  Subtitle the chart **In Millions**.

5.  Title the vertical axis **Population**.

6.  Print the chart.

7.  Save the file to your data disk as *cities* and close the file.

---

## APPLICATION 10-2

You have been running each morning to stay in shape. Over the past 10 weeks you have recorded running times along a specified route and entered times in file *app10-2.wks*. Create a line chart indicating the trend in running times over the 10-week period.

1.  Open *app10-2.wks*.

2.  Create a line chart for the data contained in A4:B12. You may select any of the following options in the Line dialog box to prepare your chart: 1, 2, 4, or 5.

3.  Title the line chart **Ten-Week Workout Program**.

4.  Title the vertical axis **Time in Minutes**.

5.  Print the chart.

6.  Save the file to your data disk as *workout* and close the file.

---

## APPLICATION 10-3

The file *app10-3.wks* contains the number of McDonald's hamburger restaurants in different regions of the world. Create a pie chart in which each slice represents a region in Column A of the spreadsheet.

1.  Open *app10-3.wks*.

2.  Create a pie chart for the data contained in A4:B8 by accessing the chart window and selecting Option 4 in the Pie dialog box.

3.  Title the pie chart **McDonald's Restaurants**.

4.  Subtitle the chart **Worldwide Locations**.

5.  Print the chart.

6.  Save the file to your data disk as *mcd* and close the file.

---

# APPLICATION 10-4

The file *app10-4.wks* contains the study time and examination scores for several students. The instructor for the course is attempting to determine if there is a relationship between study time and examination score. Create a scatter chart of the data in the spreadsheet to indicate the relationship between study time and examination scores. Then label the data points in the scatter chart with the names of the students.

1.  Open *app10-4.wks*.

2.  Create a scatter chart for the data in A4:C21 by accessing the chart window and selecting Option 1 in the XY (Scatter) dialog box.

3.  Refine the scatter chart by defining the following in the Series boxes:

    a.  The Value (Y) Series 1st should be B4:B21.
    b.  The Category (X) Series should be C4:C21.
    c.  The Value (Y) Series 2nd should not contain a range.

4.  Add data labels to the chart by entering A4:A21 in the Data Labels Value (Y) Series 1st box.

5.  Title the scatter chart **Comparison of Exam Grades to Study Time.**

6.  Title the horizontal axis **Examination Grades**.

7.  Title the vertical axis **Hours of Study**.

8.  Print the chart.

9.  Save the spreadsheet to your data disk as *study* and close the file.

# PART 4

## DATABASE

# DATABASE BASICS

## WHAT IS A DATABASE?

A *database* is an automated electronic filing system that stores and retrieves information. A database is similar to a filing cabinet that contains folders of information. However, compared to a traditional paper filing system, the database has the following advantages:

1. *Records can be retrieved quickly.* You can find the information you need by pressing keys rather than searching through folders in a file cabinet.

2. *Records can be manipulated easily.* Using simple commands, you can sort the records in a number of ways, find a particular record, or select a group of records that meet certain criteria.

3. *Records can be stored efficiently.* Databases can store large amounts of data on a disk at a low cost. File cabinets of folders can require large amounts of space and can be expensive. See Figure 11-1.

As you will see in a moment, a database looks quite similar to a spreadsheet. Both have columns and rows, a formula bar where

**FIGURE 11-1**

Records can be stored efficiently in an electronic database on a disk.

information is entered, and so on. But databases and spreadsheets differ in the way they are used. A spreadsheet is used primarily for analysis of numerical data. In Chapter 9, for example, you used a spreadsheet to calculate interest on a loan. By contrast, a database is used primarily to store and retrieve records. For example, you will create a database in this chapter to store addresses and phone numbers.

Databases are typically larger than spreadsheets because they are used for long-term storage of data. The database that keeps track of a club's membership, for example, expands as the names and addresses of new members are added. In a spreadsheet, you usually alter the existing information rather than add more data.

## ACTIVITY 11-1

### Opening an Existing Database

In this activity, you will open an existing database file.

1. Start Works. The Startup dialog box will appear.

2. Click **Open Existing File**. The Open dialog box will appear.

3. In the Drives list, click the drive containing your template disk. The files on the disk will appear in the File Name list.

4. Double-click the filename *act11-1.wdb* in the File Name list. The database will appear on the screen and should be similar to Figure 11-2.

5. Leave the file *act11-1.wdb* on your system for the next activity.

**FIGURE 11-2**
The primary parts of the
database are the entry, record,
and field.

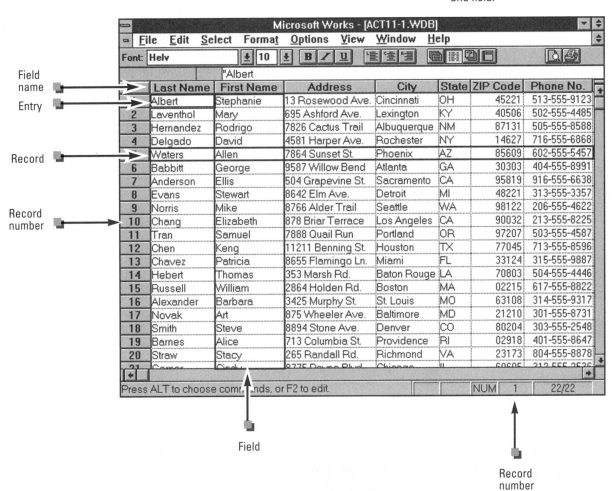

Field

Record
number

# PARTS OF A DATABASE

You will notice that many parts of the database screen look familiar.
Like the word processor and the spreadsheet screens, the database
screen shows a title bar, menu bar, scroll bars, status line, and Toolbar.
The database screen also shows a formula bar like the one you used in
the spreadsheet section.

Several features will be new to you, however, because they appear
only in the database. These features are labeled in Figure 11-2 and are
discussed below.

Figure 11-2 shows a directory of names, addresses, and phone
numbers. The data is arranged so that each kind of information is

grouped together. For example, all the last names are in one column and all the first names are in another. These categories of information are called *fields*. This database has seven fields of common information, such as last names, addresses, or ZIP codes. The *field name* at the top of the column helps you to remember what kind of information will be stored in the column.

Each piece of information entered into a field is called an *entry*. In the database shown in Figure 11-2, for example, each name in the Last Name field is an entry.

One complete set of field entries is called a *record*. Each record has a *record number* displayed on the left side of the screen. In Figure 11-2, Record 1 consists of the name, address, city, state, ZIP code, and phone number for Stephanie Albert.

# VIEWING A DATABASE

As you become more familiar with databases, you will realize that they can become very large—too large for you to view all records at once. Fortunately, Works allows several options for displaying the data you need on screen.

## List and Form View

**FIGURE 11-3A**
A database may be displayed in List view, as here, or in or Form view.

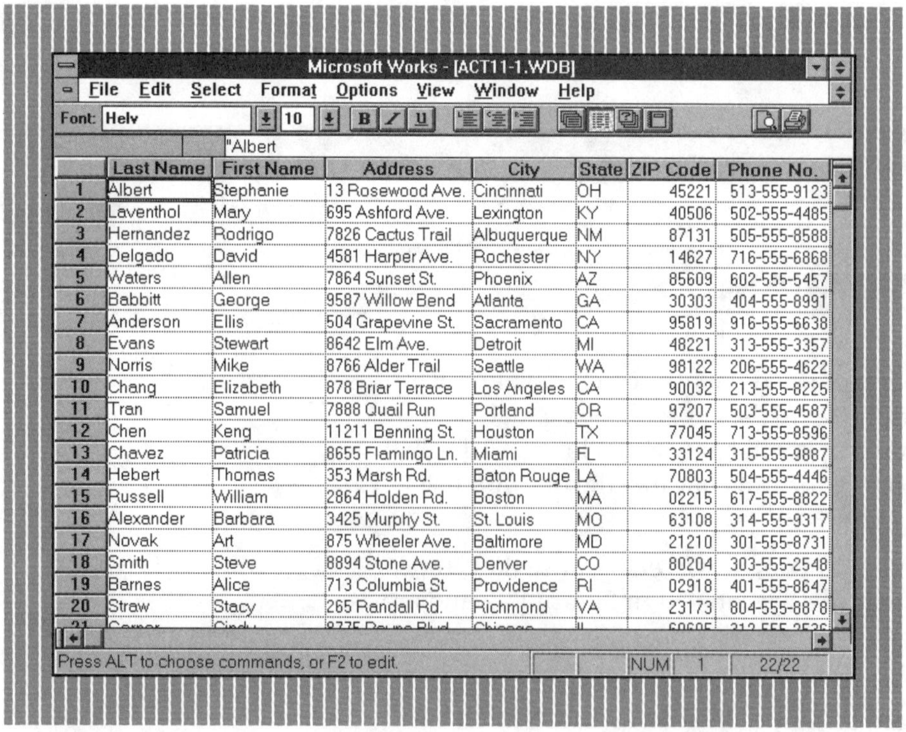

A database may be displayed on screen in List view or Form view. The database now on your screen is in *List view,* which is similar in appearance to the spreadsheet. List view is most appropriate when you want to display several records at once. *Form view,* on the other hand, displays one record at a time. It is most appropriate for entering or editing a specific record. List and Form view are shown in Figures 11-3A and 11-3B.

You may switch between List and Form views in three ways:

1. By choosing the Form or List command from the View menu (see Figure 11-4).

**FIGURE 11-3B**
A database may be displayed in List view or in Form view, as here.

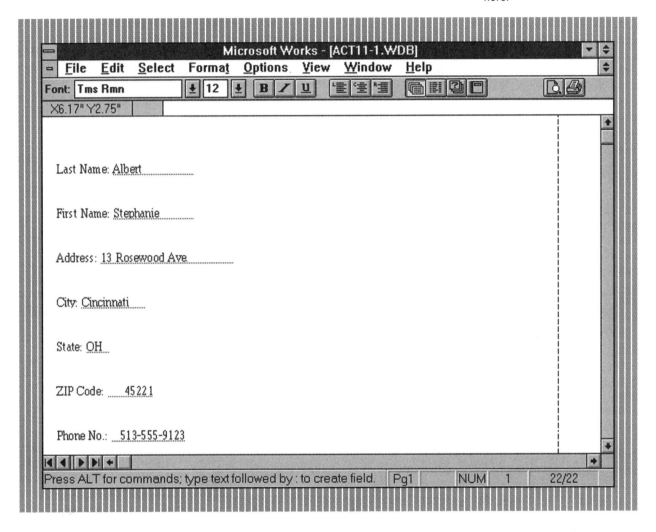

2. By pressing the F9 key.
3. By clicking the Form View or List View button on the Toolbar.

Form View button

List View button

**FIGURE 11-4**
You can switch between List and Form view from the View menu.

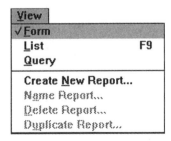

ACTIVITY 11-2

## Switching between List and Form View

In this activity, you will switch between List and Form views in the database. The file *act11-1.wdb* is currently in List view on your screen. Switch between views by following these steps:

1. From the **View** menu, choose **Form**. The database will appear in Form view.
2. Press **F9**. The database will return to List view.
3. Click the **Form View** button on the Toolbar.
4. Click the **List View** button on the Toolbar.
5. Leave the file *act11-1.wdb* on your screen for the next activity.

## Splitting the Screen

If a database is very large, you may want to view several parts of the database on the screen at the same time by ***splitting*** the screen. Sections of a split window are called ***panes***. By creating panes in the window, you may view as many as four parts of the database at once. For example, the database in Figure 11-5 has been split horizontally to display the records at the top and bottom of the database. The database in Figure 11-6 has been split into four panes. The split screen shows the Phone No. field, which was originally at the extreme right side of the screen, next to the names.

**FIGURE 11-5**
Splitting the screen horizontally enables you to view the top and bottom of a database simultaneously.

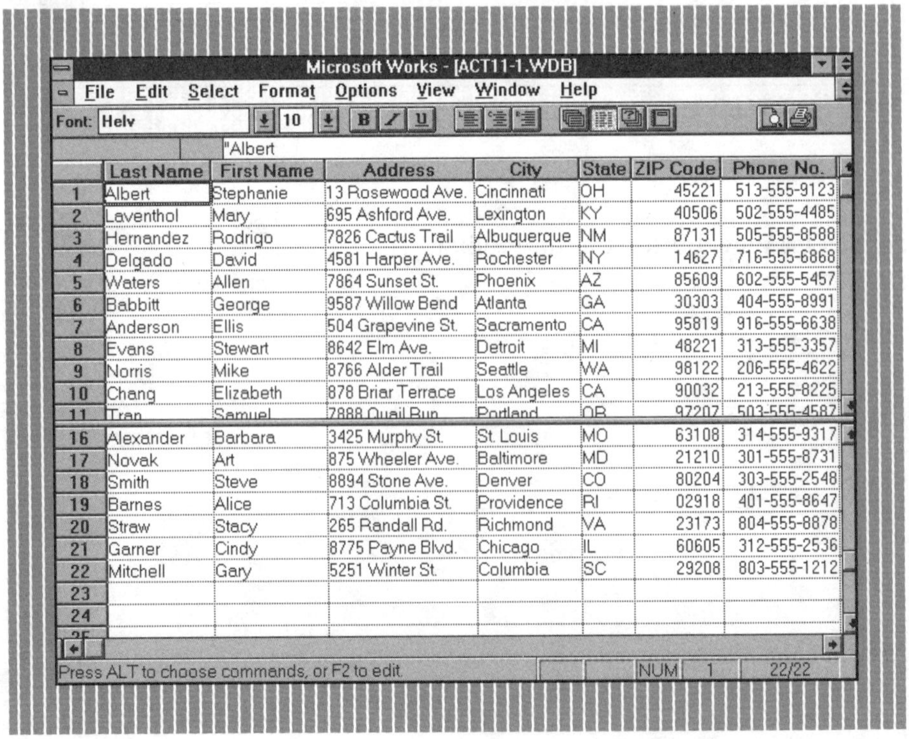


| | Last Name | First Name | Address | City | State | ZIP Code | Phone No. |
|---|---|---|---|---|---|---|---|
| 1 | Albert | Stephanie | 13 Rosewood Ave. | Cincinnati | OH | 45221 | 513-555-9123 |
| 2 | Laventhol | Mary | 695 Ashford Ave. | Lexington | KY | 40506 | 502-555-4485 |
| 3 | Hernandez | Rodrigo | 7826 Cactus Trail | Albuquerque | NM | 87131 | 505-555-8588 |
| 4 | Delgado | David | 4581 Harper Ave. | Rochester | NY | 14627 | 716-555-6868 |
| 5 | Waters | Allen | 7864 Sunset St. | Phoenix | AZ | 85609 | 602-555-5457 |
| 6 | Babbitt | George | 9587 Willow Bend | Atlanta | GA | 30303 | 404-555-8991 |
| 7 | Anderson | Ellis | 504 Grapevine St. | Sacramento | CA | 95819 | 916-555-6638 |
| 8 | Evans | Stewart | 8642 Elm Ave. | Detroit | MI | 48221 | 313-555-3357 |
| 9 | Norris | Mike | 8766 Alder Trail | Seattle | WA | 98122 | 206-555-4622 |
| 10 | Chang | Elizabeth | 878 Briar Terrace | Los Angeles | CA | 90032 | 213-555-8225 |
| 11 | Tran | Samuel | 7888 Quail Run | Portland | OR | 97207 | 503-555-4587 |
| 16 | Alexander | Barbara | 3425 Murphy St. | St. Louis | MO | 63108 | 314-555-9317 |
| 17 | Novak | Art | 875 Wheeler Ave. | Baltimore | MD | 21210 | 301-555-8731 |
| 18 | Smith | Steve | 8894 Stone Ave. | Denver | CO | 80204 | 303-555-2548 |
| 19 | Barnes | Alice | 713 Columbia St. | Providence | RI | 02918 | 401-555-8647 |
| 20 | Straw | Stacy | 265 Randall Rd. | Richmond | VA | 23173 | 804-555-8878 |
| 21 | Garner | Cindy | 8775 Payne Blvd. | Chicago | IL | 60605 | 312-555-2536 |
| 22 | Mitchell | Gary | 5251 Winter St. | Columbia | SC | 29208 | 803-555-1212 |
| 23 | | | | | | | |
| 24 | | | | | | | |

A split box appears on the left side of the horizontal scroll bar and at the top of the vertical scroll bar (see Figure 11-7). As you point to the split box, the mouse pointer will turn into two parallel lines with a double-headed arrow through them ( ⯭ ). To split the screen, drag from the split box to the point where the screen is to be split (or you may split the screen in half by simply double-clicking the split box). After you have split the screens, you may scroll within each of the panes by clicking in the pane and dragging the scroll box.

**FIGURE 11-6**

Splitting the screen vertically enables you to view the left and right side of a database simultaneously.

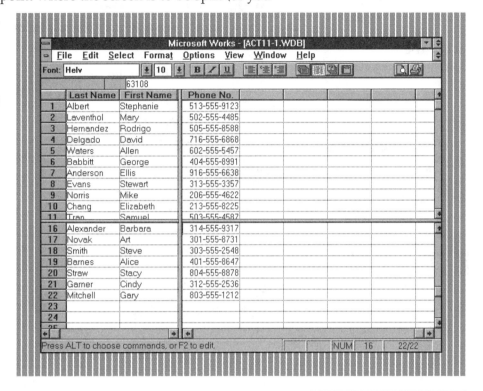

**FIGURE 11-7**

A database screen is split by dragging from the split boxes.

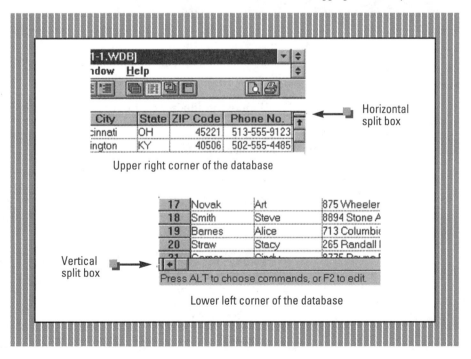

# ACTIVITY 11-3

**FIGURE 11-8**
Splitting the screen allows you to view several parts of the database at the same time.

## Splitting a Database Screen

In this activity, you will split the screen into four panes. The file *act11-1.wdb* is currently on your screen in List view.

1.  Double-click the horizontal split box in the upper right part of the screen. The screen should split horizontally.

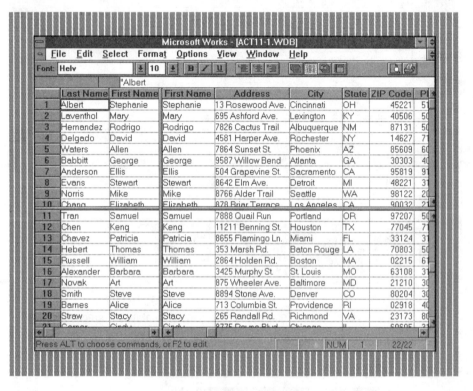

2.  Drag from the vertical split box to the right edge of the First Name field. Your screen should appear similar to the screen in Figure 11-8.

3.  Click anywhere in the lower right pane of the window.

4.  Using the horizontal scroll bar, scroll to the left in the pane until the Phone No. field is next to the First Name field on the other side of the split bar. Your screen should look similar to Figure 11-6.

5.  Return the screen to a single pane by double-clicking the lines that split the window.

6.  Leave the file *act11-1.wdb* on the screen for the next activity.

*Note:* You may also split a spreadsheet in the same way you split the database.

# MOVING THE HIGHLIGHT IN THE DATABASE

In either Form view or List view, the easiest way to move the highlight is by simply clicking that area with the mouse. You can also move the highlight using key commands. Keystroke commands to move the highlight are different in List view and Form view.

## Moving the Highlight in Form View

In Form view, you may scroll only within the form of a single record. You will only need to scroll when the record exceeds the size of the screen. Table 11-1 shows the keystrokes for moving the highlight in Form view if you prefer not to use the mouse.

The *navigation buttons,* shown in Figure 11-9, allow you to move to other records in the database. The buttons are located in the left part of the status line and are useful for moving to the first, previous, next, or last record in the database. You can also move from record to record using the key combinations shown in Table 11-2.

**TABLE 11-1**
Keystrokes move the highlight within a record in Form view.

| To Move | Press |
|---|---|
| Up one line | Up Arrow |
| Down one line | Down Arrow |
| Up one window | Page Up |
| Down one window | Page Down |
| To the next field | Tab |
| To the previous field | Shift+Tab |
| To the left edge of the form | Home |
| To the right edge of the form | End |

**FIGURE 11-9**
Navigation buttons move the highlight from record to record while in Form view.

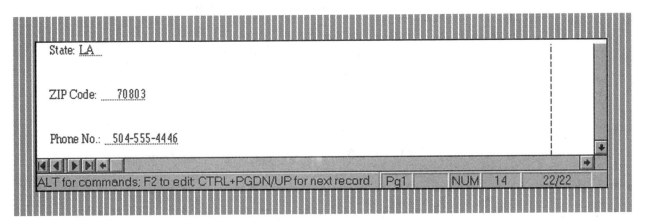

## Moving the Highlight in List View

Moving the highlight in List view is similar to moving it in the spreadsheet. You may scroll throughout the database using the mouse to drag the scroll bars as you learned in Chapter 1.

You can also move the highlight by pressing certain keys or key combinations. Table 11-3 shows how to move the highlight with keystrokes while in List view.

**TABLE 11-2**
Keystrokes may be used to
move the highlight to other
records in Form view.

| To Move | Press |
|---|---|
| To the first record | Ctrl+Home |
| To the last record | Ctrl+End |
| To the next record | Ctrl+Left Arrow |
| To the previous record | Ctrl+Right Arrow |

**TABLE 11-3**
Moving the highlight in List
view is similar to moving the
highlight in the spreadsheet.

| To Move | Press |
|---|---|
| Left one field | Left Arrow |
| Right one field | Right Arrow |
| Up one record | Up Arrow |
| Down one record | Down Arrow |
| To the first field of a record | Home |
| To the last field of a record | End |
| To the first record | Ctrl+Home |
| To the last record | Ctrl+End |
| Up one window | Page Up |
| Down one window | Page Down |
| Left one window | Ctrl+Page Up |
| Right one window | Ctrl+Page Down |

## Using the Go To Command to Move in the Database

In the spreadsheet, the Go To command is used to move the highlight to a specific cell by indicating the cell reference (for example, B13). Because cell references are not available in the database, the Go To command asks for a field name instead. After you select the Go To command from the Select menu, each field in the database will be displayed in the Go To dialog box. When you double-click the field name, Works will place the highlight in that field. The Go To command is available in both Form and List view.

## Moving the Highlight in the Database

In this activity, you will move the highlight in a database. Your screen now shows the database *act11-1.wdb* in List view.

1. Press **Ctrl+Home** to move the highlight to the first entry in the database.

2. Press **Ctrl+End** to move to the last record in the database. The highlight will move to the lower right side of the database.

3. Press **Home** to move to the first entry of the last record in the database. The highlight should appear in an entry with the name *Mitchell*.

4. Press **Up Arrow** to move the highlight up one record. The highlight will appear in an entry containing the name *Garner*.

5. Move to the ZIP Code field by using the Go To command:

   a. From the **Select** menu, choose **Go To**.

   b. Double-click **ZIP Code** in the Names box. The highlight will appear in an entry containing *60605* in the ZIP Code field.

6. Press **F9** to switch to Form view.

7. Click the **First Record** navigation button to move to the first record in the database. The highlight will appear in an entry containing *45221*.

8. Press **Shift+Tab** to move to the previous field. The highlight will appear in an entry containing *OH*.

9. Press **Ctrl+Page Down** to move to the next record.

10. Click the **Last Record** navigation button to move to the last record in the database. In Form view, the last record will be blank and ready to receive new data.

11. Leave this blank record on the screen for the next activity.

# ADDING AND DELETING RECORDS IN THE DATABASE

Once a database has been created, it is simple to add new records to it or to delete records that you no longer need. New records may be entered in either Form or List view. Because Form view displays one record at a time, single records are usually entered in Form view.

Records that are no longer useful may be deleted from the database. To delete a record in Form view, display the record to be deleted on the screen and select the Delete Record command from the Edit menu. To delete a record in List view, select the entire record and choose Delete Record/Field from the Edit menu.

## ACTIVITY 11-5

### Adding and Deleting Records

In this activity, you will add a new record to the database *act11-1.wdb*. Your screen should now contain a blank record in Form view.

1. Click the line beside the **Last Name** field. The entry will be highlighted.

2. Key **Chester**.

3. Press **Tab**. The highlight will move to the right of the colon beside the **First Name** field.

4. Key **Tom**.

5. Continue to Tab to the next fields and enter the following data:

   | | |
   |---|---|
   | Address: | **3584 Daisy St.** |
   | City: | **Washington** |
   | State: | **DC** |
   | ZIP Code: | **20549** |
   | Phone No: | **202-555-8789** |

6. Press **Enter**.

7. Click the **First Record** navigation button in the lower left part of the Form view screen. The record for Stephanie Albert of Cincinnati will appear.

8. From the **Edit** menu, choose **Delete Record**. The record for Stephanie Albert will disappear and the record for Mary Laventhol of Lexington will appear in place of the deleted record.

Activity 11-5 continued

9. Switch to List view by pressing **F9** or by clicking the **List View** button on the Toolbar.

10. Select the record for Keng Chen of Houston by clicking Record Number **11**. Selecting the record number highlights the entire record.

11. From the **Edit** menu, choose **Delete Record/Field**. The record will be deleted from the database. When you complete the activity, your screen should appear similar to Figure 11-10.

12. Leave the file *act11-1.wdb* on your screen for the next activity.

**FIGURE 11-10**
It is simple to add and delete records in the Works database.

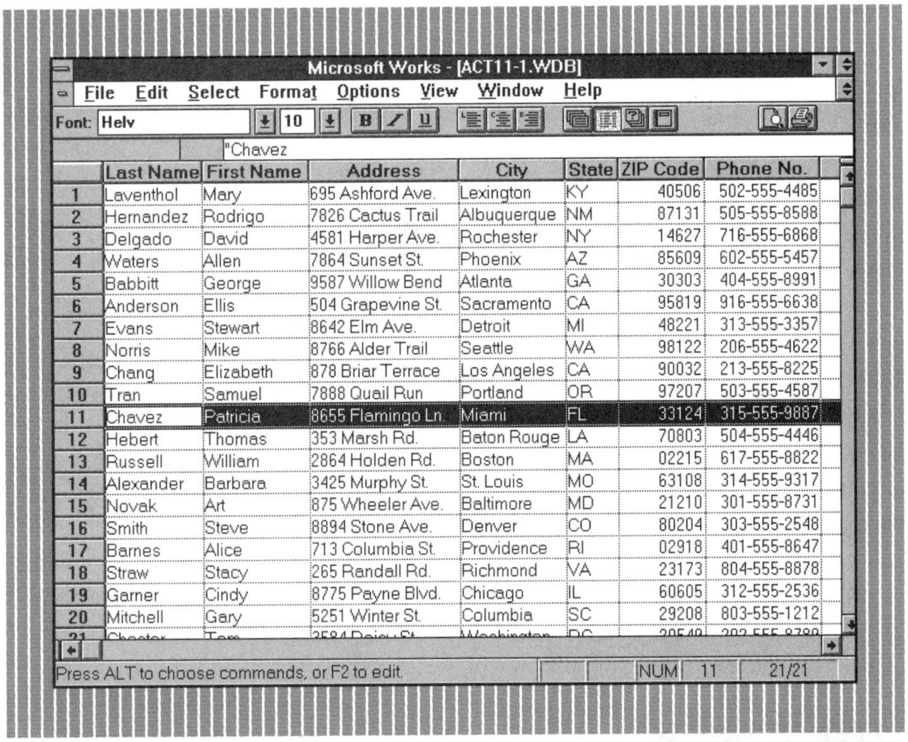


| | Last Name | First Name | Address | City | State | ZIP Code | Phone No. |
|---|---|---|---|---|---|---|---|
| 1 | Laventhol | Mary | 695 Ashford Ave. | Lexington | KY | 40506 | 502-555-4485 |
| 2 | Hernandez | Rodrigo | 7826 Cactus Trail | Albuquerque | NM | 87131 | 505-555-8588 |
| 3 | Delgado | David | 4581 Harper Ave. | Rochester | NY | 14627 | 716-555-6868 |
| 4 | Waters | Allen | 7864 Sunset St. | Phoenix | AZ | 85609 | 602-555-5457 |
| 5 | Babbitt | George | 9587 Willow Bend | Atlanta | GA | 30303 | 404-555-8991 |
| 6 | Anderson | Ellis | 504 Grapevine St. | Sacramento | CA | 95819 | 916-555-6638 |
| 7 | Evans | Stewart | 8642 Elm Ave. | Detroit | MI | 48221 | 313-555-3357 |
| 8 | Norris | Mike | 8766 Alder Trail | Seattle | WA | 98122 | 206-555-4622 |
| 9 | Chang | Elizabeth | 878 Briar Terrace | Los Angeles | CA | 90032 | 213-555-8225 |
| 10 | Tran | Samuel | 7888 Quail Run | Portland | OR | 97207 | 503-555-4587 |
| 11 | Chavez | Patricia | 8655 Flamingo Ln. | Miami | FL | 33124 | 315-555-9887 |
| 12 | Hebert | Thomas | 353 Marsh Rd. | Baton Rouge | LA | 70803 | 504-555-4446 |
| 13 | Russell | William | 2864 Holden Rd. | Boston | MA | 02215 | 617-555-8822 |
| 14 | Alexander | Barbara | 3425 Murphy St. | St. Louis | MO | 63108 | 314-555-9317 |
| 15 | Novak | Art | 875 Wheeler Ave. | Baltimore | MD | 21210 | 301-555-8731 |
| 16 | Smith | Steve | 8894 Stone Ave. | Denver | CO | 80204 | 303-555-2548 |
| 17 | Barnes | Alice | 713 Columbia St. | Providence | RI | 02918 | 401-555-8647 |
| 18 | Straw | Stacy | 265 Randall Rd. | Richmond | VA | 23173 | 804-555-8878 |
| 19 | Garner | Cindy | 8775 Payne Blvd. | Chicago | IL | 60605 | 312-555-2536 |
| 20 | Mitchell | Gary | 5251 Winter St. | Columbia | SC | 29208 | 803-555-1212 |



# PRINTING PART OF A DATABASE

Large databases are not usually printed. You can probably imagine how many pages it would take to print a database with thousands of records. Instead large databases are usually summarized and printed in reports. You will learn about reporting in Chapter 14. However, you may want to print a small database or an individual record in a database.

## Printing a Small Database from List View

Small databases may be printed as they appear in List view. In other words, rows of records will be printed in the order that they appear on screen. To print a database from List view, choose the Print command from the File menu or click the Print button on the Toolbar. If you desire, you can preview the printed database by choosing the Print Preview command from the File menu or by clicking the Print Preview button on the Toolbar. If you desire to adjust margins or page characteristics, you can do so by choosing the Page Setup & Margins command from the File menu.

**FIGURE 11-11**

To print an individual record, click *Current record only* in the Page Setup & Margins dialog box.

## Printing Records from Form View

You may also print records as they appear in Form view. Records will be printed, one per page, with fields in the same position as they appear on the screen. To print individual records from Form view, you must first click *Current record only* in the Page Setup & Margins dialog box, which is shown in Figure 11-11. Otherwise, Works will print a page for every record in the database (quite a printing task if your database contains many records!). You may then print the record that appears on screen by choosing the Print command from the File menu or by clicking the Print button on the Toolbar.

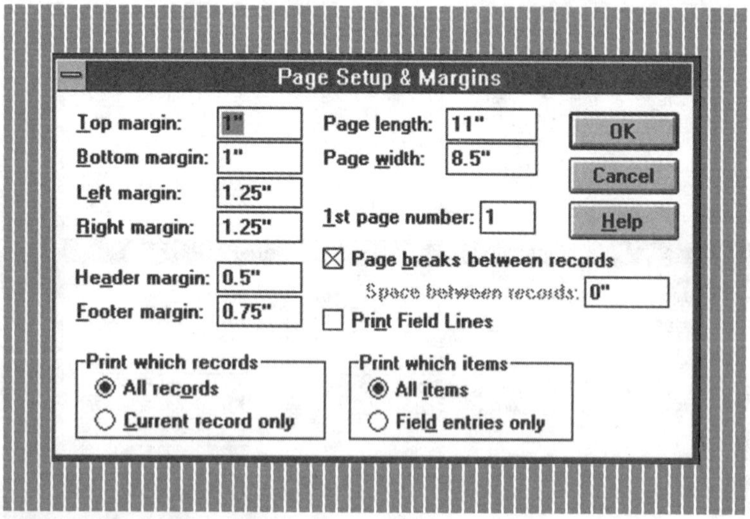

**ACTIVITY 11-6**

### Printing a Database

In this activity you will print the database *act11-1.wdb* from List view and print an individual record from Form view. Your screen now shows the database *act11-1.wdb* in List view.

1. From the **File** menu, choose **Print Preview**. The database will appear on screen as it would be printed.

2. Click **Print**. The Print dialog box will appear.

3. Click **OK**. The database will print.

4. Select the record for Rodrigo Hernandez (Record Number 2).

5. Press **F9** to switch to Form view.

6. From the **File** menu, choose **Page Setup & Margins**.

Activity 11-6 continued

7.   Click **Current record only**.

8.   Click **OK**.

9.   From the **File** menu, choose **Print**. The Print dialog box will appear.

10.   Click **OK**. Your printed pages should appear similar to the printed pages shown in Figure 11-12.

11.   Leave the database *act11-1.wdb* on your screen for the next activity.

**FIGURE 11-12**

You may print the entire database as it appears in List view or individual records as they appear in Form view.

| | | | | | | |
|---|---|---|---|---|---|---|
| Laventhol | Mary | 695 Ashford Ave. | Lexington | KY | 40506 | 502-555-4485 |
| Hernandez | Rodrigo | 7826 Cactus Trail | Albuquerque | NM | 87131 | 505-555-8588 |
| Delgado | David | 4581 Harper Ave. | Rochester | NY | 14627 | 716-555-6868 |
| Waters | Allen | 7864 Sunset St. | Phoenix | AZ | 85609 | 602-555-5457 |
| Babbitt | George | 9587 Willow Bend | Atlanta | GA | 30303 | 404-555-8991 |
| Anderson | Ellis | 504 Grapevine St. | Sacremento | CA | 95619 | 916-555-6638 |
| Evans | Stewart | 8642 Elm Ave. | Detroit | MI | 48221 | 313-555-3357 |
| Norris | Mike | 8766 Alder Ave. | Seattle | WA | 98122 | 206-555-4622 |
| Chang | Elizabeth | 878 Briar Terrace | Los Angeles | CA | 90032 | 213-555-8225 |
| Tran | Samuel | 7888 Quail Run | Portland | OR | 97207 | 503-555-4587 |
| Chavez | Patricia | 8655 Flamingo Ln. | Miami | FL | 33124 | 315-555-9887 |
| Hebert | Thomas | 353 Marsh Rd. | Baton Rouge | LA | 70803 | 504-555-4446 |
| Russell | William | 2864 Holden Rd. | Boston | MA | 02215 | 617-555-8822 |
| Alexander | Barbara | 3425 Murphy St. | St. Louis | MO | 63108 | 314-555-9317 |
| Novak | Art | 875 Wheeler Ave. | Baltimore | MD | 21210 | 301-555-8731 |
| Smith | Steve | 8894 Stone Ave. | Denver | CO | 80204 | 303-555-2548 |
| Barnes | Alice | 713 Columbia St. | Providence | RI | 02918 | 401-555-8647 |
| Straw | Stacy | 265 Randall Rd. | Richmond | VA | 23173 | 804-555-8878 |
| Garner | Cindy | 8775 Payne Blvd. | Chicago | IL | 60605 | 312-555-2536 |
| Mitchell | Gary | 5251 Winter St. | Columbia | SC | 29208 | 803-555-1212 |
| Chester | Tom | 3584 Daisy St. | Washington | DC | 20549 | 202-555-8789 |

Last Name:  Hernandez
First Name:  Rodrigo
Address:  7826 Cactus Trail
City:  Albuquerque
State:  NM
ZIP Code:       87131
Phone No.:    505-555-8588

## Saving and Exiting a Database

You save a file and exit the database in the same way you perform these operations in the word processor or the spreadsheet. Both the Save command and the Close command appear in the File menu.

**ACTIVITY
11-7**

### Saving and Closing a Database

In this activity you will save and exit the file *act11-1.wdb,* which is now on your screen in Form view.

1.  From the **File** menu, choose **Save As**. The Save As dialog box will appear.

2.  Insert your data disk and key the appropriate drive letter in the File Name box.

3.  Key **address**.

4.  Click **OK**. An hourglass will appear momentarily while the file is being saved.

5.  From the **File** menu, choose **Close**. The database will disappear from the screen.

## Designing Fields

The arrangement of a database is critical to its usefulness. At the beginning of this chapter, you learned that one advantage of using a database is that it allows you to find information easily. You also learned that records may be sorted quickly in a database. The efficiency of these operations depends on whether the fields of the database have been designed carefully.

### Creating Fields

You can create fields in either List view or Form view. When you are creating fields for a new database, you will probably want to do so in Form view because you can quickly key several field names and locate them easily just where you want them. To add a single new field to an existing database, you can use the Insert Record/Field command from the Edit menu in List view. In this section, new fields will be created in Form view.

To create a field, type the field name and a colon. After you press Enter, a dialog box will appear and ask you to specify the size of the field. Fields created in Form view will also appear in List view.

You may enter a new field name anywhere in the record. To locate the field name, click the area where you want the field name to appear. Your new field name can then be entered at the cursor. If you would like to move field names, you can drag them to a new location within the record. Works will show you the position of the field name in the formula bar.

**ACTIVITY
11-8**

## Creating a New Field

In this activity, you will create a new field for the database *act11-8.wdb*. This database contains information on national parks in the United States. You would like to use this database to advise travelers of activities available in these parks. Enter an additional field to this database to indicate whether fishing is available in the park by following these steps:

1. Open the file *act11-8.wdb* from the template disk. A database in Form view will appear.

2. Click two lines below the *A* in the **ACRES (000)** field.

3. Key **FISHING:**. (Remember to include the colon.)

4. Press **Enter**. The Field Size dialog box will appear.

5. Click **OK**.

6. Press **F9** to switch to List view.

7. Enter the following data in the newly created FISHING field:

| | |
|---|---|
| Acadia | Yes |
| Badlands | No |
| Big Bend | Yes |
| Carlsbad Caverns | No |
| Denali | Yes |
| Everglades | Yes |
| Glacier | Yes |
| Grand Canyon | Yes |
| Haleakala | No |

Actifvity 11-8 continued

| Hot Springs | No | Shenandoah | Yes |
| Isle Royale | Yes | Yellowstone | Yes |
| Mammoth Cave | Yes | Yosemite | Yes |
| Olympic | Yes | Zion | No[1] |
| Rocky Mountain | Yes | | |

8.  Leave the database *act11-8.wdb* on your screen in List view for the next activity.

## Field Size

In the last activity, you accepted the default field size of 20 characters. However, sometimes you will not be able to determine the field size until you enter data into the field. The field size may be adjusted in either List or Form view.

In List view, the field size is adjusted in the same way a column width is adjusted in the spreadsheet. If numerical data is wider than the column, a series of number signs (######) will appear in the entry. Alphabetical data will be truncated (deleted at the end) if the field is too narrow. You can widen a field by placing the mouse pointer on the boundary of the right edge of the field name. The pointer will turn into a vertical bar with a double-headed arrow, as shown in Figure 11-13. Widen the column by dragging the double-headed arrow to the right until the column is wide enough to show all of the data.

**FIGURE 11-13**

In List view, field width may be adjusted by dragging the double-headed arrow at the right edge of the field name.

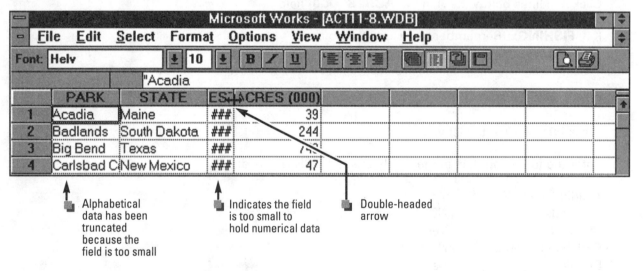

[1]Source: Michael Frome, *The Leading National Park Guide* (Chicago:  Rand McNally, 1987); and National Park Service, *National Park System Map and Guide* (Washington, D.C.: U.S. Department of the Interior, 1989).

In Form view, the field size is adjusted by clicking the field and pointing to the Field Size box in the lower right corner of the field, as shown in Figure 11-14. When the pointer turns into a double-headed arrow, drag it to the field size you desire. The field size will be changed for all records.

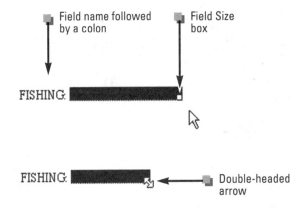

Field name followed by a colon

Field Size box

FISHING:

Double-headed arrow

**ACTIVITY 11-9**

## Changing the Size of a Field

In this activity, you will decrease the size of the FISHING field in Form view of *act11-8.wdb*. *Act11-8.wdb* is currently on your screen in List view.

1.  Press **F9** to switch to Form view.

2.  If the contents of the FISHING field are not already highlighted, click the line to the right of the field name to highlight them.

3.  Point to the Field Size box in the lower right corner of the field. The pointer will turn into a double-headed arrow.

4.  The contents of the FISHING field will contain a maximum of three letters (for the word *Yes*). Drag the double-headed arrow to the left until the field is large enough to fit approximately five letters.

5.  Leave the database *act11-8.wdb* on your screen in Form view for the next activity.

## Moving a Field in Form View

A field in Form view may be moved to any part of the record. To change the location of the field, click the field name and the pointer will turn into a hand, as shown in Figure 11-15. Then drag the field to the location you desire. Changing the location of the field in Form view will not affect the location of the field in the List view.

**FIGURE 11-15**

In Form view, the position of a field may be changed by dragging the field to a new location.

The location of the field will be displayed in the formula bar. (See Figure 11-15.) The number after the *X* indicates where the field appears horizontally, and the number after the *Y* indicates where the field appears vertically.

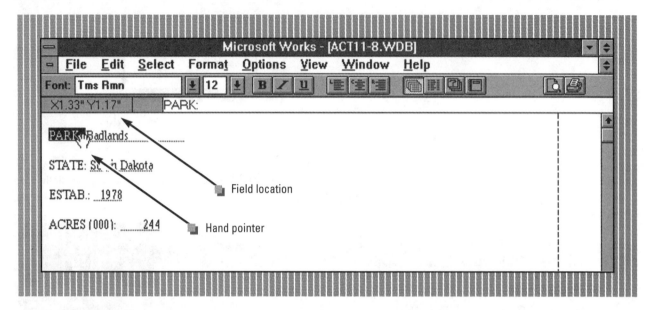

ACTIVITY
11-10

## Moving a Field

In this activity, you will move a field. The file *act11-8.wdb* is currently on your screen in Form view.

1. Move the locations of the fields so that each field appears vertically (Y) every one-half inch.

2. Arrange the fields horizontally so that all fields are 1.5 inches (or as close to 1.5 inches as possible) from the left margin.

3. Leave the database *act11-8.wdb* on your screen in Form view for the next activity.

## Field Alignment

Left alignment button

Center alignment button

Works will automatically align alphabetical characters to the left side of the field and numerical characters to the right side of a field. You may change the alignment of field data by highlighting the field (or a field

entry) and clicking one of the alignment buttons on the Toolbar. When
an alignment button is clicked, all the data in the field will be aligned.
The alignment will occur in both Form and List view.

 Right alignment button

**ACTIVITY
11-11**

## Aligning Entries in a Field

In this activity, you will center the data in the FISHING field of database
*act11-8.wdb. Act11-8.wdb* is currently on your screen in Form view.

1.   Select the contents of the FISHING field.

2.   Click the **Center** alignment button on the Toolbar. The contents of
     the entry should move to the center.

3.   Press **F9** to switch to List view. The contents of the FISHING field
     should be centered.

4.   Leave the database *act11-8.wdb* on your screen in List view for the
     next activity.

## Font Style

B   **Bold**

The font style of entries may be changed to be bold, italicized, or
underlined. To change the font style of a field, highlight the field (or a
field entry) and click one of the font style buttons on the Toolbar. When
a style button is clicked, all the data in the field will be changed in both
Form and List view.

I   **Italic**

U   **Underline**

## Database Fonts and Font Sizes

Font box

The font and font size can affect the readability of a database on the
screen. The number of fonts available is determined by the printer you
are using. Works allows only one font in either List or Form view of the
database.

Font Size
box

   To change the font of the database, click the Font box arrow on the
Toolbar and choose the name of the font you desire. Use the same
procedure to specify the font size by clicking the Font Size box arrow.

# Hiding Fields and Records

**FIGURE 11-16**
Fields and records are hidden and redisplayed by choosing the Field Width command from the Format menu. Records are hidden by choosing the Hide Record command and redisplayed by choosing the Show All Records command from the Select menu.

When databases become large, you may find it easier to view only a portion of the database. Hiding fields and records removes data from view but does not delete data from the database.

## Hiding Fields

It is more convenient to hide a field in List view than in Form view. Hide a field by dragging the right border of the field to the left until the field name disappears from view. Or you may hide a field by choosing the Field Width command from the Format menu and typing 0 as the field width. To redisplay a field that has been hidden, choose the Go To command from the Select menu (or press F5) and choose the field name. Then choose the Field Width command and increase the field width (which is currently 0). (See Figure 11-16.)

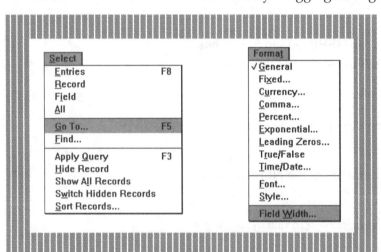

## Hiding Records

Records may be hidden from List view or Form view. In List view, select the record or records you want to hide and choose the Hide Record command from the Select menu.

In Form view, you may hide the record currently on the screen by choosing the Hide Record command from the Select menu. From Form view, you can hide records only one at a time. To redisplay hidden records, choose Show All Records from the Select menu.

## ACTIVITY
## 11-12

### Hiding Fields and Records

In this activity, you will hide and redisplay fields and records. The file *act11-8.wdb* is currently on your screen in List view.

1.   Hide the ESTAB. field following these steps:

   a.   Point to the right side of the ESTAB. field. The pointer will turn into a double-headed arrow.

Activity 11-12 continued

    b.    Drag the double-headed arrow to the left until it reaches the left edge of the field. The field's grid line also moves to show the changing field width. Release the mouse button. The ESTAB. field is now hidden.

2.    Hide the records for Haleakala and Hot Springs (Records 9 and 10) by following these steps:

    a.    Drag from Record 9 to Record 10 along the left side of the screen to select the records for Haleakala and Hot Springs.

    b.    From the **Select** menu, choose **Hide Record**. Records 9 and 10 will be hidden.

3.    Redisplay the ESTAB. field by following these steps:

    a.    From the **Select** menu, choose **Go To**. The Go To dialog box will appear.

    b.    Double-click **ESTAB.** in the Names list. You will be returned to List view.

    c.    From the **Format** menu, choose **Field Width**. The Field Width dialog box will appear.

    d.    Enter **10** in the Width list.

    e.    Click **OK**. The ESTAB. field will be restored.

4.    Redisplay Records 9 and 10 by choosing **Show All Records** from the **Select** menu.

5.    Print the entire database from List view.

6.    Save the file to your data disk as *parks* and close the file.

# SUMMARY

A database is an automated electronic filing system that stores and retrieves information. It is comprised of rows, called *records*, and columns, called *fields*. A database typically contains larger amounts of information and involves less computation than a spreadsheet.

A database can be viewed in two ways. List view shows several records at once and has a format similar to a spreadsheet. While in List view, a database screen may be split to view several parts of the database on the screen at the same time. Form view displays one record at a time. Records may be added and deleted from a database in either List or Form view.

The design of fields in a database is critical to its usefulness. Field size, entry style (bolding, italicizing, and underlining), and field alignment (left, center, and right justification) may be adjusted to accommodate the needs of the database user.

Selected fields and records may be hidden to make it easier to read a large database. Hiding removes the data from view on the screen but does not delete the data from the database.

# CHALLENGES

## TRUE/FALSE

Circle **T** or **F** to show whether the statement is true or false.

| | | | |
|---|---|---|---|
| T | F | 1. | The ability to sort records quickly is an advantage of using an electronic database. |
| T | F | 2. | Databases usually contain less data than a spreadsheet. |
| T | F | 3. | A record is a row of entries in the database. |
| T | F | 4. | A field is the smallest unit in a database and contains one piece of information. |
| T | F | 5. | The List view of the database shows one record at a time. |
| T | F | 6. | While in Form view, pressing F9 will switch the screen to List view. |
| T | F | 7. | While in Form view, choosing the List command in the View menu will switch the screen to List view. |
| T | F | 8. | A database screen may be split into either two or four panes. |
| T | F | 9. | Works allows only one font in List view and one font in Form view of a database. |
| T | F | 10. | Hiding a field in the database will erase the field. |

# COMPLETION

Write the correct answer in the space provided.

1. What is a row of field entries in a database called?

_____

2. What is a column of database information called?

_____

3. In Form view, what buttons are clicked to move to the first, previous, next, or last record in the database?

_____

4. In Form view, what combination of keys is pressed to move to the first record in a database?

_____

5. In Form view, what punctuation indicates that keyed characters are a field name?

_____

6. When moving a field in Form view, in what shape does the mouse pointer appear?

_____

7. When widening a field in the database, in what shape does the mouse pointer appear?

_____

8. What is the effect of setting a field width at 0 (zero)?

_____

9. What command in the Select menu will hide a record in a database?

_____

10. What command restores hidden records in a database?

_____

# APPLICATIONS

## APPLICATION 11-1

In the blank space, write the letter of the keystroke that matches the highlight movement in <u>Form</u> view of the database.

| | Highlight Movement | | Keystroke |
|---|---|---|---|
| ___ | 1. Up one line | a. | Shift+Tab |
| ___ | 2. Down one line | b. | Up Arrow |
| ___ | 3. Up one window | c. | Ctrl+End |
| ___ | 4. Down one window | d. | Down Arrow |
| ___ | 5. To the next field | e. | Tab |
| ___ | 6. To the previous field | f. | Ctrl+Left Arrow |
| ___ | 7. To the left edge of form | g. | Page Up |
| ___ | 8. To the right edge of form | h. | Ctrl+Right Arrow |
| ___ | 9. First record | i. | Ctrl+Home |
| ___ | 10. Last record | j. | End |
| ___ | 11. Next record | k. | Home |
| ___ | 12. Previous record | l. | Page Down |

## APPLICATION 11-2

In the blank space, write the letter of the keystroke that matches the highlight movement in <u>List</u> view of the database.

| | Highlight Movement | | Keystroke |
|---|---|---|---|
| ___ | 1. Left one field | a. | Ctrl+End |
| ___ | 2. Right one field | b. | Ctrl+Page Down |
| ___ | 3. Up one record | c. | Down Arrow |
| ___ | 4. Down one record | d. | Left Arrow |

_____ 5. To the first field of a record        e. End

_____ 6. To the last field of a record        f. Home

_____ 7. To the first record        g. Ctrl+Page Up

_____ 8. To the last record        h. Page Up

_____ 9. Up one window        i. Right Arrow

_____ 10. Down one window        j. Ctrl+Home

_____ 11. Left one window        k. Up Arrow

_____ 12. Right one window        l. Page Down

---

# APPLICATION 11-3

In the blank space, write the letter of the appropriate database key or mouse procedure that matches the database operations. You may use the items in the right column more than once if necessary. For some questions, more than one answer may be correct; however, you are required to identify only one of the correct answers.

**Database Operation**

_____ 1. Open an existing database file

_____ 2. Switch to Form view

_____ 3. Switch to List view

_____ 4. Split the List view

_____ 5. Move to the next record in Form view

_____ 6. Move to the first record while in Form view

_____ 7. Move up one record in List view

_____ 8. Move to the last record in List view

_____ 9. Widen a field in List view

_____ 10. Widen a field in Form view

_____ 11. Hide a field in List view

_____ 12. Redisplay a record in List view

_____ 13. Save a database file

**Key or Mouse Procedure**

a. Press the F9 key

b. Click a navigation button

c. Press Ctrl+Left Arrow

d. Double-click the split box

e. Press Ctrl+End

f. Drag from the Field Size box

g. Click a button on the Toolbar

h. Press Ctrl+Home

i. Choose a command from the Format menu

j. Press Up Arrow

k. Choose a command from the File menu

l. Press Ctrl+Right Arrow

*Application 11-3 continues on next page*

___ 14. Exit Works1

m. Drag from the right side of the field name

n. Choose a command from the Select menu

---

# APPLICATION 11-4

The file *app11-4.wdb* is a database of population statistics for selected countries. The database currently contains the following fields:

Country
Population (for the year 1990)
Birth Rate (per 1,000 of the population)
Death Rate (per 1,000 of the population)

   Perform the following operations to change the fields of the database:

1.   Open *app11-4.wdb*.
2.   Narrow the entries to the right of the field names in the Form view to eliminate excess space.
3.   Switch to List view and widen the fields to show all field names and entry contents if necessary.
4.   Add a new field entitled *Life Expectancy* and enter the following data in the field:

| Country | Life Expectancy |
| --- | --- |
| Australia | 76 |
| Brazil | 66 |
| China | 70 |
| Cuba | 74 |
| Egypt | 63 |
| Ethiopia | 43 |
| France | 76 |
| India | 60 |
| Indonesia | 58 |
| Italy | 76 |
| Mexico | 70 |
| Nigeria | 52 |
| Poland | 71 |
| Turkey | 66 |
| United Kingdom | 76 |
| United States | 76 |
| USSR | 70 |
| West Germany | 75 |
| Zaire | 54 |

Source: *United Nations Population Fund (UNFPA), The State of the World Population 1990* (1990).

5. Center the contents of the Birth Rate, Death Rate, and Life Expectancy fields.
6. Print the database.
7. Save the file to your data disk as *popula* and close the file.

# APPLICATION 11-5

In this application, you will enter additional records and delete obsolete records from the file created in Application 11-4.

1. Retrieve the file *popula.wdb* created in Application 11-4.
2. The countries of West Germany and the USSR no longer exist in their present form. Delete these records from the database.
3. Add the following record for the unified Germany to the bottom of the database:

| Country | Population | Birth Rate | Death Rate | Life Expectancy |
|---------|-----------|-----------|-----------|-----------------|
| Germany | 77,188,000 | 10 | 11 | 75 |

4. Print the individual record for Germany from Form view.
5. Save and close the file.

# APPLICATION 11-6

The file *app11-6.wdb* is a database of dog breeds and their characteristics. The purpose of the database is to assist in selecting a breed for a pet. The database exceeds the size of the screen. Perform the following operations to make viewing the database more manageable:

1. Open *app11-6.wdb*.
2. Center the contents of the Height and Weight fields.
3. Split the screen horizontally so that the top and bottom of the database may be viewed simultaneously.
4. Suppose you are not interested in the height of the breed. Hide this field from view.
5. Suppose you are not interested in breeds in the Toy Group. Hide the records in the Toy Group.
6. Save the database to your data disk as *short*.
7. Print the shortened database from List view.
8. Restore the hidden records and fields.
9. Save the database to your data disk as *long* and exit Works.

Source: Patricia Sylvester, ed., *The Reader's Digest Illustrated Book of Dogs,* rev. ed. (The Readers' Digest Association, Inc., 1989); heights and weights are minimums required by various kennel associations.

<br>

CHAPTER

# 12

# STRENGTHENING DATABASE SKILLS

## LEARNING OBJECTIVES

**When you complete this chapter, you will be able to:**

1. Create a new database.
2. Copy data to other entries.
3. Insert a record in the database.
4. Move data to other entries.
5. Format a database field.
6. Insert dates and times in a database.
7. Perform calculations in a database.
8. Protect parts of the database.

In Chapter 11, you learned the basics of a database. In this chapter, you will strengthen your database skills by creating and refining a database. In the chapter activities, you will create and refine a database that records the membership of a student organization called the Future Entrepreneurs.

## CREATING A NEW DATABASE

A new database is created by clicking the Database button in the Startup dialog box shown in Figure 12-1. If Works is already running, you can create a new database by choosing the Create New File command from the File menu and then clicking the Database icon. In either case, an empty database will appear in Form view. When you save the database, you will have created a new database file.

**FIGURE 12-1**
Click the Database button in the Startup dialog box to create a new database.

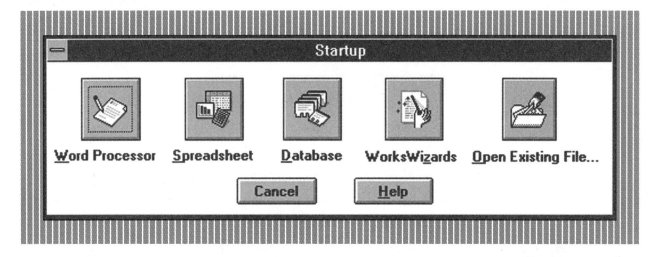

ACTIVITY
12-1

## Creating a New Database

In this activity, you will create a new database for membership records for the Future Entrepreneurs by following these steps:

1.  Start Works on your computer. The Startup dialog box will appear.

2.  Click the **Database** button. An empty database will appear in Form view.

3.  Create the following fields using the techniques you learned in Chapter 11. (Do not forget to key a colon after each field name.)

| Field Name | Width |
| --- | --- |
| Last Name | 15 |
| First Name | 15 |
| Address | 20 |
| City | 10 |
| ZIP Code | 10 |
| Interest | 20 |

Activity 12-1 continued

4.  When you select a field, its location will be displayed at the left side of the formula bar. Move the fields to the following X and Y locations in Form view. If your cursor does not snap to these exact locations, place the fields in approximate locations. When you have entered the fields, your screen should look similar to Figure 12-2.

| Field Name | X | Y |
| --- | --- | --- |
| Last Name | 1.33" | 1.17" |
| First Name | 3.67" | 1.17" |
| Address | 1.33" | 1.50" |
| City | 3.67" | 1.50" |
| ZIP Code | 5.08" | 1.50" |
| Interest | 1.33" | 2.00" |

5.  Switch to List view.

6.  Enter the data on the next page in the database. Do not enter any data for the city at this time.

**FIGURE 12-2**
Form view is ideal for creating fields for a new database.

7.  Adjust the field width in List view so that all entry contents are visible on screen. Your screen should appear similar to Figure 12-3.

8.  Save the database to your data disk as *feclub*.

9.  Leave *feclub* on the screen for the next activity.

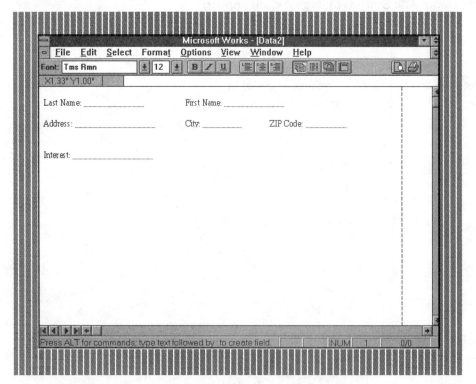

Activity 12-1 continued

| Last Name | First Name | Address | ZIP Code | Interest |
|-----------|-----------|---------|----------|----------|
| Berry | Kevin | 5902 Sierra St. | 80231 | Plumbing |
| Cheng | Lan | 618 Poplar Point | 80266 | Insurance |
| Fisher | Carl | 87 Stone Drive | 80244 | Furniture |
| Fleming | Jane | 2816 Indigo St. | 80255 | Appliance Repair |
| Foley | David | 1254 Cherry Dr. | 80274 | Locksmith |
| Gordon | Tony | 265 Briar Lane | 80206 | Clothing |
| Johnston | Betty | 7822 West Ave. | 80231 | Restaurant |
| Knight | Curt | 2822 Echo Lane | 80266 | Bakery |
| Mathews | Alan | 846 Center Ave. | 80240 | Frozen Foods |
| Mitchell | Jose | 762 Hill St. | 80255 | Convenience Stores |
| Padilla | Phillip | 630 Rosebud St. | 80245 | Restaurant |
| Ross | Ernest | 8401 Harbor Rd. | 80244 | Cabinetry |
| Simon | Harold | 879 Clear Creek Dr. | 80228 | Dry Cleaning |

**FIGURE 12-3**

List view displays the entire database.

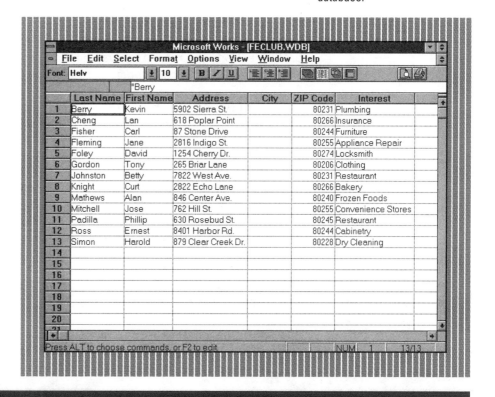

**FIGURE 12-4**
The Edit menu contains all copying commands. The most frequently used copying commands in the database are Copy, Paste, and Fill Down.

| Edit | |
|---|---|
| Cut | Ctrl+X |
| Copy | Ctrl+C |
| Paste | Ctrl+V |
| Clear Field Entry | |
| Delete Record/Field | |
| Insert Record/Field | |
| Fill Right | |
| Fill Down | |
| Fill Series... | |
| Delete Page Break | |
| Insert Page Break | |
| Field Name... | |
| Headers & Footers... | |

# COPYING DATA

Repetitive typing is unnecessary if you copy common data from one entry to another. Just as you learned in the spreadsheet chapters, you can copy data using either Copy and Paste or Fill Down.

## Copying and Pasting

The first way to copy data from one part of the database to another is to use the Copy and Paste commands located in the Edit menu, shown in Figure 12-4. Copying and pasting in the database are the same operations as copying and pasting in the word processor or the spreadsheet.

## ACTIVITY 12-2

### Copying and Pasting

In this activity, you will copy a record in the database that you have just created. Your screen now shows the database you saved as *feclub* in List view. David Foley's brother John recently joined the Future Entrepreneurs club. His address, phone, and interest are the same as his brother's. Copy the record for David Foley and change the first name to John by following these steps:

1.  Select **Record 5** (David Foley) by clicking **5** in the Record Number box. The entire record will be highlighted.

2.  From the **Edit** menu, choose **Copy**.

3.  Click **14** in the Record Number box to select the empty record at the bottom of the database. The empty record will be highlighted.

4.  From the **Edit** menu, choose **Paste**. The record for David Foley will be copied into Record 14.

5.  Click the First Name field of Record 14. (The field contains the name David.)

6.  Enter **John** in the First Name field.

7.  Leave *feclub* on the screen for the next activity.

## Filling Down

*Filling down* copies data from an original entry to an entry or entries directly below the original. Filling down is performed by selecting the entry containing the original data and dragging over the entries to be filled with the copied data. When the Fill Down command is selected from the Edit menu, shown in Figure 12-5, the contents of the original will be copied to the empty entries.

**FIGURE 12-5**

The Fill Down command copies data from an original cell to cells below the original.

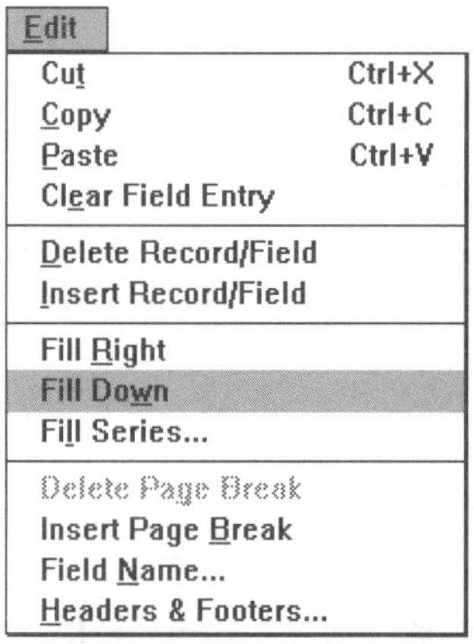

| Edit | |
|---|---|
| Cut | Ctrl+X |
| Copy | Ctrl+C |
| Paste | Ctrl+V |
| Clear Field Entry | |
| Delete Record/Field | |
| Insert Record/Field | |
| Fill Right | |
| Fill Down | |
| Fill Series... | |
| Delete Page Break | |
| Insert Page Break | |
| Field Name... | |
| Headers & Footers... | |

**ACTIVITY 12-3**

## Filling Down

In this activity, you will use the Fill Down command to copy an entry into several fields. Your screen now shows the database *feclub* in List view. Copy the name of the city throughout the entire field by following these steps:

1. Highlight the entry in the City field of Record 1.

2. Enter **Denver**.

3. Drag from the entry in which you entered data to the last entry (Record 14) of the City field.

4. From the **Edit** menu, choose **Fill Down**. The name *Denver* will appear in the empty entries.

5. Leave *feclub* on your screen for the next activity.

## INSERTING A RECORD

In the last chapter, you learned to enter a record at the bottom of a database. You may, however, want to insert a record within the List view of the database. Choosing the Insert Record/Field command from the Edit menu, shown in Figure 12-6, will place an empty record above a selected record in the database.

**FIGURE 12-6**

The Insert Record/Field command is located in the Edit menu.

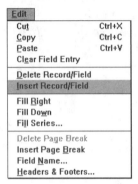

## ACTIVITY 12-4

**FIGURE 12-7**

The Insert Record/Field command places an empty record above the highlighted record.

# Inserting a Record in List View

In this activity, you will insert an empty record in the database that you have created. Your screen now shows the database *feclub* in List view. Follow these steps to insert a record in List view:

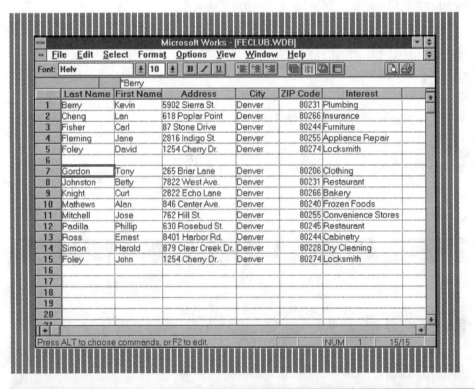

1. Select **Record 6** (Tony Gordon) by clicking **6** in the Record Number box. The entire record will be highlighted.

2. From the **Edit** menu, choose **Insert Record/Field**. An empty record will appear as Record 6. The record for Tony Gordon will be moved down to Record 7, as shown in Figure 12-7.

3. Leave *feclub* on the screen for the next activity.

# MOVING DATA

To move data, choose the Cut command and then the Paste command from the Edit menu. The process is similar to the copy and paste process you learned earlier except the Cut command removes data from its original position in the database.

**ACTIVITY
12-5**

### Moving Data in a Database

In this activity, you will move the record for John Foley from the bottom of the database to the empty record (Record 6) in the middle of the database.

1.  Select the contents of Record 15 (John Foley) by dragging from the name *Foley* to the interest *Locksmith* or by clicking **15** in the Record Number box.

2.  From the **Edit** menu, choose **Cut**. The record will disappear.

3.  Click the Last Name field of Record 6 (the empty record).

4.  From the **Edit** menu, choose **Paste**. The record for John Foley will appear in Record 6.

5.  Leave *feclub* on the screen for the next activity.

# FIELD FORMATS

*Field formats* determine how data is presented in a column of a database. The formats available are the same as those available in the spreadsheet. However, in the spreadsheet you were able to format individual cells; in a database, all entries within a field must have the same format.

## Formats in the Database

The default format is called *general format*, which works with both text and numerical data. Other available formats are shown in Table 12-1. To format a field, select an entry within the field and choose one of the commands from the Format menu shown in Figure 12-8. A field may be formatted in either Form or List view.

**TABLE 12-1**
Fields of a database may be formatted in several ways.

| Format | Description |
|---|---|
| *General* | The default format; displays both text and numerical data as keyed |
| *Fixed* | Displays numerical data with a fixed amount of places to the right of the decimal point |
| *Currency* | Displays numerical data preceded by a dollar sign |
| *Comma* | Displays numerical data with commas every third decimal place |
| *Percent* | Displays numerical data followed by a percent sign |
| *Exponential* | Displays numerical data in scientific notation |
| *Leading zeros* | Displays numerical data with a specified number of decimal places to the left of the decimal |
| *True/False* | Displays the word *True* for all non-zero number values and *False* for zero |
| *Time/Date* | Displays text and numerical data as times or dates |

**FIGURE 12-8**
The commands in the Format menu determine the appearance of data in an entry.

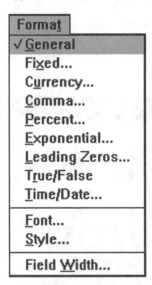

## ACTIVITY 12-6

### Formatting a Database Field

In this activity, you will create fields for the dues owed to the club and dues paid to the club. You will then format the fields for currency. Your screen now shows the database *feclub* in List view.

Activity 12-6 continued

1. Switch to Form view and create the following fields:

| Field | Field Width | Location (or Approximate Location) in the Form |
|---|---|---|
| Dues Owed | 10 | X 1.33", Y 2.50" |
| Dues Paid | 10 | X 1.33", Y 2.83" |
| Balance | 10 | X 1.33", Y 3.17" |

2. Click the area to the right of the colon in the Dues Owed field. A darkened box will appear to indicate the field is selected.

3. From the **Format** menu, choose **Currency**. The Currency dialog box will appear and will request the number of decimal places to be shown in the field.

4. Click **OK** to indicate that 2 is the appropriate number of decimal places.

5. Switch to **List view**.

6. Scroll to the three new fields you have created and adjust the column widths so that the entire headings can be seen on screen.

7. Select the **Dues Paid** and **Balance** fields by dragging the field names at the top of the columns.

8. From the **Format** menu, choose **Currency**. The Currency dialog box will appear and will request the number of decimals to be shown in the field.

9. Click **OK** to indicate that 2 is the appropriate number of decimal places.

10. Enter the following data in the Dues Owed and Dues Paid fields. You will enter data into the Balance field in another activity.

| Record Number | Dues Owed | Dues Paid |
|---|---|---|
| 1 | $20.00 | $20.00 |
| 2 | $20.00 | $20.00 |
| 3 | $20.00 | $20.00 |

Activity 12-6 continued

| Record Number | Dues Owed | Dues Paid |
|---|---|---|
| 4 | $20.00 | $0.00 |
| 5 | $20.00 | $20.00 |
| 6 | $10.00 | $10.00 |
| 7 | $20.00 | $0.00 |
| 8 | $20.00 | $10.00 |
| 9 | $20.00 | $20.00 |
| 10 | $20.00 | $20.00 |
| 11 | $20.00 | $20.00 |
| 12 | $20.00 | $20.00 |
| 13 | $20.00 | $20.00 |
| 14 | $20.00 | $0.00 |

**FIGURE 12-9**

Currency format places a dollar sign in front of the data and designates the number of decimal places you desire.

11. Split the screen so that the names and dues amounts may be viewed at the same time. Your screen should appear similar to Figure 12-9.

12. Leave *feclub* on the screen for the next activity.

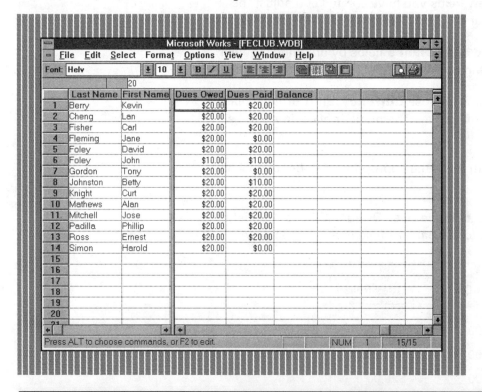

# TIME AND DATE FORMATS

Times and dates are sometimes entered as data in a database. Works has special formats for times and dates that permit them to be used in formulas and to be displayed in formats shown in Table 12-2. Format a field in the database for a time or date by selecting a field and choosing the Time/Date command from the Format menu. When the Time/Date dialog box appears (see Figure 12-10), click the display format you desire.

**TABLE 12-2**
Times and dates can be displayed in several ways.

| TIME FORMATS | | |
| --- | --- | --- |
| **This Format** | | **Will Display** |
| 12 hours | Hour, minute, second | 3:00:00 PM |
| | Hour, minute | 3:00 PM |
| 24 hours | Hour, minute, second | 15:00:00 |
| | Hour, minute | 15:00 |

| DATE FORMATS | | |
| --- | --- | --- |
| **This Format** | | **Will Display** |
| Long | Month, day, year | September 15, 1995 |
| | Month, year | September 1995 |
| | Month, day | September 15 |
| | Month only | September |
| Short | Month, day, year | 9/15/95 |
| | Month, year | 9/95 |
| | Month, day | 9/15 |

**FIGURE 12-10**
The Time/Date dialog box designates the way times and dates will be displayed in the database.

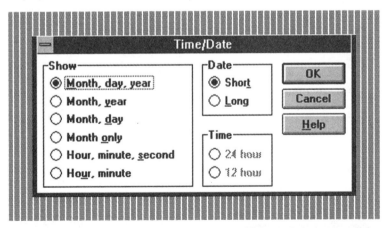

## ACTIVITY 12-7

### Entering Times and Dates in a Database

In this activity, you will enter a field formatted for dates in the database that you have created. Your screen now shows the database *feclub* in List view.

Activity 12-7 continued

**FIGURE 12-11**

The Date Joined field may be formatted for long or short dates, as shown in Table 12-2.

1.   Switch to Form view and create a field located at X  1.33", Y  3.67" entitled *Date Joined*. Set the field width to 20 spaces. Your screen should look similar to Figure 12-11.

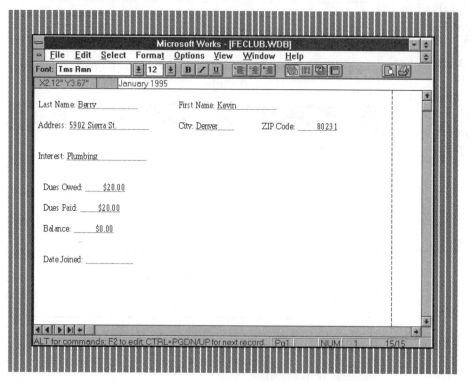

2.   Switch to List view and enter the data given in the table below in the Date Joined field. You may have to adjust field widths to make the field name or field contents visible.

3.   Click the **Date Joined** field name to select the field.

4.   Format the Date Joined field by following these steps:

  a.   From the **Format** menu, choose **Time/Date**. The Time/Date dialog box will appear.

| Record Number | Date Joined |
| --- | --- |
| 1 | 1/11/95 |
| 2 | 2/15/95 |
| 3 | 9/30/95 |
| 4 | 1/11/95 |
| 5 | 7/18/95 |
| 6 | 2/1/96 |
| 7 | 9/2/95 |
| 8 | 1/11/95 |
| 9 | 1/11/95 |
| 10 | 2/15/95 |
| 11 | 1/11/95 |
| 12 | 3/25/95 |
| 13 | 1/11/95 |
| 14 | 11/4/95 |

Activity 12-7 continued

    b.   The **Month, day, year** button in the Show list should be selected. If it is not, click the button now.

    c.   Click **Long** in the Date list.

    d.   Click **OK**. The field is formatted for a long date. You may need to widen the field in List view to accommodate the long date.

5.   Delete the day from the format by following these steps:

    a.   From the **Format** menu, choose **Time/Date**. The Time/Date dialog box will appear.

    b.   Click **Month, year** in the Show list.

    c.   Click **OK**. The field is formatted for month and year.

6.   Leave *feclub* on the screen for the next activity.

## Current Times and Dates

Most computers contain an internal clock that keeps track of the current time and date. Works will insert the current time or date in your database or spreadsheet. To do this, select an entry or cell and perform the following keystrokes:

| To Enter the Current | Press |
|---|---|
| Time | Ctrl+Shift+; |
| Date | Ctrl+; |

## CALCULATING IN THE DATABASE

The database is not used as extensively for calculation as the spreadsheet is. However, the same mathematical and function formulas available for use in the spreadsheet are also available in the database.

Because the database does not use cell references, formulas in the database use field names to calculate values. For example, Figure 12-12 shows a database containing product prices, sales volumes, and the amount of total sales. Total sales were calculated by a formula designating the product of the price and volume (=Price*Volume). The formula is displayed in the formula bar. The formula results are displayed in the Sales field. Note that an equal sign is entered first, just as in the spreadsheet, to tell Works to expect a formula.

**FIGURE 12-12**

The values in the Sales field were determined by the product of the values in the Price and Volume fields.

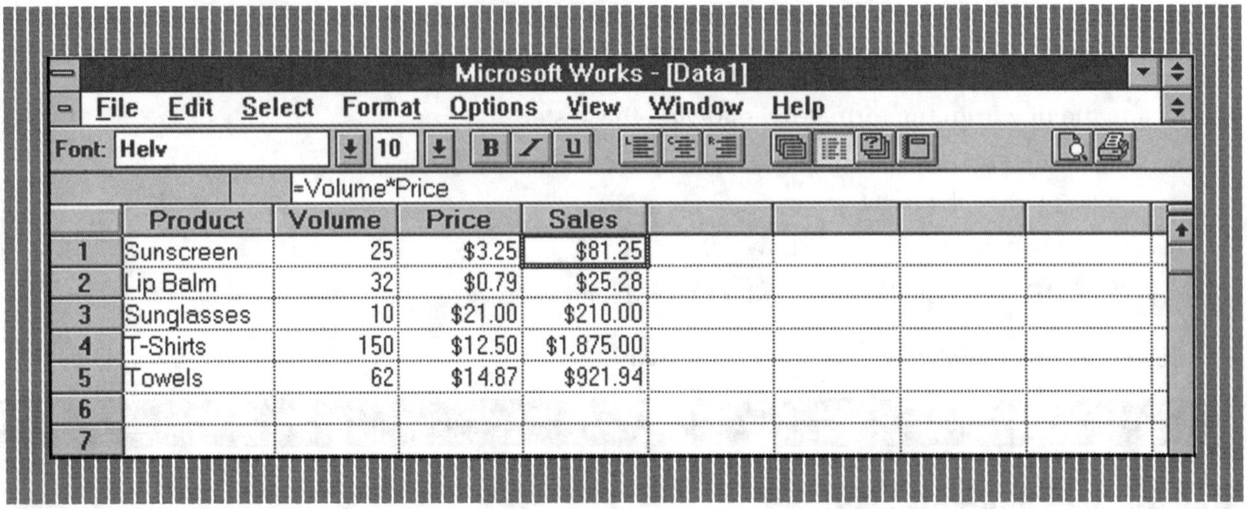

A database formula consists of two types of characters: operands and operators. An *operand* is the field name used in formulas. An *operator* tells Works what to do with the operands. The operators used in formulas are shown in Table 12-3. The sequence in which a formula will perform calculations is the same as the order followed for formulas in the spreadsheet.

```
Microsoft Works - [Data1]
File  Edit  Select  Format  Options  View  Window  Help
Font: Helv        10    B  Z  U
=Volume*Price
```

| | Product | Volume | Price | Sales | | | |
|---|---|---|---|---|---|---|---|
| 1 | Sunscreen | 25 | $3.25 | $81.25 | | | |
| 2 | Lip Balm | 32 | $0.79 | $25.28 | | | |
| 3 | Sunglasses | 10 | $21.00 | $210.00 | | | |
| 4 | T-Shirts | 150 | $12.50 | $1,875.00 | | | |
| 5 | Towels | 62 | $14.87 | $921.94 | | | |
| 6 | | | | | | | |
| 7 | | | | | | | |

**TABLE 12-3**

Operators tell Works what to do with operands.

| Operator | Operation |
|---|---|
| + | Addition |
| - | Subtraction |
| * | Multiplication |
| / | Division |
| ^ | Exponentiation |

**ACTIVITY 12-8**

### Calculating in a Database

In this activity, you will enter a field formula to calculate the balance of the dues owed by each member to the club. Your screen now shows the database *feclub* in List view.

1. Place the highlight in any entry in the Balance field.

2. Key **=Dues Owed-Dues Paid**.

Activity 12-8 continued

3.  Press **Enter**. The calculated values will appear in the Balance field. Your completed database should appear similar to Figure 12-13.

4.  Leave *feclub* on the screen for the next activity.

**FIGURE 12-13**
The formula has calculated the amounts due in the Balance field.

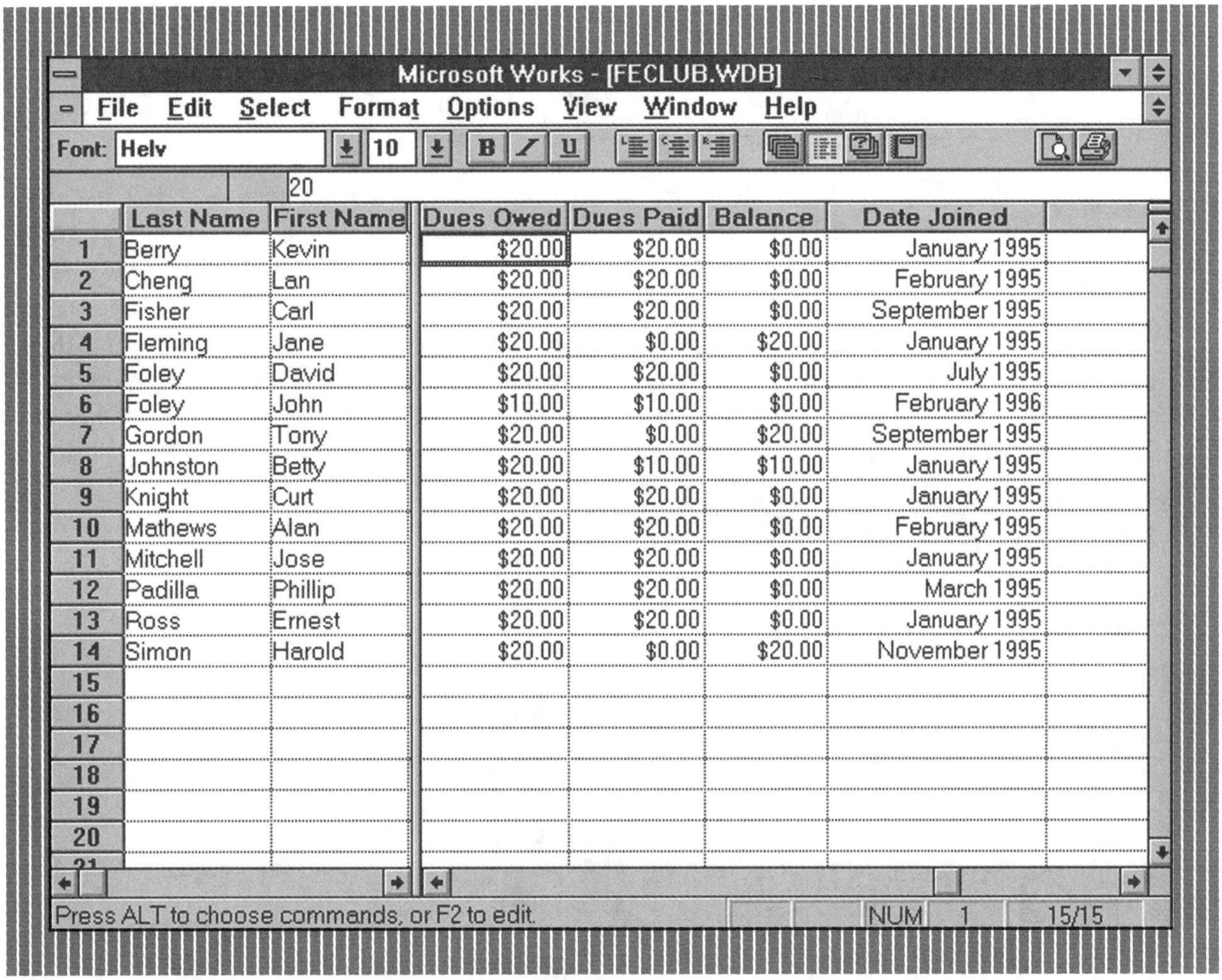

| | Last Name | First Name | Dues Owed | Dues Paid | Balance | Date Joined |
|---|---|---|---|---|---|---|
| 1 | Berry | Kevin | $20.00 | $20.00 | $0.00 | January 1995 |
| 2 | Cheng | Lan | $20.00 | $20.00 | $0.00 | February 1995 |
| 3 | Fisher | Carl | $20.00 | $20.00 | $0.00 | September 1995 |
| 4 | Fleming | Jane | $20.00 | $0.00 | $20.00 | January 1995 |
| 5 | Foley | David | $20.00 | $20.00 | $0.00 | July 1995 |
| 6 | Foley | John | $10.00 | $10.00 | $0.00 | February 1996 |
| 7 | Gordon | Tony | $20.00 | $0.00 | $20.00 | September 1995 |
| 8 | Johnston | Betty | $20.00 | $10.00 | $10.00 | January 1995 |
| 9 | Knight | Curt | $20.00 | $20.00 | $0.00 | January 1995 |
| 10 | Mathews | Alan | $20.00 | $20.00 | $0.00 | February 1995 |
| 11 | Mitchell | Jose | $20.00 | $20.00 | $0.00 | January 1995 |
| 12 | Padilla | Phillip | $20.00 | $20.00 | $0.00 | March 1995 |
| 13 | Ross | Ernest | $20.00 | $20.00 | $0.00 | January 1995 |
| 14 | Simon | Harold | $20.00 | $0.00 | $20.00 | November 1995 |
| 15 | | | | | | |
| 16 | | | | | | |
| 17 | | | | | | |
| 18 | | | | | | |
| 19 | | | | | | |
| 20 | | | | | | |

Microsoft Works - [FECLUB.WDB]

File  Edit  Select  Format  Options  View  Window  Help

Font: Helv   10   B  /  U

Press ALT to choose commands, or F2 to edit.          NUM    1    15/15

# PROTECTING PARTS OF THE DATABASE

Protecting data is particularly important in the database because you may want to store data for a long period of time without making any changes to it. By protecting your data, you prevent anyone from making changes accidentally. In other words, the entry becomes "locked" until someone removes the protection. In the database, there are two ways of protecting data. You can protect fields or you can protect the form you created for the database.

## Protecting Fields

To protect fields in the database, choose the Protect Data command from the Options menu. To use the Protect Data command, you must first select the fields you want to protect and turn on the Locked check box in the Style dialog box from the Format menu, as shown in Figure 12-14. After the Locked option is on, you may protect the field by choosing the Protect Data command from the Options menu, shown in Figure 12-15.

Works locks the entire database as a default option, so it is a good practice to "unlock" all the fields and then "lock" only those you want to protect before choosing the Protect Data command. Otherwise, the entire database will be protected.

If you attempt to change the data in the entries of a field after they have been protected, Works will display a dialog box telling you the data cannot be changed (see Figure 12-16). If you intend to change the data, you must first unprotect it.

**FIGURE 12-14**
The Style dialog box is displayed when the Style command in the Format menu is chosen. The dialog box contains the Locked check box used to designate data to protect.

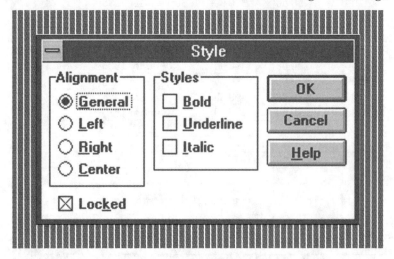

**FIGURE 12-15**
Data in a field is protected by choosing the Protect Data command from the Options menu.

**FIGURE 12-16**
Works displays a dialog box if you attempt to change data in a field that has been protected.

**ACTIVITY
12-9**

## Protecting Fields

In this activity, you will protect the Last Name and First Name fields in the database. Your screen now shows the database *feclub* in List view.

1.   Unlock all the fields of the database:

   a.   Select the entire database by clicking the box above the record number for Record 1. The entire contents of the database will darken.

   b.   From the **Format** menu, choose **Style**.

   c.   Click the Locked check box until it becomes blank.

   d.   Click **OK**.

2.   Select the Last Name and First Name fields by dragging the field names.

3.   Lock the fields:

   a.   From the **Format** menu, choose **Style**.

   b.   Click the Locked check box until an *X* appears.

   c.   Click **OK**.

4.   From the **Options** menu, choose **Protect Data**. The Last Name and First Name fields are now protected.

5.   Check the protection of the fields by attempting to enter data in the Last Name field. A dialog box should appear indicating that the field is locked.

6.   Leave *feclub* on the screen for the next activity.

**FIGURE 12-17**
The Protect Form command is located in the Options menu in Form view.

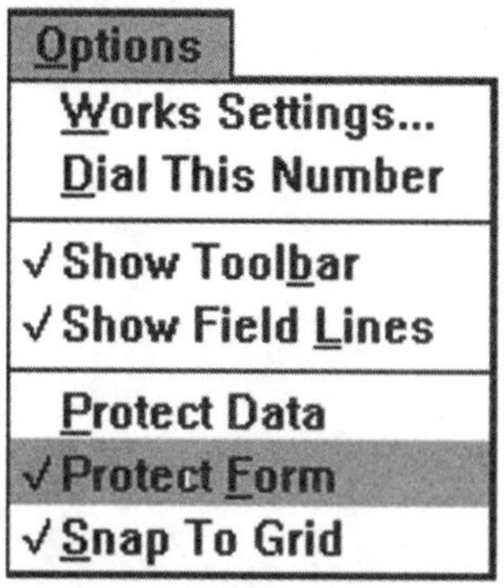

| Options |
|---|
| <u>W</u>orks Settings... |
| <u>D</u>ial This Number |
| √ Show Tool<u>b</u>ar |
| √ Show Field <u>L</u>ines |
| <u>P</u>rotect Data |
| √ Protect <u>F</u>orm |
| √ <u>S</u>nap To Grid |

## Protecting Forms

After you have worked with a particular database, you may become comfortable with the database form. To prevent the form from being changed, you may select the Protect Form command from the Options menu while in Form view, as shown in Figure 12-17. If someone attempts to add, delete, or move a field, a message will indicate the database form is protected.

**ACTIVITY
12-10**

### Protecting a Database Form

In this activity, you will protect the form you used to create the database. Your screen now shows the database *feclub* in List view.

1.  Switch to Form view.

2.  From the **Options** menu, choose **Protect Form**.

3.  Check the protection of the form by attempting to create a new field. A message should appear indicating that the form is protected.

4.  Save and close the file.

# SUMMARY

Data can be moved or copied in the database by using the Cut, Copy, Paste, and Fill Down commands from the Edit menu. These commands save time by eliminating repetitive keying.

Field formats determine the appearance of data in a column of a database. These formats are designed to accommodate alphabetical data, numerical data (such as money and percentages), times of day, and dates. A field format will apply to all entries within the field.

The same mathematical and function formulas available in the spreadsheet are also available to determine calculated values in the database. Because the database does not contain cell references, variables in a database formula are represented by the field name.

Fields in the database may be protected from accidental change by choosing the Protect Data command from the Options menu. In addition, a database form may be protected from alteration by choosing the Protect Form command from the Options menu in Form view. Both fields and forms may be unprotected if changes are necessary.

# CHALLENGES

## TRUE/FALSE

Circle **T** or **F** to show whether the statement is true or false.

T  F  1. When the Database icon is clicked in the Startup dialog box, a database in List view will appear.

T  F  2. The original data will not be affected when the Copy command is chosen.

T  F  3. The Fill Down command copies data to entries directly below the original data.

T  F  4. The Insert Record/Field command will place an empty record directly below a record selected in a database.

T  F  5. The Cut command is used to move data in the database.

T  F  6. Fields may be formatted in Form view of the database but not in List view.

T  F  7. General format may be used for alphabetical data only.

T  F  8. Short date formats will show the name of the month spelled out rather than in numerical form.

T  F  9. In a database, the field names act as operands in a field formula.

T  F  10. The Protect Form command will prevent data from being entered in a locked field.

# COMPLETION

Write the correct answer in the space provided.

1. What command will cause data that has been copied or cut to appear?

_____

2. What command will copy data to entries directly below the original data?

_____

3. What command may be used to place an empty record in the middle of a database?

_____

4. What two commands are used to move data in a database?

_____

5. Which field format will place a dollar sign in front of numerical data in the database?

_____

6. Which field format is a default format that accommodates both alphabetical and numerical data?

_____

7. Which field format may be used to convert an entry of 1/3/95 to January 3, 1995?

_____

8. What keystrokes will insert the current date in an entry of a database?

_____

9. What term describes the field names contained in a field formula of a database?

_____

10. What operation must occur before a field can be protected with the Protect Data command from the Options menu?

_____

# APPLICATIONS

## APPLICATION 12-1

You have been collecting compact discs (CDs) for your stereo for the last year. The CDs have ranged in cost from $4.99 to $12.87. Each CD may have as many as 21 tracks (songs). Your interest in music includes rock 'n' roll, country, classical, and other types of music.

You would like to create a database to keep track of the CDs you own. The database should contain at least five fields that will distinguish your CDs from one another.

1. In the Field Name column, identify fields you would include in the database.

2. In the Field Format column, designate which field format you would use.

| Field Name | Field Format |
| --- | --- |
| _____ | _____ |
| _____ | _____ |
| _____ | _____ |
| _____ | _____ |
| _____ | _____ |
| _____ | _____ |
| _____ | _____ |

## APPLICATION 12-2

The file *app12-2.wdb* contains financial data for a small corporation. In this application, you will format fields, create a field formula, and add new records.

1. Retrieve the file *app12-2.wdb*.

2. Format the Assets, Sales, and Expenses fields for currency. There should be no digits to the right of the decimal point.

3. Add a new field called *Income* to the right of the Expenses field.

4. Create a field formula to determine the value in the Income field. Income is determined by the difference between Sales and Expenses.

5. Format the Income field for currency with no digits to the right of the decimal point.

6. Add a record for the most current year, 1994:

| | |
| --- | --- |
| Assets | 20,123 |
| Sales | 55,876 |
| Expenses | 50,629 |

7.   Insert a record for the missing year, 1986:

     Assets        3,104
     Sales         8,456
     Expenses      7,821

8.   Print the database.

9.   Save the file to your data disk as *income*.

10.  Close the file.

# APPLICATION 12-3

In this application, you will prepare a database to help you decide which college you would like to attend.

1.   Open an untitled database.

2.   Enter and format the following fields:

| Field Contents | Field Name | Format | Alignment |
|---|---|---|---|
| College or University | School | General | Left |
| Miles from Home | Miles | Comma | Right |
| Tuition per Semester | Tuition | Currency | Right |
| Dorm Fee per Semester | Dorm | Currency | Right |
| Quality of School | Quality | General | Center |
| Friends at School | Friends | General | Center |

3.   Enter the following data into the database:

| School | Miles | Tuition | Dorm | Quality | Friends |
|---|---|---|---|---|---|
| Univ. of Aston | 15 | $  500 | $1,500 | C | 5 |
| Bering Univ. | 100 | $1,500 | $3,000 | A | 2 |
| Cochise St. | 150 | $1,000 | $2,000 | B | 1 |
| Denton College | 60 | $2,000 | $2,000 | C | 7 |
| Univ. of Elgin | 300 | $1,000 | $1,000 | A | 0 |
| Franklin College | 20 | $ ·750 | $1,200 | B | 3 |

4.   Print the database.

5.   Save the database to your data disk as *college*.

6.   Close the file.

# APPLICATION 12-4

Create a database of the addresses and telephone numbers of some of your friends and relatives.

1. Create a database containing the following fields: Last Name, First Name, Address, City, ZIP Code, Phone No.
2. Enter the names, addresses, and phone numbers of six of your friends or relatives.
3. Print the database.
4. Save the database to your data disk as *dir*.
5. Close the file.

## CHAPTER

# 13

# ADVANCED DATABASE OPERATIONS

### LEARNING OBJECTIVES

**When you complete this chapter, you will be able to:**

1. Search a database.
2. Sort data in a database.
3. Query a database.

As a database becomes large, you will not be able to see the entire database on screen at once. As a result, you may find it difficult to find the specific records you want to work with. Fortunately, Works has three ways to manipulate the information in a database to help you find the records you need: searching, sorting, and querying.

To find specific data in the database when you are not sure of its location, you use the search function. To arrange records in a specific order, such as alphabetically or from largest to smallest, you use the sort function. To display on the screen a record or group of records that match the criteria you have specified, you use the query function. In this chapter, you will practice searching, sorting, and querying using a database containing prices and specifications of computers.

## SEARCHING A DATABASE

*Searching* locates specific data in a database. For example, in a directory of names and addresses, you may want to search for someone whose last name is Johnson and who lives in the ZIP Code area of 77042. Search criteria are specified in the Find dialog box, shown in Figure 13-1, and accessed by choosing the Find command from the Select menu, shown in Figure 13-2.

Works will perform two types of searches in a database. A *Next Record search* finds the first record after the highlight in which the specified data is present. An *All Records search* displays on the screen only those records containing the specified data.

**FIGURE 13-1**
Search criteria are specified in the Find dialog box.

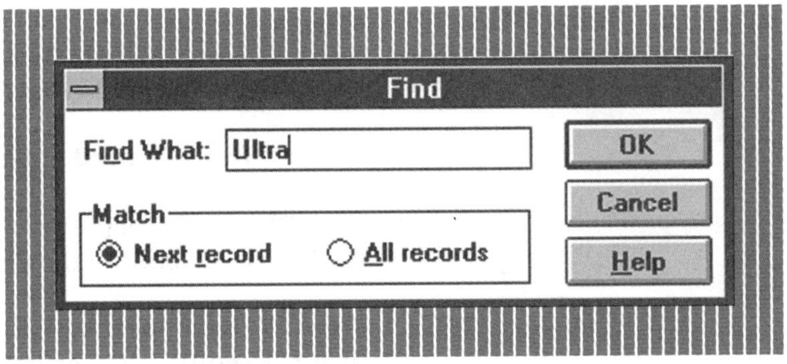

## Searching Next Records

A Next Record search looks for entries that match data specified in the Find What box of the Find dialog box. Works looks for the first occurrence of the data following the highlight. Therefore, if you want to search the entire database, you should begin the search by placing the highlight in the first entry of the database.

You may repeat a Next Record search by pressing F7, the Repeat key. The Find dialog box will not appear because Works assumes you are searching for the same data keyed in the Find What box in the previous search.

**FIGURE 13-2**
The Find dialog box is accessed by choosing the Find command from the Select menu.

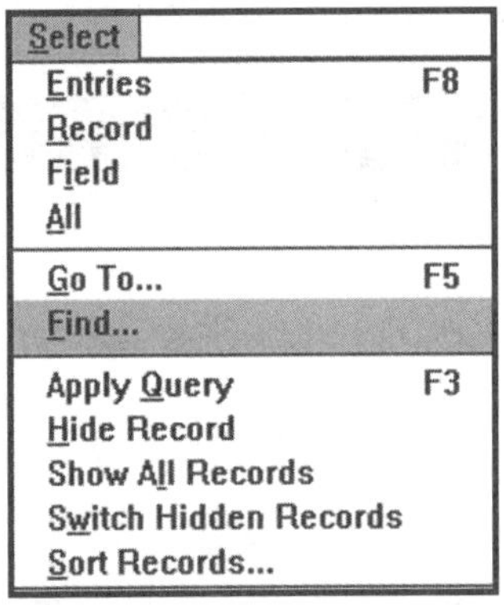

## ACTIVITY 13-1

### Searching Next Records

In this activity, you will practice Next Record searches. The file *act13-1.wdb* contains prices and specifications of several computer products listed for sale. The database contains fields for brand, model, price, CPU (central processing unit), RAM (random access memory), clock speed, hard disk storage, and availability of a mouse. Find the records of computers with the brand name Ultra by following these steps:

1. Open the file *act13-1.wdb* from your template disk.

2. Place the highlight in the first entry of the Brand field if it is not there already.

3.  From the **Select** menu, choose **Find**. The Find dialog box will appear.

4.  Key **Ultra** in the Find What box.

5.  Click the **Next Record** option button if it is not already selected.

6.  Click **OK**. The highlight will appear in the Brand field of Record 22, the first occurrence of the word Ultra in the database.

7.  Press **F7** (the Repeat key). The highlight will appear in the Brand field of Record 23, the second occurrence of the word *Ultra* in the database.

8.  Press **F7** again. The highlight will appear in the Brand field of Record 24, the third occurrence of the word *Ultra* in the database.

9.  Leave the database *act13-1.wdb* on your screen for the next activity.

## Searching All Records

An All Records search will display all records containing data specified in the Find What box. Records not containing the specified data will be hidden. After you have completed the search, you can see what portion of the records is displayed by looking at the far right of the status line. The fraction at the right side of the status line indicates the number of records displayed and the total number of records in the database.

## ACTIVITY 13-2

## Searching All Records

In this activity, you will practice searching all records. Your screen now shows the database *act13-1.wdb*. Suppose you want to view on the screen only those records of computers with a 450-S CPU. Perform an All Records search by following these steps:

1.  From the **Select** menu, choose **Find**.

2.  Key **450-S** in the Find What box.

3.  Click the **All Records** option button.

Activity 13-2 continued

4.  Click **OK**. Your screen should appear similar to Figure 13-3. All records containing 450-S appear on screen. Records that do not contain 450-S are hidden from view. The fraction 6/29 at the right side of the status line indicates that there are 29 records in the database and that 6 of those records are currently displayed.

**FIGURE 13-3**
The fraction in the status line indicates that 6 of the 29 records in the database are displayed.

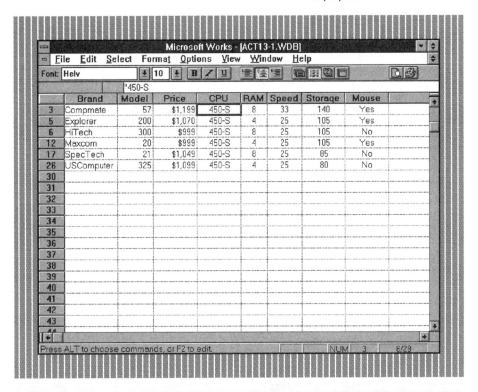

5.  Leave the database *act13-1.wdb* on the screen for the next activity.

## Redisplaying Records

Hidden records may be redisplayed in two ways. The Switch Hidden Records command from the Select menu will hide records currently displayed and display those records hidden. The Show All Records command from the Select menu will display all the records contained in the database.

**ACTIVITY 13-3**

### Redisplaying Hidden Records

In this activity, you will redisplay hidden records. Your screen now shows the database *act13-1.wdb*. Suppose you want to view records currently hidden. Redisplay the hidden records by following these steps:

Activity 13-3 continued

1. From the **Select** menu, choose **Switch Hidden Records**. The records that do not contain 450-S will be displayed on screen. The fraction 23/29 should appear in the status line to indicate that 23 of the 29 records in the database are displayed on screen.

2. From the **Select** menu, choose **Show All Records**. All the records in the database will be displayed. The fraction 29/29 should appear in the status line.

3. Leave the database *act13-1.wdb* on the screen for the next activity.

## Searching with Wildcards

Suppose you want to find a particular record in your database but cannot remember enough information to use the Search command. For example, you know the last name of the person is either Jenson or Jonson. Rather than perform two searches to try to find the record, you can use a *wildcard* character to help you retrieve the record you want.

**TABLE 13-1**
Wildcard searches look for data similar to but not exactly like the search characters.

The Works wildcard character is an asterisk (*). It can represent one or several characters—either letters or numbers—and may be placed in any part of a word for a search. To find the record mentioned above, you would key J*nson in the Find What box. Works will find all names that begin with J and end with *nson*. It will find not only Jenson and Jonson but also Johanson and Johnson. Table 13-1 shows examples of how the wildcard character may be used to search for data.

| These Wildcard Searches | Will Find |
| --- | --- |
| Will* | William, Will, Willy, Willard |
| *ness | kindness, tenderness, selfishness |
| b*p | bump, bishop, blimp |

## ACTIVITY 13-4

### Wildcard Searches

In this activity, you will perform a wildcard search. Your screen now shows the database *act13-1.wdb*. Suppose you want to view records of computers priced in the range of $2,000 to $2,999. Search for these records by following these steps:

Activity 13-4 continued

1. From the **Select** menu, choose **Find**. The Find dialog box will appear.

2. Key **$2*** in the Find What box.

3. Click the **All Records** option button.

4. Click **OK**. All records containing computers in the price range of $2,000 to $2,999 will appear on the screen.

5. From the **Select** menu, choose **Show All Records**. All the records of the database will be redisplayed.

6. Leave the database *act13-1.wdb* on the screen for the next activity.

## SORTING A DATABASE

*Sorting* arranges records in a specific sequence. For example, a directory of names, addresses, and phone numbers may be sorted in many ways. Directories, including telephone directories, are usually sorted in alphabetical order according to last names. However, you may want to sort a directory in other ways. You could sort a directory geographically by state or by ZIP Code. If birthdays are entered in a directory, you could sort the directory by the age of the person described in the record.

You sort a database by selecting the Sort Records command from the Select menu, shown in Figure 13-4. When the Sort Records dialog box appears, the sort field and order (ascending or descending) are designated (see Figure 13-5). A second field may be designated if more than one record contains the same data in the first field. For example, if you would like to sort a directory geographically, you could sort first by the state. Because some records may contain the same state, a second field sort will order by the city within each state. Table 13-2 shows the order in which records will be sorted. In an ascending sort, text will be sorted from A to Z and numerical data from smallest to largest. In a descending sort, text will be sorted from Z to A and numerical data from largest to smallest. Works will also sort times and dates.

**FIGURE 13-4**

The Sort Records command is located in the Select menu.

**FIGURE 13-5**

The sort field and sort order are designated in the Sort Records dialog box.

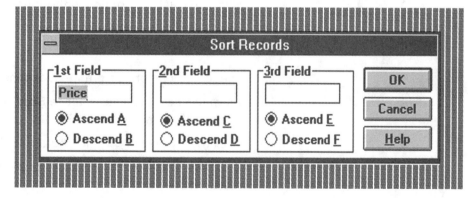

**TABLE 13-2**
The Ascend or Descend option buttons determine the order of the sort.

| Sort | Data | Direction of Sort |
|------|------|-------------------|
| Ascending | Text | A to Z |
|  | Times | Earlier to later |
|  | Numbers | Smaller to larger |
|  | Dates | Past to recent |
| Descending | Dates | Recent to past |
|  | Numbers | Larger to smaller |
|  | Times | Later to earlier |
|  | Text | Z to A |

## ACTIVITY 13-5

### Sorting a Database

In this activity, you will sort the database in several different orders. Your screen now shows the database *act13-1.wdb* in List view. To help you decide which computer to purchase, you want to sort the records in certain orders based on the contents of certain fields.

1. Sort the records by price from least expensive to most expensive:

   a. From the **Select** menu, choose **Sort Records**.

   b. Key **Price** in the 1st Field box.

   c. Click the **Ascend A** option button in the 1st Field box if it is not already selected. (The underlined A indicates that A may be keyed to select the option without using the mouse.)

   d. Click **OK**. The records will be sorted from least expensive to most expensive.

2. Sort the records by price from most expensive to least expensive:

   a. From the **Select** menu, choose **Sort Records**. Price should already be keyed in the 1st Field box.

   b. Click the **Descend B** option button in the 1st Field box.

   c. Click **OK**. The records will be sorted from most expensive to least expensive.

3.  Sort the records by most to least hard disk storage:

    a.  From the **Select** menu, choose **Sort Records**.

    b.  Key **Storage** in the 1st Field box.

    c.  Click the **Descend B** option button in the 1st Field box if it is not already selected.

    d.  Click **OK**. The records will be sorted from most storage to least storage.

4.  Sort the records by brand name and then by model number:

    a.  From the **Select** menu, choose **Sort Records**.

    b.  Key **Brand** in the 1st Field box.

    c.  Click the **Ascend A** option button in the 1st Field box.

    d.  Key **Model** in the 2nd Field box.

    e.  Click the **Ascend C** option button in the 2nd Field box if it is not already selected.

    f.  Click **OK**. The records will be sorted by brand name and model number within the brand name.

5.  Leave the database *act13-1.wdb* on your screen for the next activity.

# QUERYING A DATABASE

Database *queries* display records meeting specific criteria. Queries differ from All Records searches in two ways. First, queries look for a match in a specific field, whereas searches look for matches in any part of the database. Second, queries can match records that fit into a range. For example, in a database of names and addresses, you may request all records with a ZIP Code greater than 50000 or last names beginning with the letters G through K. Wildcards may be used in queries in the same way they are used in searches.

To query the database, choose the Query command from the View menu (see Figure 13-6) or click the Query button in the Toolbar. The screen will appear in *Query view*, as shown in Figure 13-7. Query view is similar to Form view except the word *QUERY* will appear at the right side of the status line. After keying query instructions in the fields of the Query view, the List view will show only the records meeting the criteria of the query.

Works allows you to make several kinds of queries: exact match, numerical, alphabetical, or complex. These queries are discussed in the following sections.

**FIGURE 13-6**

Begin a query either by choosing the Query command from the View menu or by clicking the Query button in the Toolbar.

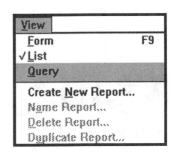

   Query button

**FIGURE 13-7**
Query data is specified in
Query view.

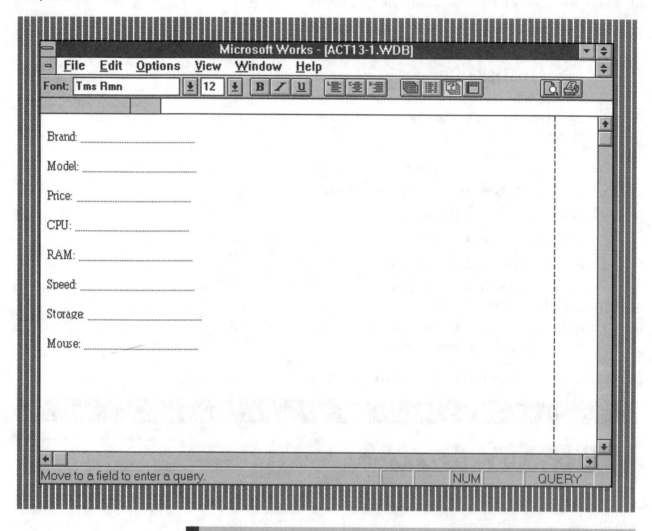

## Exact Match Queries

An exact match query will search for data in a field just as it appears in
Query view.

**ACTIVITY
13-6**

### Querying an Exact Match

In this activity, you will display only the records of computers listed in
*act13-1.wdb* that have a speed of 33 by following these steps:

1.   Click the **Query** button in the Toolbar. The screen will appear in
     Query view.

2.   Key **33** to the right of the Speed field name.

Activity 13-6 continued

3.  Press **Enter**.

4.  Switch to **List view**. Only the records showing a speed of 33 appear. The fraction at the bottom of the page in the status line should be 12/29, indicating that 12 of 29 records have a speed of 33.

5.  Leave the database *act13-1.wdb* on the screen for the next activity.

## Numerical Queries

Numerical queries may request exact matches or data occurring within a range. For example, you may request records with data meeting requirements specified by the operators in Table 13-3. Table 13-4 shows how queries may search for exact matches or numerical data within a range.

**TABLE 13-3**
Operators indicate the characteristics of the data in a query.

| Operator | Function |
|----------|----------|
| = | Equal to |
| <> | Not equal to |
| > | Greater than |
| < | Less than |
| >= | Greater than or equal to |
| <= | Less than or equal to |
| ~ | Not |
| \| | Or |
| & | And |

**TABLE 13-4**
Numerical requests can search for exact data or data within a specified range.

| Field | Query Request | Searches for Records Of |
|-------|---------------|-------------------------|
| Age | =18 | Those whose age is 18 |
| Weight | >135 | Those whose weight is greater than 135 |
| Cost | <100 | Products costing less than $100* |
| Size | <>8 | Objects that are not Size 8 |
| ZIP Code | =340* | Addresses with ZIP Codes beginning with 340 |

* Dollar signs are not included in query requests.

**ACTIVITY
13-7**

## Querying a Numerical Range

In this activity, you will display only the records of computers costing less than $1,500. Your screen now shows the database *act13-1.wdb* in List view.

1.  Click the **Query** button in the Toolbar. The screen will appear in Query view.

2.  Delete the existing query in the Speed field.

3.  Key **<1500** in the Price field. (Do not include the dollar sign in the query.)

4.  Press **Enter**.

5.  Switch to **List view**. Only the records with computers costing less than $1,500 appear. The fraction at the bottom of the page in the status line should be 16/29, indicating that 16 of 29 computers cost less than $1,500.

6.  Leave the database *act13-1.wdb* on the screen for the next activity.

## Alphabetical Queries

**TABLE 13-5**
Alphabetic requests can search for exact data or data within a specified range.

Alphabetical queries may also designate matches of data occurring within a range. For example, you may request records with names occurring within a certain part of the alphabet, such as A through E. Table 13-5 shows how alphabetical queries are used to search for exact matches or for data within a range. In an alphabetical query, characters must be enclosed in quotation marks.

| Field | Query Request | Searches for Records Of |
|---|---|---|
| City | ="Detroit" | Addresses in Detroit |
| Part | <>"Tire" | Parts that are not tires |
| Color | ~"Red" | Objects whose color is not red |
| First Name | ="D*" | Those whose first name begins with D |
| Last Name | <"N" | Those whose last name is in the first half of the alphabet |
| Last Name | >"X" | Those whose last name begins with Y or Z |

## Querying Alphabetical Characters

In this activity, you will display only the records of computers that cost less than $1,500 and include a mouse in the purchase price. Your screen now shows the database *act13-1.wdb* in List view.

1. Click the **Query** button in the Toolbar. The screen will appear in Query view.

2. Key **="Yes"** in the Mouse field. Do not delete the data currently in the Price field.

3. Press **Enter**.

4. Switch to **List view**. Only the records of computers that have a mouse and that cost less than $1,500 appear. The fraction at the bottom of the page in the status line should be 7/29, indicating that 7 of 29 computers cost less than $1,500 and include a mouse.

5. Leave the database *act13-1.wdb* on the screen for the next activity.

## Complex Queries

A *complex query* will make several comparisons simultaneously in the database. These queries may include operators AND (&) or OR (|) to display records with very specific qualities. Table 13-6 shows examples of complex queries that include AND and OR operators. It is not necessary to make a complex query within a specific field because the name of the field is specified within the query request. In a complex query, alphabetical characters must appear within quotation marks. Works recognizes words not enclosed in quotation marks as field names.

**TABLE 13-6**
Complex queries include operators AND (&) or OR (|) in the query request.

| Query Request | In the Field | Searches for Records With |
|---|---|---|
| ="Joe"\|="Joseph" | First Name | A first name of either Joe or Joseph |
| ="Jones"\|="Jacobs" | Last Name | Last names of either Jones or Jacobs |
| >"S"&<"V" | Last Name | Last names beginning with T or U |
| >21&<50 | Age | Ages greater than 21 but less than 50 |

## ACTIVITY 13-9

### Complex Queries

In this activity, you will query database *act13-1.wdb* to identify the computers meeting very specific qualities. Suppose you have decided you would like to buy a computer with the following characteristics:

1.  The computer should have at least 8 megabytes of RAM.

2.  The speed of the computer should be either 33 or 50 megahertz.

3.  The hard disk should have at least 100 megabytes of storage.

4.  If the computer has a mouse, you would be willing to pay up to $1,699; if the computer does not have a mouse, you would be willing to pay up to $1,599.

   Display the records of computers meeting these criteria by following these steps:

1.  From the **Select** menu, choose **Show All Records**.

2.  Switch to **Query view**.

3.  Clear the existing query requests in the Price and Mouse fields.

4.  Enter a query request to show only records of computers with at least 8 megabytes of RAM:

    a.  Key **>=8** in the RAM field.

    b.  Press **Enter**.

5.  Enter a query request to show only records of computers with a speed of either 33 or 50 megahertz:

    a.  Key **=Speed=33I=50** in the Speed field.

    b.  Press **Enter**.

6.  Enter a query request to show only records of computers with at least 100 megabytes of storage:

    a.  Key **>=100** in the Storage field.

    b.  Press **Enter**.

7.  Enter a query request to show only records of computers costing less than $1,700 if the computer has a mouse and less than $1,600 if the computer does not have a mouse:

    a.  Key **=(Price<1700&Mouse="Yes")I(Price<1600&Mouse="No")** in the Price field.

    b.  Press **Enter**.

Activity 13-9 continued

When you have finished, the Query view screen should appear similar to Figure 13-8.

8. Switch to **List view**. Only the records with computers meeting your criteria should appear. The fraction at the bottom of the page should be 10/29, indicating that 10 of 29 computers meet your needs.

9. Save the database to your data disk as *comp* and close the file.

**FIGURE 13-8**
Complex queries may be specified in any field of the Query view screen. For example, the Price field of this screen has query specifications for the Mouse field.

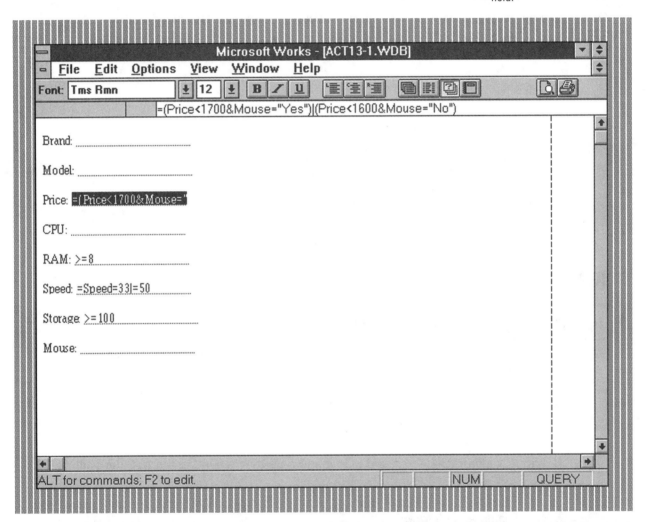

# SUMMARY

As a database becomes large, it is impossible to see the entire database on screen at once. Searching locates specific data in a database when you are not sure of its location. You may search for the next record in the database containing data you specify using a Next Record search. An All Records search will display only the records containing data specified.

Sorting a database arranges records in the database in a specific order (such as alphabetical or largest to smallest). Database sorts can also arrange times and dates.

Querying a database displays only records with certain qualities. Queries differ from All Records searches by matching data to a specific field and by matching records that fit into arange.

# CHALLENGES

## TRUE/FALSE

Circle **T** or **F** to show whether the statement is true or false.

| | | | |
|---|---|---|---|
| T | F | 1. | A Next Record search will hide all records that do not contain specific data. |
| T | F | 2. | A record search may be repeated by pressing the F9 key. |
| T | F | 3. | An All Records search will display all records in the database. |
| T | F | 4. | The Show All Records command in the Select menu will redisplay all hidden records. |
| T | F | 5. | Wildcard characters aid in locating data that is similar, but not identical, to the data in the search. |
| T | F | 6. | If child* is entered in the Find What box, Works will search for both the words *child* and *children*. |
| T | F | 7. | Sorting will locate specific data within a database. |
| T | F | 8. | A descending sort arranges dates from the most recent to the past. |
| T | F | 9. | In a numerical query, data must be placed within quotation marks. |
| T | F | 10. | The query ="Red"|"Black" will display records that have either the word *red* or the word *black* in the record. |

## COMPLETION

Write the correct answer in the space provided.

1. What kind of search indicates the first record after the highlight in which specified data is present?

_____

2. What kind of search displays on the screen only those records containing the specified data?

_____

3. What command will display records previously hidden and hide records previously displayed?

_____

4. What command will display all the records in the database?

_____

5. What key will repeat a Next Record search?

_____

6. What is the effect of specifying a second sort field?

_____

7. What type of sort will arrange alphabetical data from Z to A?

_____

8. How is Query view accessed?

_____

9. What query statement will display all records of those with ages greater than 21 in the Age field?

_____

10. What does the fraction 7/52 in the status line of the List view in a database indicate?

_____

# APPLICATIONS

## APPLICATION 13-1

The file *app13-1.wdb* is a database[1] of the planets in our solar system containing some statistics about each planet.

Perform the following database sorts to answer the following questions:

1. Open *app13-1.wdb* from your template disk.

   a. Sort the database by **distance** in ascending order. Which planet is closest to the sun?

   _____

   b. Sort the database by **distance** in descending order. Which planet is farthest from the sun?

   _____

   c. Sort the database by **revolution** in descending order. Which planet takes longest to revolve around the sun?

   _____

   d. Sort the database by **rotation** in ascending order. Which planet takes the shortest time to rotate around its axis?

   _____

   e. Sort the database by **diameter** in descending order. Which planet is the largest?

   _____

   f. Sort the database by **moons** in descending order. Which planet has the most moons?

   _____

2. Close the file without saving.

## APPLICATION 13-2

The file *app13-2.wdb* is a database of zoo animals, their classification, and their continent of origin. The database also contains the location of the animals in the zoo (W is west, E is east, C is central, N is north, S is south) and the number of animals in the exhibit.

1. Open *app13-2.wdb* from your template disk.

_____

[1]Source: *Hammond World Atlas* (Hammond Inc., 1984), 352.

2. Sort the database in the following orders:

   a. Alphabetically by **animal**. What is the first animal in alphabetical order?

   _____

   b. Alphabetically by **classification**. What is the first classification to be listed in the database?

   _____

   c. Alphabetically by **zoo location**. What is the first zoo location to be listed?

   _____

   d. Decreasing order of the **number** of animals in the exhibit. What is the most common animal in the zoo?

   _____

   e. Increasing order of the **number** of animals in the exhibit.  How many animals in the zoo occur in twos?

   _____

   f. Alphabetically by **zoo location** and alphabetically by **animal** within zoo location. How many different animals are in the central location?

   _____

   g. Alphabetically by **continent**, then alphabetically by **classification** within continent and alphabetically by **animal** within **classification**. How many different animals are from Asia?

   _____

3. Close the file without saving.

---

# APPLICATION 13-3

The file *app13-3.wdb* is a database of restaurants in a city. The database has been developed by a hotel to aid guests in selecting a restaurant that meets their needs.

1. Open *app13-3.wdb* from your template disk.

2. Perform queries to identify the restaurants that satisfy the following guest requests:

   a. What are the names of restaurants that serve Chinese food?

   _____

   b. What are the names of restaurants in the west part of town?

   _____

c.   Is Frank's Deli open for supper?

_____

d.   What are the names of restaurants that serve either barbecue or hamburgers?

_____

e.   Are there any inexpensive restaurants downtown?

_____

f.   What restaurants serve lunch in the south or southwest section of town?

_____

3.   Close the file without saving.

# APPLICATION 13-4

The file *app13-4.wdb* is a database for a mail order catalog business called The Night Shop. The store specializes in bedding and night clothes. Many merchandise requests come over the telephone and require quick answers. Use search, sort, and query techniques to respond to the following customer requests:

1.   Open *app13-4.wdb* from your template disk.

a.   How much does item 21-74-3 cost? (*Hint:* Do a Next Record search by item no.)

_____

b.   How many of Item No. 18-73-2 are available? (*Hint:* Do a Next Record search by item no.)

_____

c.   What types of items are available in pink? (*Hint:* Do an All Records search for pink.)

_____

d.   What are the least expensive items in the store? (*Hint:* Sort by ascending price.)

_____

e.   What sizes of sheets are available in a solid blue? (*Hint:* Query the database for names equal to solid sheets and color equal to blue.)

_____

f.   What types of sheets are available in gray? (*Hint:* Query the database for articles equal to sheets and color equal to gray.)

g.  What sizes of terry robes are available in white? (*Hint:* Query the database for articles equal to robe and color equal to white.)

2.  Close the file without saving.

# APPLICATION 13-5

In Application 12-4, you created a directory of friends and relatives and saved the database as *dir*.

1.  Open the database *dir* that you created.
2.  Sort the directory of friends and relatives by the last name as a 1st Field and first name as a 2nd Field.
3.  Close the file without saving.

# DATABASE REPORTING

## LEARNING OBJECTIVES

**When you complete this chapter, you will be able to:**

1. Create a database report.
2. Change the appearance of a database report.
3. Sort and group records in a database report.
4. Preview and print a database report.
5. Name a database report.
6. Save a database report.

Databases can become large as additional records are added. Because of its size, an entire database is rarely printed. By creating a *database report*, you may organize, summarize, and print a portion of the database. The report organizes by placing records, or portions of records, in a certain order or in groups. Reports can summarize data by inserting subtotals, totals, and statistics between groups or at the end of reports. For example, the report in Figure 14-1 was created from the database in Figure 14-2. The report contains six of the nine fields in the database. The report also sums the contents of two of the fields.

A number of reports may be created from one database. For example, in this chapter you will create and print several database reports from the inventory of a bicycle shop named Mike's Bikes (see Figure 14-3). The bicycle shop uses database reports to inform:

▶ The owner of when to order more bicycles from the manufacturer

▶ Salespersons of whether a specific model is in stock

▶ The accountant of the value of the bicycle inventory

▶ Customers of the price of the bicycles in stock

## CREATING A DATABASE REPORT

Database reports are created in the New Report dialog box and the Report Statistics dialog box. The New Report dialog box specifies the fields to be included in a report. The Report Statistics dialog box specifies statistics (such as sums, averages, minimums, and maximums) that summarize numerical data in the database report.

**FIGURE 14-1**

Database reports organize, summarize, and print a portion of a large database.

### REORDER REPORT

| Manufacturer | Model | Color | Quant | Order | Cost |
|---|---|---|---|---|---|
| Bye-cycles | 50 | Blue | 7 | 5 | $112.50 |
| Bye-cycles | 50 | Red | 8 | 4 | $112.50 |
| Bye-cycles | 70 | Blue | 5 | 4 | $142.50 |
| Bye-cycles | 70 | Red | 4 | 4 | $142.50 |
| Two Wheeler | Sizzle | Green | 3 | 4 | $125.00 |
| Two Wheeler | Sizzle | Red | 2 | 4 | $125.00 |
| Two Wheeler | Zip | Blue | 3 | 4 | $135.00 |
| Two Wheeler | Zip | Red | 3 | 4 | $135.00 |
| Spokes | 101 | Green | 4 | 3 | $157.50 |
| Spokes | 101 | Red | 2 | 3 | $157.50 |
| Spokes | 103 | Green | 1 | 3 | $187.50 |
| Spokes | 103 | Red | 3 | 3 | $187.50 |
| Spokes | 103 | Blue | 6 | 3 | $187.50 |
| Edison | Dart | Orange | 5 | 5 | $180.00 |
| Edison | Dart | Yellow | 7 | 5 | $180.00 |
| Edison | Sierra | Green | 2 | 5 | $190.00 |
| Edison | Sierra | Red | 3 | 5 | $190.00 |
| Edison | Sierra | Orange | 2 | 5 | $190.00 |
| Star | Spica | Black | 10 | 8 | $220.00 |
| Star | Mira | Yellow | 6 | 8 | $230.00 |
| | | **TOTAL** | 86 | 86 | |

## Choosing Fields for a Report

**FIGURE 14-2**

A database report is created from an existing database.

The New Report dialog box is accessed by choosing the Create New Report command from the View menu (see Figure 14-4). The New Report dialog box, shown in Figure 14-5, has two purposes. First, you can title your report by keying a name in the Report Title box. Second, you can designate the fields to be included in the report by selecting each field from the column on the left and clicking the Add>>> button. If you change your mind about a field you have already added, select the field in the right column and click the Remove button.

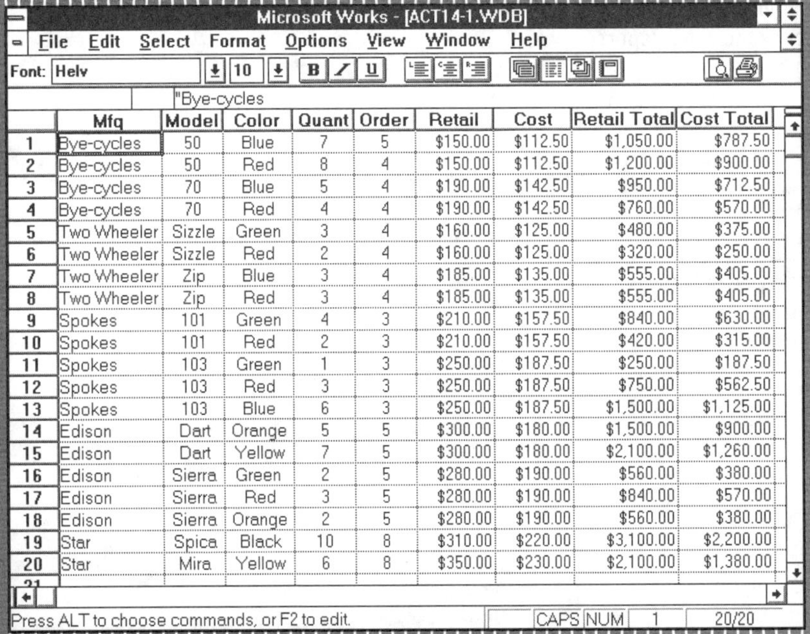

| | Mfg | Model | Color | Quant | Order | Retail | Cost | Retail Total | Cost Total |
|---|---|---|---|---|---|---|---|---|---|
| 1 | Bye-cycles | 50 | Blue | 7 | 5 | $150.00 | $112.50 | $1,050.00 | $787.50 |
| 2 | Bye-cycles | 50 | Red | 8 | 4 | $150.00 | $112.50 | $1,200.00 | $900.00 |
| 3 | Bye-cycles | 70 | Blue | 5 | 4 | $190.00 | $142.50 | $950.00 | $712.50 |
| 4 | Bye-cycles | 70 | Red | 4 | 4 | $190.00 | $142.50 | $760.00 | $570.00 |
| 5 | Two Wheeler | Sizzle | Green | 3 | 4 | $160.00 | $125.00 | $480.00 | $375.00 |
| 6 | Two Wheeler | Sizzle | Red | 2 | 4 | $160.00 | $125.00 | $320.00 | $250.00 |
| 7 | Two Wheeler | Zip | Blue | 3 | 4 | $185.00 | $135.00 | $555.00 | $405.00 |
| 8 | Two Wheeler | Zip | Red | 3 | 4 | $185.00 | $135.00 | $555.00 | $405.00 |
| 9 | Spokes | 101 | Green | 4 | 3 | $210.00 | $157.50 | $840.00 | $630.00 |
| 10 | Spokes | 101 | Red | 2 | 3 | $210.00 | $157.50 | $420.00 | $315.00 |
| 11 | Spokes | 103 | Green | 1 | 3 | $250.00 | $187.50 | $250.00 | $187.50 |
| 12 | Spokes | 103 | Red | 3 | 3 | $250.00 | $187.50 | $750.00 | $562.50 |
| 13 | Spokes | 103 | Blue | 6 | 3 | $250.00 | $187.50 | $1,500.00 | $1,125.00 |
| 14 | Edison | Dart | Orange | 5 | 5 | $300.00 | $180.00 | $1,500.00 | $900.00 |
| 15 | Edison | Dart | Yellow | 7 | 5 | $300.00 | $180.00 | $2,100.00 | $1,260.00 |
| 16 | Edison | Sierra | Green | 2 | 5 | $280.00 | $190.00 | $560.00 | $380.00 |
| 17 | Edison | Sierra | Red | 3 | 5 | $280.00 | $190.00 | $840.00 | $570.00 |
| 18 | Edison | Sierra | Orange | 2 | 5 | $280.00 | $190.00 | $560.00 | $380.00 |
| 19 | Star | Spica | Black | 10 | 8 | $310.00 | $220.00 | $3,100.00 | $2,200.00 |
| 20 | Star | Mira | Yellow | 6 | 8 | $350.00 | $230.00 | $2,100.00 | $1,380.00 |

Microsoft Works - [ACT14-1.WDB]

File  Edit  Select  Format  Options  View  Window  Help

Font: Helv   10   B  I  U

"Bye-cycles

Press ALT to choose commands, or F2 to edit.   CAPS NUM   1   20/20

**FIGURE 14-3**
More than one report may be
created from one database.

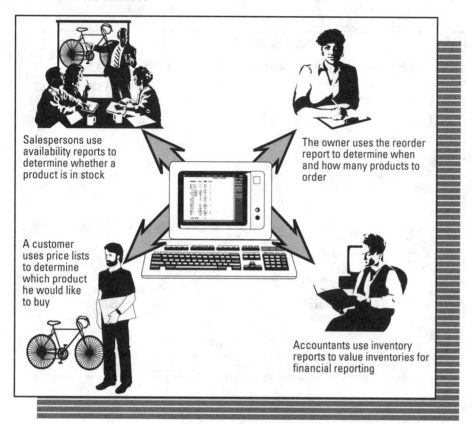

Salespersons use
availability reports to
determine whether a
product is in stock

The owner uses the reorder
report to determine when
and how many products to
order

A customer
uses price lists
to determine
which product
he would like
to buy

Accountants use inventory
reports to value inventories for
financial reporting

**FIGURE 14-4**
Choose the Create New Report
command from the View menu
to access the New Report
dialog box.

| View | |
|---|---|
| **Form** | **F9** |
| √ List | |
| Query | |
| **Create New Report...** | |
| Name Report... | |
| Delete Report... | |
| Duplicate Report... | |

**FIGURE 14-5**

The New Report dialog box is used to title the report and to designate fields to be included in the report.

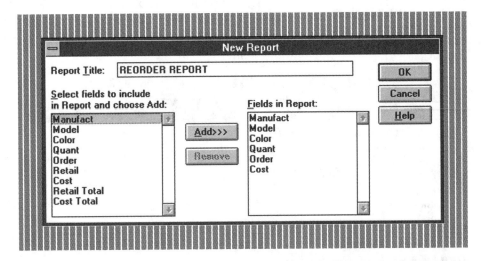

**ACTIVITY
14-1**

## Creating a New Report

In this activity, you will create a database report. The file *act14-1.wdb* is a database that contains an inventory for a bicycle shop. You will create an Availability Report to help the salespeople determine which bicycles are available for sale. Title the report and designate the fields to be included in the report by following these steps:

1. Open *act14-1.wdb*.

2. From the **View** menu, Choose **Create New Report**.

3. Key **AVAILABILITY REPORT** in the Report Title box. (Do not press the Enter key after you enter the title.)

4. Select **Manufact** if it is not already selected.

5. Click **Add>>>**. Manufact will appear in the right column.

6. Include **Model**, **Color**, and **Quant** in the report by selecting and clicking the **Add>>>** button.

7. Click **OK**. The Report Statistics dialog box will appear.

8. Leave the Report Statistics dialog box on screen for the next activity.

## Placing Statistics in a Report

Statistics summarize numerical data. The Report Statistics dialog box, shown in Figure 14-6, is used to specify descriptive statistics for numerical data in the report. For example, at the bottom of a report containing the salaries of employees of a department, you may want to show the number of employees, the average salary, the largest salary, and the smallest salary.

**FIGURE 14-6**

The Report Statistics dialog box is used to specify statistics that summarize numerical data in the database report.

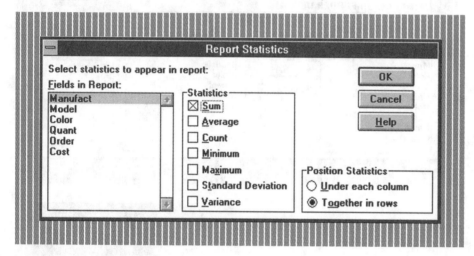

There are seven statistics available in the Statistics list of the dialog box. You may place the statistics under the column of the field or group the statistics together in rows at the bottom of the report. You may select the statistics you desire, then click OK. If you do not want summary statistics in the report, simply click OK.

## ACTIVITY 14-2

## Placing Statistics in a Report

In this activity, you will add statistics to your report. Your screen now shows the Report Statistics dialog box for the report you have created in the file *act14-1.wdb*. One of the fields, Quant, contains numerical data. You will sum the field at the bottom of the report by following these steps:

1.  Select Quant in the Fields in Report list.

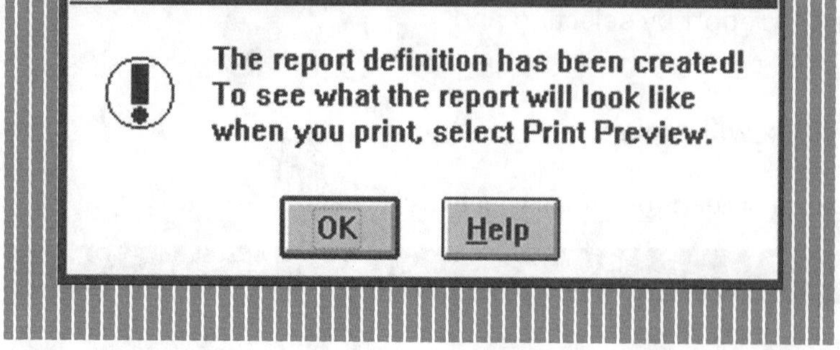

**FIGURE 14-7**

After report statistics have been defined, a message will appear indicating that the report is complete.

2.  Click the **Sum** box in the Statistics list.

3.  Click **Together in rows** in the Position Statistics box if it is not already selected to place the sum in a row at the bottom of the report.

4.  Click **OK**. A message similar to Figure 14-7 will appear.

5.  Click **OK**. Your screen is now in Report view, as indicated by

Activity 14-2 continued

the pressed Report button in the Toolbar. Report view will be
discussed in the next section.

Report button

6.  Click the **Print Preview** button in the Toolbar. The report you have
    created will appear. You may inspect the report more closely by
    using the mouse pointer as a magnifying glass. The report should
    appear similar to Figure 14-8.

**FIGURE 14-8**
The Print Preview command will
show what the database report
will look like when it is printed.

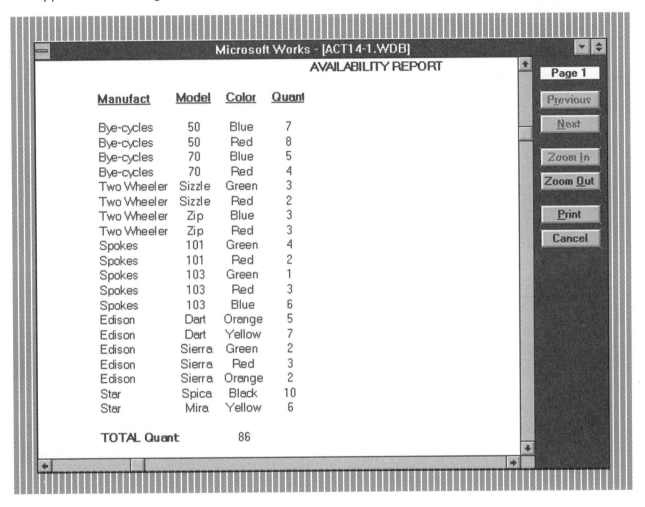

7.  Click **Cancel**. You will be returned to Report view.

8.  Leave the file *act14-1.wdb* on the screen in Report view for the next
    activity.

# CHANGING THE APPEARANCE OF A DATABASE REPORT

You can alter the appearance of the database report by making changes
in the *Report view* of the database, an example of which is shown in

Figure 14-9. The Report view determines what information will be included in the report, how the information will be presented, and how the information will be printed.

The *row labels* that appear on the left side of the Report view instruct Works on how the report will appear. The report in Figure 14-9 and the report you just created have row labels for the title, headings, records, and summaries. Table 14-1 describes the purpose of each row label available in Report view.

**FIGURE 14-9**

The appearance of a database report is changed in Report view.

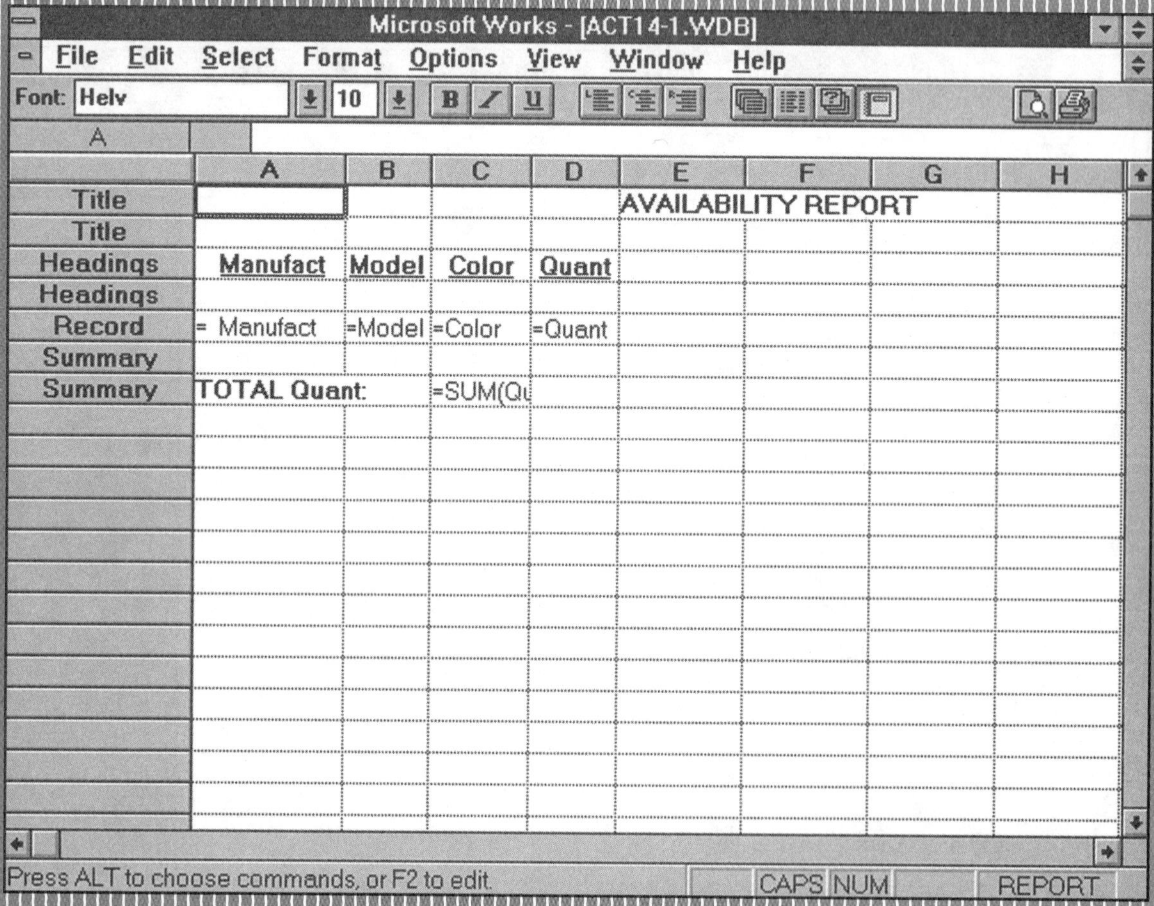

**Placing Additional Titles in a Report**

The New Report dialog box permits you to enter one title line in the database report. For example, in Activity 14-1, you entered AVAILABILITY REPORT in the Report Title box. If you would like to change that title or add an additional title, you may do so in Report view. Titles are added and changed in rows with *Title* labels.

**TABLE 14-1**
Row labels determine the
format of a database report.

| Row Label | Function |
|---|---|
| Title | Prints a title on the first page of the report |
| Headings | Prints a heading at the top of each column |
| Record | Indicates which fields will be printed in the report |
| Summary | Indicates which statistic will be printed at the bottom of the report |
| Intr *field name* | Inserts a blank row or heading between groups of records in a sorted report |
| Summ *field name* | Indicates which statistics will be printed after each group of records in a sorted report |

**ACTIVITY
14-3**

## Inserting Additional Titles in a Report

In this activity, you will insert an additional title in file *act14-1.wdb* and insert a blank line under the title by following these steps:

1. In the second row, select the entry in Column E.

2. Key **Mike's Bikes**.

3. Press **Enter**.

4. Click the first appearance of the word *Headings* in the row label column in the left part of the screen. The entire row will be highlighted.

5. From the **Edit** menu, choose **Insert Row/Column**. The Insert Row dialog box will appear.

6. Click **Title**.

7. Click **OK**. A Title row label will be inserted in the Report view screen.

8. Center the title over the data in the report by following these steps:

   a. Select the three title rows in Column E.

   b. From the **Edit** menu, choose **Cut**.

    c.   Select the first entry in Column C.

    d.   From the **Edit** menu, choose **Paste**.

9.   Leave the file *act14-1.wdb* on the screen in Report view for the next activity.

## Changing Heading Names

Heading names are contained in the rows with *Headings* row labels in Report view. The default heading will be the name of the field as it appears in the database. The field name is often abbreviated to fit the limited space in the database. If you prefer a different name, you must edit the field name as it appears in the row with the Headings row label.

## ACTIVITY 14-4

### Changing the Names of Headings

In this activity, you will change the names of the two headings in *act14-1.wdb* that are now abbreviated by following these steps:

1.   Select **Manufact** in Column A of the Headings row.

2.   Enter **Manufacturer**.

3.   Widen the column so that you can see the entire word.

4.   Select **Quant** in Column D of the Headings row.

5.   Enter **Quantity**.

6.   Select **TOTAL Quant:** in Column A of the Summary row.

7.   Enter **Total Bikes in Stock**.

8.   Widen the column so that you can see the entire entry.

9.   Examine your changes by clicking the **Print Preview** button in the Toolbar. When you have finished, click **Cancel** to return to Report view.

10.   Leave the file *act14-1.wdb* on the screen in Report view for the next activity.

## Including Additional Fields in a Report

In most cases, fields to be included in a database report will be specified in the New Report dialog box when the report is created. However, if you want to add additional fields, they may be added in Record rows in Report view.

**ACTIVITY
14-5**

### Adding an Additional Field to a Report

In this activity, you will include the retail cost of the bicycle model in the *act14-1.wdb* report.

1.  Select the entry in Column E of the Record row.

2.  Key **=Retail**.

3.  Press **Enter**.

4.  Format the report data as currency by following these steps:

    a.  From the **Format** menu, choose **Currency**.

    b.  Click **OK**.

5.  Select Column E of the first Headings row.

6.  Key **Price**.

7.  Press **Enter**.

8.  Format the Price heading by following these steps:

    a.  Click the **Bold** button in the Toolbar.

    b.  Click the **Underline** button in the Toolbar.

    c.  Click the **Center alignment** button in the Toolbar.

9.  Examine your changes by clicking the **Print Preview** button in the Toolbar. When you have finished, return to Report view.

10. Leave the file *act14-1.wdb* on the screen in Report view for the next activity.

## SORTING AND GROUPING RECORDS IN A REPORT

**FIGURE 14-10**
The Sort Records dialog box lets you indicate how to sort records in your report.

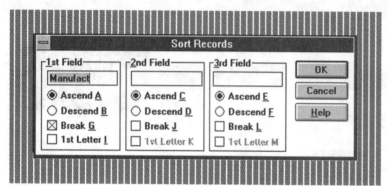

You can sort the records in a database report in the same way you would sort records in the full database. When you choose the Sort Records command from the Select menu, the Sort Records dialog box, as shown in Figure 14-10, will appear. The dialog box is the same as the Sort Records dialog box in the full database except it contains check boxes for Break options, which are described below.

*Grouping* identifies records that have similar field contents. For example, if you are sorting by color, Works will "break" between each group of colors in a sorted database report. To group records, select the *Break* option in the Sort Records dialog box. The Break option will insert a Summ *field name* row after each sorted group. This row contains statistics that are printed after each group of records.

**ACTIVITY 14-6**

### Sorting and Grouping Records in a Report

In this activity, you will sort the records in file *act14-1.wdb* by the bicycle manufacturer, group the records by manufacturer, and insert a blank row between each group by following these steps:

1. Sort the records in the report:

   a. From the **Select** menu, choose **Sort Records**.

   b. Enter **Manufact** in the 1st Field box.

   c. Click the **Ascend A** button if it is not already selected.

   d. Click **Break G**. An *X* will appear in the box.

   e. Click **OK**. A new row will appear with a row label of *Summ Manufact*. The row will contain default summary statistics for some of the fields you have included in the report. The default statistic for alphabetical field contents is COUNT; the default statistic for numerical field contents is SUM.

2. Widen the columns so that you can view all of the contents. Your screen should appear similar to Figure 14-11.

Activity 14-6 continued

3. View the database report by clicking the **Print Preview** button in the Toolbar. Notice that the database has been sorted alphabetically and grouped by manufacturer. Default statistics divide each group. For example, the COUNT statistic identifies how many types of bicycles are in each group. When you have finished viewing the report, return to Report view by clicking the **Cancel** button.

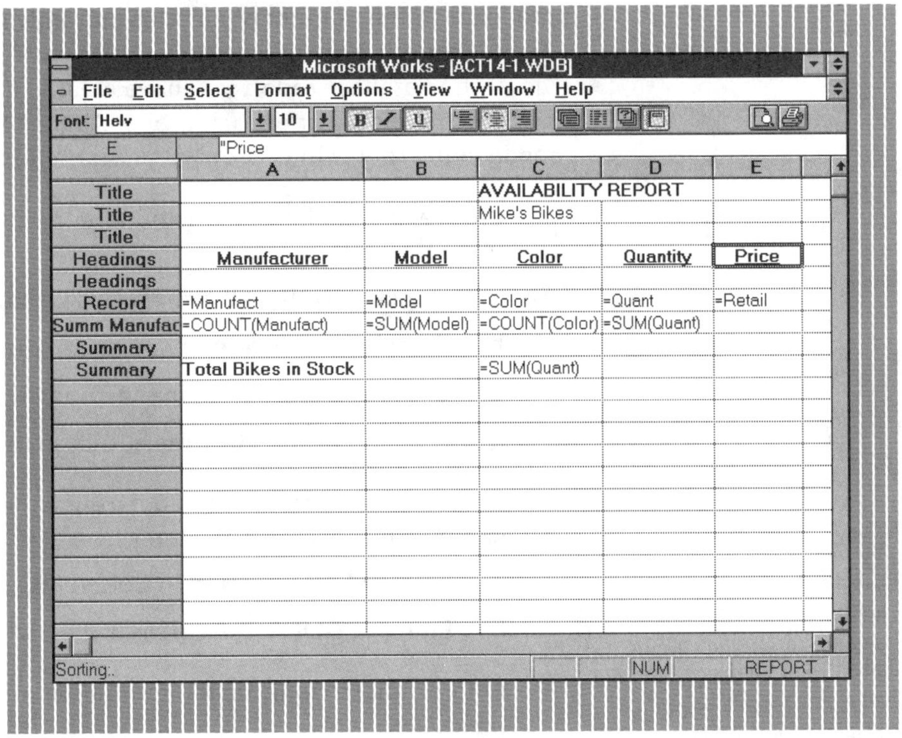
Microsoft Works - [ACT14-1.WDB]
File Edit Select Format Options View Window Help
Font: Helv 10
E "Price
A B C D E
Title AVAILABILITY REPORT
Title Mike's Bikes
Title
Headings Manufacturer Model Color Quantity Price
Headings
Record =Manufact =Model =Color =Quant =Retail
Summ Manufac =COUNT(Manufact) =SUM(Model) =COUNT(Color) =SUM(Quant)
Summary
Summary Total Bikes in Stock =SUM(Quant)
Sorting.. NUM REPORT

**FIGURE 14-11**
The Report view determines how information will appear in the database report.

4. Insert a row between each of the record groups included in the report:
   a. Select the row with the row label of *Summ Manufact* by clicking the row label.
   b. From the **Edit** menu, choose **Insert Row/Column.** The Insert Row dialog box will appear.
   c. Click **Intr Manufact**.
   d. Click **OK**. A row label of Intr Manufact will appear.

5. Examine the changes you have created by clicking the **Print Preview** button in the Toolbar. Notice that a blank row has been inserted after the summary statistic between each group. When you have finished, return to Report view by clicking the **Cancel** button.

6. Leave the file *act14-1.wdb* on the screen in Report view for the next activity.

## Creating Statistical Summaries for Groups in a Report

In Activity 14-2, you placed statistics at the end of a report by creating a Summary row. The Summ *field name* row is used to place statistics after each group of records in a sorted report.

ACTIVITY
14-7

## Placing Summary Statistics after a Group

In this activity, you will prepare statistics to indicate the number of models and the number of bicycles currently in stock for each of the manufacturers. Your screen now shows the file *act14-1.wdb* in Report view. The database report you have created now has the default summary statistics after each group. All the following entries will be made in the row with the row label *Summ Manufac.*

1. Enter a label to indicate the number of models supplied by each manufacturer:

    a. Select **=COUNT(Manufact)** in Column A.

    b. Enter **No. of Models:** in place of the existing data.

    c. Click the **Bold** button in the Toolbar.

    d. Click the **Right alignment** button in the Toolbar.

2. Enter summary statistics to determine the number of models supplied by each manufacturer:

**FIGURE 14-12**

The Report view in this figure contains all six types of row labels: Title, Headings, Intr *field name*, Record, Summ *field name*, and Summary.

    a. Select **=SUM(Model)** in Column B.

    b. Enter **=COUNT(Model)** in place of the existing data.

3. Enter a label to indicate the number of models supplied by each manufacturer:

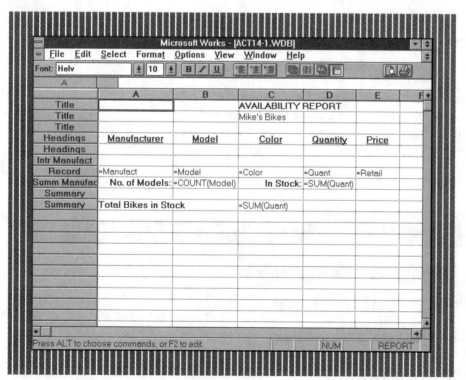

a. Select **=COUNT(Color)** in Column C.

b. Enter **In Stock:** in place of the existing data.

c. Click the **Bold** button in the Toolbar.

d. Click the **Right alignment** button in the Toolbar.

4. When you have completed the activity, the Report view screen should appear similar to Figure 14-12. You may want to

Activity 14-7 continued

examine the changes you have created once more by clicking the
**Print Preview** button.

5. Remain in the Print Preview screen for the next activity.

# PRINTING A DATABASE REPORT

Throughout this chapter, you have previewed the database you are
preparing to print. You may print the database report by clicking the
Print button in the Print Preview screen. A dialog box similar to the one
in Figure 14-13 will appear.

Several options may be selected in the Print dialog box:

**FIGURE 14-13**
Print options for the database
report are selected in the Print
dialog box.

▶ The number of copies of the
report are indicated in the
Number of Copies box.

▶ If you choose *All* in the print
range, Works will print the
entire report. By choosing *Pages*,
you may print a portion of the
database report; the page
numbers are designated in the
From and To boxes.

▶ By choosing the Draft Quality
Printing option, you may print
the report quickly but in a lower-
quality font.

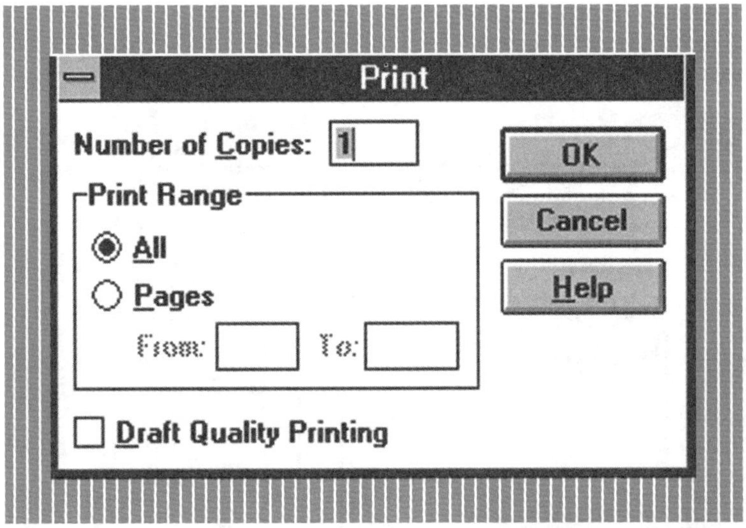

## ACTIVITY 14-8

## Printing a Report

In this activity, you will print the database report you have prepared by
following these steps:

1. Click the **Print** button. The Print dialog box will appear. The options
   now indicate that one copy of all pages will be printed.

2. Choose **OK**. The database report will be printed.

3. Leave the file *act14-1.wdb* on the screen for the next activity.

**FIGURE 14-14**
You may rename a report by choosing the Name Report command from the View menu. Existing report names appear at the bottom of the menu.

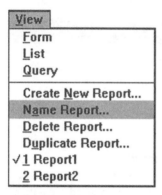

# NAMING REPORTS IN A DATABASE

Works will automatically name database reports as you create them. The first report will be called Report1, the second Report2, etc. A maximum of eight reports may be created for each database.

You may rename a report by choosing the Name Report command from the View menu, which is shown in Figure 14-14. The Name Report dialog box, shown in Figure 14-15, will appear. Select the report to be named by clicking the name in the Reports list, then type the new name in the Name box and click the Rename button. A report name is limited to 15 characters.

**FIGURE 14-15**
The Name Report dialog box contains a list of all reports existing for the database.

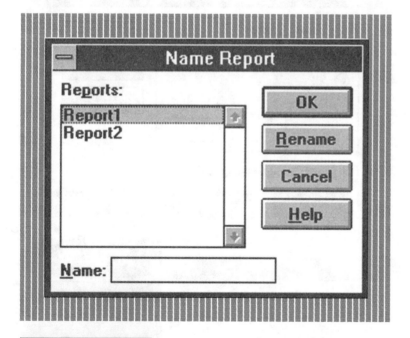

**ACTIVITY
14-9**

### Naming a Database Report

In this activity, you will name the database report you have prepared by following these steps:

1. From the **View** menu, choose **Name Report**. The Name Report dialog box will appear and Report1 will be highlighted in the Reports list.

Activity 14-9 continued

2. Click the **Name** box.

3. Key **Avail Report** in the Name box.

4. Click **Rename**.

5. Click **OK**.

6. Click **View** in the menu bar. Notice the name Avail Report appears at the bottom of the menu. You may access the Report view for any report you have created by clicking the report name in the View menu.

7. Leave the file *act14-1.wdb* on the screen for the next activity.

## SAVING REPORTS IN A DATABASE

You may create and save as many as eight reports per database. When you save the database, you will save all of the database reports you have created from the database. You need not return to the full database to save.

The database reports you save become an integral part of the database. In other words, the report depends on the data saved in the database. If the database is changed, the presentation of the report will also be changed to reflect the new data in the database.

**ACTIVITY 14-10**

### Saving Reports in a Database

In this activity, you will save the database and report you created in the database by following these steps:

1. Save the file to your data disk as *mikes*. The database and the report you have created will be saved.

2. Close the file.

# SUMMARY

Entire databases are rarely printed because of their large size. Instead, database reports, which organize and summarize database information, are printed. Database reports are created in the New Report dialog box and Report Statistics dialog box. The New Report dialog box specifies the fields to be included in the report. The Report Statistics dialog box summarizes numerical data in the database report. The new database report may be changed in the Report view of the database.

Records in a database report may be sorted in the same way you would sort records in the full database. Sorted database reports may also be grouped, with a row containing statistics printed after each group of records in a sorted report.

Database reports are printed by choosing Print in the Print Preview screen or by clicking the Print button in the Toolbar.

You may create and save as many as eight reports per database. Each report may be named to indicate what is contained in the report. Otherwise, Works will automatically name the database report as it is created. When you save the database, you will save all of the database reports you have created from the database.

# CHALLENGES

## TRUE/FALSE

Circle **T** or **F** to show whether the statement is true or false.

T  F  1. The purpose of the database report is to print the entire database as it appears on screen.

T  F  2. You may create as many reports as you like from a single database.

T  F  3. Statistics summarizing the data in a report may be placed under the column in which the data appears or grouped together in rows at the bottom of the report.

T  F  4. Row labels determine the type of information that will appear in a database report.

T  F  5. The Headings row label indicates the title that will be printed at the top of the database report.

T  F  6. The Summary row label indicates which statistic will be printed at the bottom of the report.

T  F  7. The procedure to sort records in a database report is similar to the way records are sorted in a full database.

T    F    8.    The Break option in the Sort Records dialog box will stop the sort sequence.

T    F    9.    Works will automatically name database reports if you do not assign a name.

T    F    10.    Database reports must be saved separately before you exit a database.

---

## COMPLETION

Write the correct answer in the space provided.

1. Which menu is accessed to perform database reporting functions, such as creating and naming a database?

_____

_____

_____

2. Identify two operations that take place in the New Report dialog box.

_____

_____

_____

3. Identify two statistics that may be used in a database report.

_____

_____

_____

4. Which view button on the Toolbar is used to make changes to a database report?

_____

_____

_____

5. Which Report view row label determines the title appearing at the top of the first page of a database report?

_____

_____

_____

6. Which Report view row label determines which fields will be printed in the report?

_____

_____

_____

7. Once a new database report has been created, how may additional fields be added to a database report?

_____

_____

_____

8. What command will place records in a database report in a specified order?

_____

_____

_____

9. Which option in the Sort Records dialog box will insert statistics after each group of records in a sort?

_____

_____

_____

10. What is the maximum number of database reports that may be saved with a single database?

_____

_____

_____

# APPLICATIONS

## APPLICATION 14-1

The file *app14-1.wdb* contains a database of bicycles for Mike's Bikes (similar to the database used in the chapter). In this application, you will prepare a database report that answers the questions of the accountant for Mike's Bikes. Specifically, the accountant would like to know the number of bicycles in the inventory and the value of the inventory at cost.

1.   Open *app14-1.wdb*.

2.   In the New Report dialog box, designate the following (*Hint:* The New Report dialog box is obtained by choosing Create New Report from the View menu):

   a.   Title the Report "Year End Inventory."
   b.   Include the following fields in the report: Manufact, Model, Quant, Cost, and Cost Total.

3.   In the Report Statistics dialog box, perform the following operations (*Hint:* The Report Statistics dialog box is obtained by clicking OK in the New Report dialog box):

   a.   Create a SUM statistic for the Quant field.
   b.   Create a SUM statistic for the Cost Total field.
   c.   Position the statistics under each column.

4.   From Report view, perform the following steps:

   a.   Change the Manufact heading to Manufacturer.
   b.   Change the Quant heading to Quantity.
   c.   Widen the columns to fit the expanded headings.
   d.   Change the Summary title in Column C to No. of Bicycles:
   e.   Change the Summary title in Column E to Value of Inventory:

5.   Print the report.

6.   Name the report *INVENTORY*. (*Hint:* The Name Report command is in the View menu.)

7.   Save the database to your data disk as *invent*.

8.   Close the file.

9.   Using the information on your printed report, answer the following questions asked by the accountant:

   a.   How many bicycles are in the year-end inventory?

   _____

   b.   What is the value of the inventory at cost?

   _____

----------------------------------◼----------------------------------

# APPLICATION 14-2

The file *app14-2.wdb* contains a database of bicycles for Mike's Bikes (similar to the database used in the chapter). In this application, you will prepare a database report that will be provided to customers so that they may know the retail prices for each bicycle model.

1.   Open *app14-2.wdb* and prepare a database report with the following characteristics:

   a.   The report title will be PRICE LIST.
   b.   The fields to be included in the report include Manufact, Model, Color, and Retail.
   c.   The report should contain no summary statistics.
   d.   The records should be sorted by price (the Retail field), from the most inexpensive to the most expensive.

e. The heading for Manufact should be changed to Manufacturer.

f. The title of the Report should be centered over the report contents. (*Hint:* Move the title from Column E to Column C in Report view.)

2. Name the report *price list*.

3. Print the report.

4. Save the database to your data disk as *price*.

5. Close the file.

---

# APPLICATION 14-3

The file *app14-3.wdb* contains grades recorded for three tests and a final examination by a course instructor. The database is currently sorted by grades made on the final examination.

1. Prepare a report that indicates test averages, the highest grade for each test, and the lowest grade for each test. The database report should be entitled EXAMINATION SUMMARY and appear similar to the following:

## EXAMINATION SUMMARY

| Name | Test 1 | Test 2 | Test 3 | Final Exam |
|------|--------|--------|--------|------------|
| Appleby | 85 | 86 | 90 | 91 |
| Barnett | 95 | 92 | 87 | 90 |
| Chandler | 77 | 74 | 73 | 70 |
| Dawson | 68 | 66 | 71 | 66 |
| Ellington | 75 | 74 | 78 | 72 |
| Fowler | 81 | 83 | 85 | 90 |
| Getz | 83 | 84 | 85 | 85 |
| Harrington | 74 | 78 | 76 | 79 |
| Ingram | 72 | 71 | 73 | 77 |
| Jones | 75 | 80 | 75 | 85 |
| Kinslow | 82 | 81 | 89 | 87 |
| Lowe | 74 | 75 | 76 | 79 |
| Martinez | 95 | 98 | 94 | 88 |
| Newsom | 83 | 88 | 90 | 82 |
| | AVG: | AVG: | AVG: | AVG: |
| | 79.93 | 80.71 | 81.57 | 81.50 |
| | MIN: | MIN: | MIN: | MIN: |
| | 68 | 66 | 71 | 66 |
| | MAX: | MAX: | MAX: | MAX: |
| | 95 | 98 | 94 | 91 |

*Hints:*

a. Make sure you position the report statistics under each column.

b. Format the test averages as fixed with two decimal digits.

    c.  Move the title of the report to Column C.

    d.  Sort the database report alphabetically by name.

2.    Name the report *stats*.

3.    Print the database report.

4.    Save the file to your data disk as *exam*.

5.    Close the file.

---

# APPLICATION 14-4

In this application, you will create a report from the database *dir.wdb*, which you created in Application 12-4 and Application 13-5. Feel free to add more names, addresses, and phone numbers if you desire.

1.    Open *dir.wdb*.

2.    Create a database report that acts as a phone list of your friends and relatives. The report will be named *phone dir* and have the following characteristics:

    a.  The report should include the fields Last Name, First Name, and Phone No.

    b.  The list should be sorted alphabetically by Last Name.

3.    Create a database report that lists the names and addresses of your friends and relatives by geographical area. The report should be named *addresses* and have the following characteristics.

    a.  The report should include the fields Last Name, First Name, Address, City, and ZIP Code.

    b.  The list should be sorted by ZIP Code.

4.    Print both reports.

5.    Save *dir* and close the file.

---

# PART 5

## INTEGRATION

# INTEGRATION BASICS

## LEARNING OBJECTIVES

**When you complete this chapter, you will be able to:**

1. Understand the concept of integration.
2. Cut, copy, and paste among documents.
3. Use linking to integrate documents.
4. Create a form letter.

## INTRODUCTION TO INTEGRATION

As you have already learned earlier in this text, Works is an integrated program. *Integration* refers to using more than one Works tool to create a document. This means that you can use information created in a spreadsheet to complete a report in the word processor. Or you can use information from a database to create form letters in the word processor. Tables from the word processor can become spreadsheet data. It is just as easy to transfer data from a database to a spreadsheet as to transfer it to another database document.

The value of an integrated program like Works is that sharing data among tools is easy. In this chapter, you will explore several ways to share data among the Works tools. The easiest approach is simply to cut, copy, and paste among the tools. Works also allows you to use a process called *linking* to integrate data between the spreadsheet and the word processor. When you use linking to insert data from a spreadsheet into a word processor document, any change to the spreadsheet will be reflected in the word processor document as well. Finally, you will explore how easy it is to create form letters by using database information in a word processor document.

# MOVING AND COPYING DATA BETWEEN DOCUMENTS

You have already learned how easy it is to move and copy data among documents created in any one of the Works tools using the Cut, Copy, and Paste commands. However, the process of moving data among different tools varies, depending on what tools are involved. Word processor, spreadsheet, and database documents have unique formats. For example, data from a spreadsheet are arranged in cells, information in a database is collected in fields, and text in a word processor document does not follow any particular format. When you move data among tools, Works changes the format of the information you are moving so that it may be used in the destination document.

## Spreadsheet to Word Processor

A common integration operation is to paste numbers from a spreadsheet into a word processor document. When spreadsheet data is copied to a word processor document, Works automatically uses tabs to separate the spreadsheet information into columns.

**ACTIVITY 15-1**

### Copying from the Spreadsheet to the Word Processor

Your template disk contains two files relating to a ski trip that Stephen and Gabriel are planning. In this activity, you will copy the spreadsheet data from the *skicost.wks* spreadsheet and paste it into the *skitrip.wps* letter. By integrating the documents, Stephen can send one instead of two pages to Gabriel.

1.  From your template disk, open *skitrip.wps* from the *gabriel* folder, which is in the *letters* folder.

2.  From the **File** menu, choose **Open Existing File**.

3.  Open *skicost.wks*, also in the *gabriel* folder. Your screen should resemble Figure 15-1.

4.  Highlight the data in the spreadsheet from Cell A1 to Cell C14. The window will scroll automatically, if necessary, as you highlight the cells.

5.  From the **Edit** menu, choose **Copy**.

6.  To bring the letter to Gabriel to the front, choose **SKITRIP.WPS** from the **Window** menu.

Activity 15-1 continued

7. Place the cursor between the first and second paragraphs.

8. From the **Edit** menu, choose **Paste**. The data from the spreadsheet appears in the letter.

9. Save *skitrip.wps* on your data disk as *skilettr.wps*.

10. Save *skicost.wks* on your data disk as *skidata.wks*.

11. Print *skilettr.wps*. Close *skilettr.wps*. Leave *skidata.wks* open for the next activity.

**FIGURE 15-1**

In preparation for integrating data from a spreadsheet to a word processor document, both documents are opened.

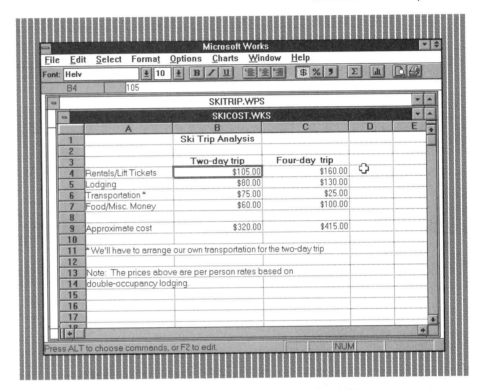

## Word Processor to Spreadsheet

Suppose you want to move data from a table in a report to the spreadsheet in order to make calculations using the data. Works handles pasting into a spreadsheet from the word processor in one of two ways. If the text from the word processor is set up as a table, with data separated by tabs, the spreadsheet will separate the text into separate cells in the spreadsheet. If the text is in a single block, all of the text will be pasted into the currently highlighted cell of the spreadsheet.

## Word Processor to Database

Suppose you have been given a list of names and addresses in a word processor file. The names need to be entered into a database. Pasting into a database from the word processor is similar to pasting into a spreadsheet from the word processor. If the text from the word processor is set up as a table, with data separated by tabs, the database will separate the text into fields. Each line will be entered as a separate record. If the text is in a single block, all of the text will be pasted into the currently highlighted field.

## Spreadsheet to Database

Pasting into a database from a spreadsheet is essentially the same as pasting from a spreadsheet to a spreadsheet. The cells cut or copied from the spreadsheet will appear in the database beginning with the highlighted entry.

## Database to Spreadsheet

When you paste into a spreadsheet from a database, the field entries will be pasted into the spreadsheet columns, and the records will be pasted into the rows.

## Database to Word Processor

Data from a database is pasted into the word processor the same way spreadsheet data is pasted into the word processor. The data is formatted with tabs when it enters the word processor. This feature could be used to create a table in the word processor, based on data in a database.

# THE MISSING LINK

Pasting data from one document into another can be useful. There will be times, however, when the data you are pasting may change periodically. Suppose it is your job as treasurer of an organization to file a monthly financial report. Your report is basically the same each month except for the month's cash flow numbers. You keep the cash flow data up to date in a spreadsheet. Using the copying and pasting techniques discussed above, you would have to copy the latest spreadsheet numbers and paste them into your word processor document each month.

There is an easier way. Instead of pasting the data manually each time, the Paste Special command can be used to link the two documents. *Linking* will automatically paste the latest figures from your spreadsheet into your report. Each time the word processor document is opened, you have the opportunity to update the document with the latest spreadsheet data.

Figure 15-2 shows the Paste Special dialog box that appears when data from a Works spreadsheet is pasted into a word processor document. The Paste Link button places the spreadsheet data into the document and creates the link to the actual spreadsheet.

Linking only works between the spreadsheet and the word processor. You can, however, link a spreadsheet chart in addition to spreadsheet data.

**FIGURE 15-2**
The Paste Special dialog box allows spreadsheet data to be pasted into a word processor document.

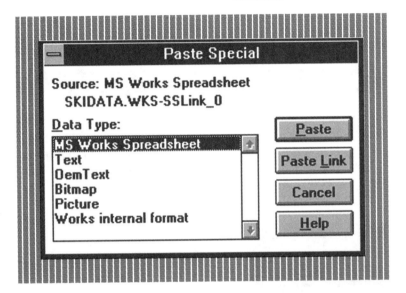

ACTIVITY
15-2

## Linking

In this activity, you will link the data from the *skidata.wks* spreadsheet into the *skitrip.wps* document. *Skidata.wks* should now be on the screen.

1.  Open *skitrip.wps* from the *gabriel* folder in the *letters* folder of your template disk.

2.  Switch to *skidata.wks* and highlight Cells A1 through C14, if they are not already highlighted. Copy the cells and switch back to *skitrip.wps*.

3.  Place the cursor between the first and second paragraphs.

4.  From the **Edit** menu, choose **Paste Special**. The Paste Special dialog box appears.

5.  Click **MS Works Spreadsheet** as the data type.

6.  Click **Paste Link**. The spreadsheet data appears in the document. The data are linked to *skidata.wks.* Any changes made to *skidata.wks* will be reflected in *skitrip.wps.*

7.  Insert one blank line above and one blank line below the linked data.

Activity 15-2 continued

8.  Save *skitrip.wps* on your data disk as *skilink.wps*.

9.  Print *skilink.wps*.

10. Save changes to *skidata.wks*. Close *skilink.wps* and *skidata.wks*.

Changes made in the *skidata.wks* spreadsheet can become a part of the *skilink.wps* letter when the letter is opened. When you open *skilink.wps*, you will have the opportunity to update the document with the latest spreadsheet data.

## ACTIVITY 15-3

## Updating a Linked Document

In this activity, you will update the *skidata.wks* spreadsheet data. You will then open *skilink.wps* and update the letter to Gabriel with the new data.

1.  Open *skidata.wks* from your data disk.

2.  Change the cost of transportation to $95 for the two-day trip and $35 for the four-day trip.

3.  Save *skidata.wks*.

4.  Open *skilink.wps* from your data disk. You will be asked whether you want to update links.

5.  Click **Yes**. *Skilink.wps* appears.

6.  Scroll down until the transportation costs are in view. You can see that the data were updated.

7.  Open *skilettr.wps*. Scroll down until the transportation costs are in view. The data were not updated in *skilettr.wps* because the data were not linked.

8.  Close all three files.

# FORM LETTERS

Another way to integrate Works tools is to print form letters. A *form letter* is a word processor document that uses information from a database in specified areas to personalize a document.

For example, you might send a letter to all of the members of a club using a form letter. The information is the same in each letter, but the names will be different in each case. Each printed letter will carry the name of a different member of the club. One letter may begin "Dear Jennifer" and another "Dear Mike."

## Creating a Form Letter

To create form letters, you integrate information from a database with a document from the word processor. Both the database and the word processor document must be open. You then insert the field names in the word processor document where you want to print information from the database. The field names you place in the word processing document are enclosed in angle brackets, as shown in Figure 15-3.

**FIGURE 15-3**
Database fields can be inserted anywhere in a word processor document.

Works ————————————————

Users of ————————————————

Maryland ════════════════════
678 Thornfield Rd.
Baltimore, MD  21229

February 13, 19--

Database fields ➤ «Title» «First Name» «Last Name»
➤ «Address»
➤ «City», «St» «ZIP Code»

➤ Dear «First Name»:

I know I do not have to tell you the benefits of membership in WUM.  The growth our group has experienced in the last year is evidence of the value WUM offers users of integrated programs.

Now WUM is an even better value!  Because of the success of the group, dues have been lowered.  You will continue to receive our award-winning newsletter, *A WUM Response*, and access to our 24-hour computer bulletin board system.  All of the quality services you have come to expect from WUM have not changed.  Only the price is on the decline.

➤ Dues this year are «Dues».  Our records indicate that you have paid «Paid» and owe a
➤ balance of «Balance».  Please remit the balance to the address on this letterhead as soon as possible.

We expect our lower dues to attract even more members.  Remember to give our new members a WUM welcome!

Yours truly,

T.J. Lau
President

## ACTIVITY 15-4

### Loading Documents for a Form Letter

In this activity, you will load a database and a word processor document to be used for form letters.

1.  Open *act15-4.wdb* from your template disk.

2.  Use the scroll bars to view all of the fields in the database.

3.  Open *act15-4.wps* from your template disk. Figure 15-3 shows where database fields have been inserted.

4.  Leave *act15-4.wps* on the screen for the next activity.

**FIGURE 15-4**

The Insert Field dialog box inserts database fields into a word processor document.

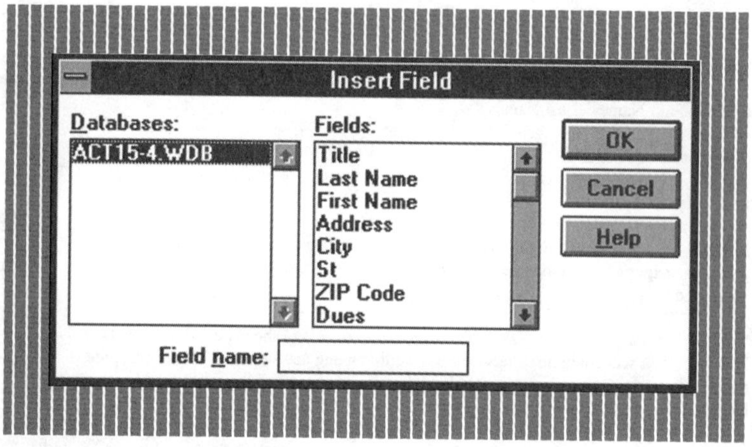

To insert a field from the database, choose the Database Field command from the Insert menu. The Insert Field dialog box will appear, as shown in Figure 15-4. The left side of the dialog box allows you to choose the database from which the form letter will draw its information. The right side of the dialog box allows you to choose which field from the database you want to insert.

Insert Field

Databases: ACT15-4.WDB

Fields: Title, Last Name, First Name, Address, City, St, ZIP Code, Dues

OK  Cancel  Help

Field name:

## ACTIVITY 15-5

### Inserting Database Fields

In this activity, you will insert additional database fields into the form letter. *Act15-4.wps* should now be on the screen.

1.  Position the cursor immediately before the word *We* in the first sentence of the last paragraph in the letter.

Activity 15-5 continued

2. Start a new paragraph before the last paragraph by keying **Dues this year are**. Key one space after the word *are*.

3. From the **Insert** menu, choose **Database Field**. The Insert Field dialog box appears.

4. Click **ACT15-4.WDB** in the Databases box. Click **Dues** in the Fields box. Click **OK** to accept. The field will appear in your document as <<Dues>>.

5. Key a period to end the sentence. Key two spaces. Key **Our records indicate that you have paid**. Key one space after the word *paid*.

6. From the **Insert** menu, choose **Database Field**. If it is not already highlighted, click **ACT15-4.WDB** in the Databases box. Scroll down in the Fields box to click **Paid**. Click **OK** to accept.

7. Key one space. Key **and owe a balance of** and key a space following the word *of*.

8. Insert the Balance field from the ACT15-4.WDB database.

9. Key a period after the Balance field. Key two spaces. Key the following sentence to complete the paragraph: **Please remit the balance to the address on this letterhead as soon as possible.**

10. Press **Enter** twice. Adjust the spacing around the paragraph if necessary. Save the document on your data disk as *WUM.wps*.

11. Leave *WUM.wps* on the screen for the next activity.

## Previewing and Printing the Form Letters

After the fields are inserted, the form letters are ready to print. You don't want to use the standard Print command. If you choose Print, Works will print the form letter word processor document, showing only the database field names. Instead, select the Print Form Letters command from the File menu. This command allows you to preview as well as print the letter with the database information included. The Print Form Letters dialog box has a Preview button and a Print button, as shown in Figure 15-5.

**FIGURE 15-5**
The Print Form Letters dialog box allows you to preview or print form letters.

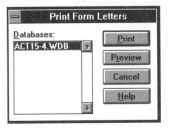

**ACTIVITY 15-6**

## Previewing Form Letters

In this activity, you will preview the form letters generated by the Print Form Letters dialog box. *WUM.wps* should now be on the screen.

1.   From the **File** menu, choose **Print Form Letters**.

**FIGURE 15-6**
Form letters can be previewed before printing.

2.   Click the **Preview** button. The first letter appears on the screen.

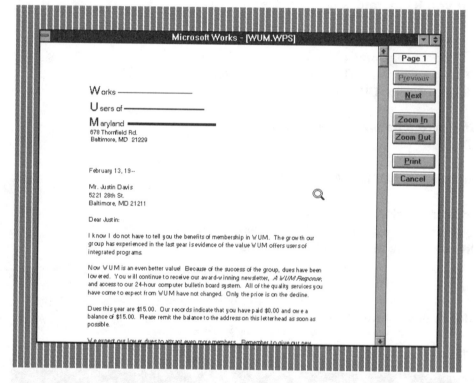

3.   Click the **Zoom In** button on the right side of the screen. Your screen should look similar to Figure 15-6.

4.   Click the **Next** button to see the next letter. Notice the name, address, and payment information changes with each letter.

5.   Click the **Next** button again to see the last letter.

6.   Click Cancel.

7.   Close *WUM.wps* and *act15-4.wdb*.

Clicking the Print button in the Print Form Letters dialog box brings up the familiar Print dialog box. Before actually printing form letters, ask your teacher.

# SUMMARY

Integration refers to using more than one of the Works tools to create a document. Data can be copied and pasted among documents or linked to ensure that data are up to date.

A common form of integration is to paste numbers from a spreadsheet into a word processor document. Data can be copied and pasted between other types of documents as well. Works performs special operations to give you the best conversion of your data.

Spreadsheet data can be linked to a word processor document using the Paste Special command. Each time the word processor document is opened, you have the opportunity to update the document with the latest spreadsheet data.

Form letters combine data from a database into word processor documents. Works allows you to insert fields from a database anywhere in a word processor document. You can then print a document for each entry in your database.

# CHALLENGES

## TRUE/FALSE

Circle **T** or **F** to show whether the statement is true or false.

| | | | |
|---|---|---|---|
| T | F | 1. | Copying spreadsheet data into a word processor is one example of integration. |
| T | F | 2. | The value of an integrated program like Works is that sharing data among the tools is easy. |
| T | F | 3. | Data can be copied and pasted among any of the Works tools. |
| T | F | 4. | Works does not change the format of data copied and pasted among the tools. |
| T | F | 5. | Linking is performed using the Copy Special command. |
| T | F | 6. | Data can be linked among any of the Works tools. |
| T | F | 7. | Linking always updates the link when the document with the link is opened. |
| T | F | 8. | Form letters get their data from spreadsheets. |
| T | F | 9. | The Insert Field dialog box is where you choose the fields to be inserted in a form letter. |
| T | F | 10. | Form letters can be previewed before being printed. |

# COMPLETION

1. What is the term for using more than one Works tool to create a document?

_____

2. Give an example of a document that could be created using integration.

_____

3. Give an example of when you might copy data from a word processor document to a spreadsheet.

_____

_____

4. Give an example of when you might copy data from a word processor document to a datadase.

_____

_____

5. What commands are used to place data from a database into a spreadsheet?

_____

6. What does Works do to spreadsheet data when it is pasted into a word processor document?

_____

7. Give an example of a document that could use linking effectively.

_____

8. What commands allow you to link spreadsheet data into a word processor document?

_____

9. What is a form letter?

_____

10. What command is used to insert a database field in a word processor document and in which menu is the command found?

_____

_____

# APPLICATIONS

## APPLICATION 15-1

In this application, you will use Cut, Copy, and Paste to move and copy data among documents.

1. Open *app15-1.wdb* from your template disk.

2. Highlight the names and addresses of both Oscar Alvarado and Marcy Bell. Do not include their titles or prizes. Highlight only the fields from First Name to ZIP Code. From the Edit menu, choose Copy.

3. Create a new word processor document. Paste the database data into the document. Notice how the fields are separated by tabs.

4. Create a new spreadsheet document. Paste the database data into the spreadsheet. Notice how each field is placed in a separate cell.

5. Close all three files. Do not save the files.

---

## APPLICATION 15-2

In this application, you will use linking to create a report for the members of a science group that is raising funds for a trip.

1. Open *app15-2.wks* from your template disk. The number in Cell D4 of the spreadsheet is the total amount of money raised for the science trip. the money is to be divided between the 11 students who are going on the trip. The spreadsheet takes the total funds raised and divides it by the number of students to calculate the portion of the trip paid for by the fundraiser. Then the remaining balance is calculated to show the students how much of the cost they will be responsible for at the current level of funding. As the total funds raised grow, each student's portion of the cost decreases.

2. Open *app15-2.wps* from your template disk.

3. Make *app15-2.wks* the active window. Highlight Cell D3. From the Edit menu, choose Copy.

4. Make *app15-2.wps* the active window. Position the cursor to the right of the word *are*. Press the space bar once. Use Paste Special to link the number from the spreadsheet.

5. Key the remainder of the first sentence to match Figure 15-7. Key the rest of the report, inserting the spreadsheet links using the same procedure followed in Steps 3 and 4. Be sure to copy the correct cells from the spreadsheet.

6. Save the word processor document as *triprep.wps* on your data disk. Save the spreadsheet as *tripfund.wks* on your data disk. Experiment with changing numbers in the spreadsheet to see the changes reflected in the report. Change the figures back to those in Figure 15-7. Print the report. Save and close both files.

**FIGURE 15-7**

**Science Trip Fund Raising Report**
12/1/--

As of today, there are [ 11 ] members planning to attend this year's science trip. Our fundraiser has raised [ $1,256.38 ] to date. Members can now expect to receive [ $114.22 ] of the [ $225.00 ] needed to pay for the trip, leaving [ $110.78 ] to be paid by each attending member.

# APPLICATION 15-3

In this application, you will draft a letter to notify customers in a database that they have won a prize in a promotional drawing. Your template disk includes a database of names, addresses, and prizes to be awarded in a file named *app15-1.wdb.* You are to complete the following.

1. Add your own name, address, and the prize you would like to be awarded to the *app15-1.wdb* database.

2. Create a form letter that notifies the customers in the database of the prizes they have been awarded. Be sure to include:

   a. name of business awarding prizes
   b. address where prize can be claimed
   c. hours of business

   Make sure you insert the database fields in all appropriate places.

3. Ask your teacher if you should print your form letters or preview them on the screen.

# APPENDIX
# A

# WORKSWIZARDS

## MEET THE WORKSWIZARDS

You have probably noticed the WorksWizards button in the Startup dialog box or the Create New File dialog box (see Figure A-1) and wondered what a WorksWizard is. *WorksWizards* are programs within Works that automate certain common Works tasks, such as creating address lists, form letters, and mailing labels. Think of a WorksWizard as an expert Works user that follows your orders to set up a database or document. The WorksWizard asks you to make some choices about your document and then, almost magically, does the work before your eyes.

---

**FIGURE A-1**
The WorksWizards button
starts the WorksWizards.

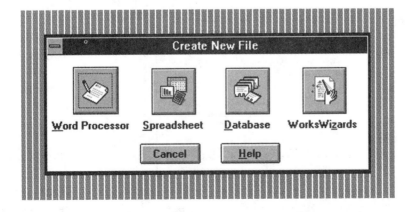

To start a WorksWizard, choose the WorksWizard button. The WorksWizards dialog box will appear and allow you to choose a WorksWizard, as shown in Figure A-2.

**FIGURE A-2**
Choose the document you want the WorksWizard to create in the WorksWizards dialog box.

# USING A WORKSWIZARD TO CREATE AN ADDRESS BOOK

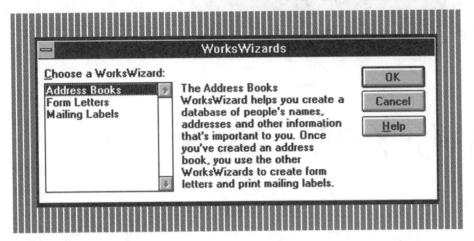

The first WorksWizard creates an address book. The Wizard will ask you some questions to customize your address book and will then create an appropriate database.

## ACTIVITY A-1

**FIGURE A-3**
This screen welcomes you to the Address Books WorksWizard.

### Using a WorksWizard

In this activity, you will use the WorksWizard that creates an address book.

1. From the **File** menu, choose **Create New File**. The Create New File dialog box appears.

2. Click the **WorksWizards** button. The WorksWizards dialog box appears.

3. Click **Address Books** if it is not already highlighted. Click **OK**. The screen shown in Figure A-3 appears.

4. Click **Next**. You are asked to choose whether you want a personal, business, or organization address book.

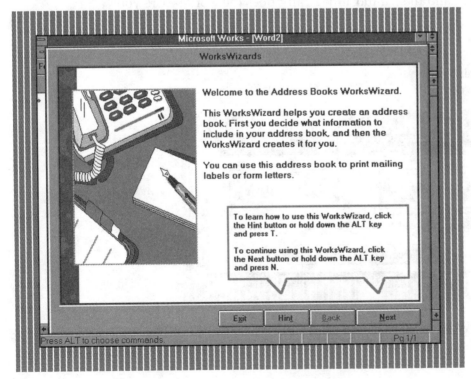

Activity A-1 continued

5.  Choose **Personal**. Click **Next**. The screen shown in Figure A-4 appears, giving you the opportunity to customize the fields in your database.

**FIGURE A-4**
The WorksWizard lets you choose what information will be in your address book.

6.  Choose **Phone**. Click **Next**. You will be asked if you want to add additional categories to the address book.

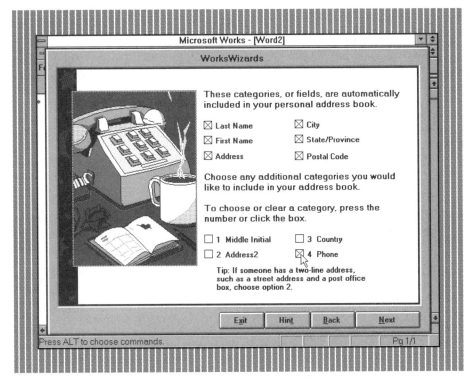

7.  Click **No**. Click **Next**. The WorksWizard is ready to create an address book database.

8.  Click **Create Address Book**. The database is created before your eyes. After the database is created, you will be asked if you want to read more information about what can be done with your database.

9.  Click **No**. Click **Next**. You will be asked if you want to save the address book. To save the database on your data disk, you will have to save it after the WorksWizard is done. Click **No**. Click **Next**.

10. The final screen will appear. Choose **Exit**. Save the database on your data disk as *addrbook*.

The database created by the WorksWizard is just like other databases you have worked with throughout the book. Add data to the address book in the same way you have in earlier chapters. Remember, the WorksWizard helps you create the database quickly, but once created, the database does not need the WorksWizard.

# ▌OTHER WIZARDS

Works also includes a WorksWizard to assist you in creating form letters and another for making mailing labels. The Form Letters WorksWizard is a way of creating form letters other than the way you learned in Chapter 15. The Form Letters WorksWizard can make it easier to create form letters, especially if you want to make form letters from an address book created with the WorksWizard. The Mailing Labels WorksWizard helps you print a sheet of mailing labels from a database. Like the address book, the other WorksWizards are easy to use.

# APPENDIX B

# MODEM TELECOMMUNICATIONS

## CONCEPTS OF MODEM TELECOMMUNICATIONS

Even working alone, a computer is a powerful tool. Your computer, however, can be made even more powerful by sharing information and files with other computers. In this chapter, you will discover how modem communication can expand the capabilities and increase the usefulness of your computer.

*Modem communication* is the process of transmitting information from computer to computer over telephone lines. Modem communication is a form of telecommunication.

The device at the heart of modem communication is the modem. A *modem* converts computer signals to and from sounds that can be transmitted over phone lines. Modems get their name from the work they do. Modems *mo*dulate a signal to be sent over a phone line and *dem*odulate a signal when receiving one. Modem is a short form of modulator/demodulator. Modems are available in different speeds and with a variety of optional features.

The speed at which a modem modulates signals is measured in *baud*. *Bits per second (BPS)*, however, is more useful because it is a measure of the usable bits that the modem sends or receives in a second. Some modems, particularly older ones, transmit one bit per baud. Because of this, many people think of baud and BPS as interchangeable. Because newer modems sometimes squeeze four or more bits into one baud, baud and BPS can no longer be thought of as the same thing.

**FIGURE B-1**

A modem can be installed inside your computer or attached to the computer with a cable.

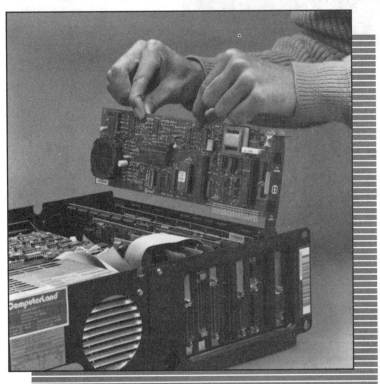

Common modem speeds are 2,400 and 9,600 baud. In its standard mode, a 2,400 baud modem can transmit about 240 characters per second, which is about 2,400 BPS. Some 2,400 baud modems, however, can transmit data at 9,600 BPS or more. The speed at which a modem can transmit data is an important factor when you are communicating over long-distance phone lines.

The modem may be installed inside the computer or connected to the computer by a cable. Modems installed inside the computer are called internal modems. An *internal modem* is a circuit card that plugs into one of the connectors inside the computer. These connectors are called *expansion slots*. An *external modem* connects to the computer by a cable that plugs into a port on the back of the computer. Figure B-1 illustrates an internal and an external modem.

# WHY COMMUNICATE?

Modem communication is available at several levels. This section will explain three common ways to communicate with other computers.

## Connecting Two Computers Directly

In one form of modem communication, two computer users connect to each other to transfer a file. Suppose that Cody has just written a letter to a college requesting information. Cody composed the letter in Microsoft Works, but he has not printed it yet. Cody's friend Kelsey, on the other side of town, volunteers to edit the letter before Cody prints it. Cody and Kelsey connect their computers over the modem, and Cody sends his letter to Kelsey's computer. Not only can Kelsey read it but she can make revisions to it and send the revised letter back to Cody.

## Bulletin Board Systems

A *bulletin board system*, commonly called a BBS, is a service run by an individual, college, club, or even a business. BBSs provide a place to post messages for other users to read. In addition, BBSs may offer private mail, files to transfer, and even on-line games. Most BBSs are local systems with one phone line used primarily by local callers. Some BBSs, however, have multiple phone lines and attract callers from all over the world.

Many BBSs are part of networks that transmit messages from local systems to other systems all over the nation and in some cases to other countries. These networks can exchange information with other computer users nationwide with a local phone call.

## On-Line Services

Larger, commercial versions of BBSs are known as *on-line services*, or electronic information services. CompuServe, Prodigy, GEnie, and America Online are four popular on-line services. These services charge for access. On-line services allow you to check stock prices and up-to-the-minute news and weather and perform encyclopedia searches. You can make airline and hotel reservations, shop for almost anything, and in some cases do your banking. You can send messages to software publishers, such as Microsoft, and sometimes get updates to software products.

# COMMUNICATING WITH WINDOWS TERMINAL

Each computer that participates in modem communication must be equipped with a modem, have access to a phone line, and have special

**FIGURE B-2**

To start Windows Terminal, double-click the Terminal program icon.

software for communication. Microsoft Works for Windows does not include a telecommunications tool. Microsoft Windows, however, includes an accessory called Terminal, which is communications software.

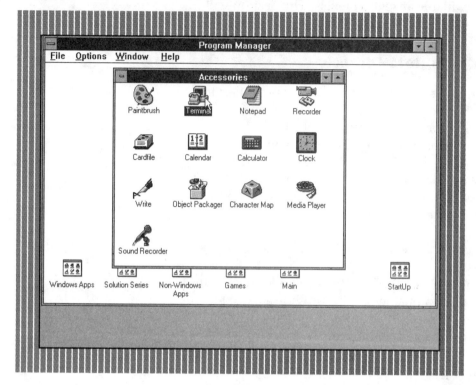

To start Terminal, open the Accessories group window from the Program Manager. Double-click on the Terminal program icon (see Figure B-2). Windows Terminal will start. Maximize the window so that you can get the maximum terminal screen size when you are connected to other computers.

Terminal is a program that makes your computer act as a terminal for a host computer. A *terminal* is a screen and keyboard used to interact with a host computer. A *host computer* is the computer to which the terminal is connected. Most large *mainframe computers* have many terminals that can do nothing unless connected to the mainframe computer. These terminals are known as dumb terminals. Because a microcomputer has a screen and keyboard, it can be used as a terminal. A microcomputer, unlike a dumb terminal, can do processing independent of a host computer.

Before you connect to a host computer, you must set up the terminal software to dial the number and to communicate with the other computer. You will configure Terminal for your system using the Settings menu. Adjusting Terminal's settings is explained in the Microsoft Windows User's Guide. In addition, Terminal has an extensive help system.

## CONNECTING

After the modem commands are set up correctly, you can place the call and connect to the other computer. The modem will dial the phone and wait for a connection. Your modem should have a speaker that lets you listen to the dialing and connection. When the computer you are calling answers, you will hear a mixture of tones coming from both ends of the line. After the connection is made, the speaker will turn off and you will see text on the screen coming from the computer you have called.

Most BBSs and on-line services will prompt you for your name and a password for identification. Entering this information is called *logging on* to a system. In most cases, the process of logging on will be followed by a menu to guide your use of the system.

## SENDING AND RECEIVING FILES

Much of what you do while on a BBS or on-line service is directed by the host computer. Reading and posting messages is done by sending text back and forth between your computer and the host. If you want to send a program or data file to the host computer, however, a special process known as a *file transfer* is used. During a file transfer, data is sent over the modem that does not appear on your screen. The communications software directs the transfer. After the file is transferred, the operation returns to normal.

## DISCONNECTING AND EXITING TERMINAL

The final modem communication step is disconnecting and exiting Windows Terminal. If you are connected to a friend's computer rather than to a BBS or an on-line service, you can simply choose Hangup from the Phone menu to disconnect. If you are connected to a BBS or an on-line service, however, you should follow the disconnect procedure provided by the system you have called. Disconnecting is sometimes referred to as *logging off* or signing off.

It is more courteous to log off rather than just hang up. Logging off ensures that the host system properly resets for the next caller. In addition, if you are paying for access to the host system, logging off ensures that you are not charged for time after you hang up.

To exit Terminal and return to the Program Manager, choose Exit from the File menu.

# GLOSSARY

## A

**absolute cell references** contain row numbers and column letters preceded by a dollar sign ($). They do not adjust to the new cell location when copied or moved.

**active cell** a highlighted cell ready for data entry.

**active window** the window that is on the front of the screen; text can only be entered into an active window.

**All Records search** a database search that displays on the screen only those records containing the specified data.

**application window** the window containing a program.

**argument** a value, cell reference, range, or text that acts as an operand in a function formula of a spreadsheet or database. The argument is enclosed in parentheses after the function name. If a function formula contains more than one argument, the arguments are separated by commas.

**ASCII** American Standard Code for Information Interchange. Provides a standard for communication between different types of computer programs.

## B

**Backspace key** the key that deletes characters to the left of the cursor.

**bar chart** rectangles of varying heights used to illustrate values in a spreadsheet.

**baud** the measurement of modem speed. A 2,400-baud modem transfers about 240 characters per second.

**bits per second (BPS)** the rate at which usable bits of information are sent via modem.

**bookmark** a hidden marker that is inserted into a document to mark a specific place.

**borders** single, double, or bold lines that surround a paragraph and are used to emphasize the text.

**Break** operation for database reports in which records are grouped and a row summarizing the data in the group is inserted between groups.

**bulletin board system (BBS)** a service, usually run by an individual, college, club, or business, that provides modem communication services such as messaging and file transfers.

## C

**cell** the intersection of a row and column in a spreadsheet.

**cell reference** identifies a cell by the column letter and row number (for example, A1, B2, C4).

**chart** graphical representation of data contained in a spreadsheet

**Chart window** a Works window used to create, refine, and print charts prepared from spreadsheet data.

**clip-art** graphics that are already drawn and available for use in your documents.

**Clipboard** the area in memory that holds text or graphics that have been cut or copied until the item can be pasted.

**close** removing a document or window from the screen.

**columns** appear vertically in a spreadsheet and are identified by letters at the top of the spreadsheet window.

**comma format** displays numerical data with commas every third decimal place.

**complex query** a database operation that displays records that meet several comparisons simultaneously.

**Control-menu box** the icon that serves as a header for the Control menu.

**currency format** displays numerical data preceded by a dollar sign.

**cursor** the short blinking vertical line that marks your place in the text and represents the point where the next keyed text will be inserted.

## D

**database** an automated electronic filing system that stores and retrieves information.

**database report** allows you to organize, summarize, and print a portion of the database.

**Delete key** the key that deletes selected characters or characters to the right of the insertion point.

**directory** a list of files grouped on a disk.

**document window** the window within the application window that contains the word processing document.

**Draft View** an option in which the text of a document appears in one font and size.

## E

**end-of-file marker** the horizontal line at the left of the document window that marks the last line entered.

**entry** the smallest unit in a database, consisting of one piece of information.

**expansion slots** a connector inside the computer that circuit cards are plugged into.

**exponential format** displays numerical data in scientific notation.

**external modem** a modem that connects to the computer by a cable.

## F

**field** a category of information in a database.

**field formats** determine the appearance of data in a column of a database.

**field name** label that appears at the top of a database column that describes the kind of information to be stored in the column.

**file transfer** the process of sending a file from one computer to another over a modem.

**filling down** copies data from an original cell or entry to cells or entries directly below the original.

**financial functions** function formulas used to analyze loans and investments. The primary financial functions are future value, present value, and payment.

**fixed format** displays numerical data with a fixed amount of places to the right of the decimal point.

**font** refers to the shape of characters belonging to a particular family of type.

**footer** text that repeats at the bottom of a page.

**footnote** text that is used to document text that you do not want to include in the body of your document.

**form letter** a word processor document that uses information from a database in specified areas to personalize a document.

**formula** an equation that calculates a new value from existing values in a spreadsheet or database.

**formula bar** appears directly below the Toolbar in the spreadsheet. The formula bar will display a formula when the cell of a spreadsheet or entry of a database contains a calculated value.

**Form view** a window in the database that displays one record at a time. Form view is most appropriate for entering or editing a specific record.

**function formulas** spreadsheet formulas that do not use operators to calculate a result.

**function name** identifies the operation to be performed in a function formula of a spreadsheet or database. A function name is usually two to seven characters.

## G

**general format** displays both text and numerical data as keyed. The general format is the default format.

**graphical user interface (GUI)** a way of interacting with a computer that involves pictures.

**graphics** pictures in your document that help illustrate the meaning of text or make the page more attractive or functional.

**grid snap** the feature that aligns objects in Draw to the nearest grid line.

**grouping** database reporting process that inserts a Summ *field name* row after each sorted group.

## H

**handles** small squares that appear around an object to indicate that the object is selected.

**hanging indent**   an indent in which the first line of text begins at the left margin and the remaining lines are indented.

**hardware**   the physical components of a computer.

**header**   text that repeats at the top of a page.

**highlight**   the entry point of a spreadsheet or database. A highlighted cell is indicated by a dark border.

**host computer**   the computer that receives the call and uses the calling computer as a terminal.

## I

**I-beam**   the mouse pointer that appears similar to the letter *I* when moved through text in a document window.

**icon**   a graphical representation of an item or object.

**indent**   a space set between text and a document's margin.

**insertion point**   see *cursor*.

**integrated software package**   a computer program that combines common tools into one program.

**integration**   the process of using more than one Works tool to create a document.

**internal modem**   a modem installed inside the computer.

## J

**justification**   determines how text is aligned at the margins.

## L

**landscape orientation**   refers to a page that, when printed, is wider than it is long.

**leading zeros format**   displays numerical data with a specified number of decimal places to the left of the decimal point.

**line chart**   uses points connected by a line to illustrate values in a spreadsheet. The line chart is ideal for illustrating trends of data over time.

**linking**   the process of integrating data between the spreadsheet and the word processor.

**List view**   a window in the database that is similar in appearance to the spreadsheet. List view is most appropriate when you want to display several records at once.

**logging off**   disconnecting from a host computer.

**logging on**   providing a name and password for access to a host computer.

## M

**mainframe computer**   a large multiuser computer system that uses terminals to interact with users.

**margin**   the amount of space between the edge of a page and the printed or written text in a document.

**mathematical functions**   a type of function formula that manipulates quantitative data in a spreadsheet or database. Examples include summing, finding the square root, and rounding numbers to a specific number of decimal places.

**Maximize button**   the button at the right side of the title bar that enlarges a window to its maximum size.

**menu bar**   the horizontal bar below the title bar that contains the names of the program's menus.

**mixed cell reference**   cell references containing both relative and absolute references.

**Minimize button**   the button at the right side of the title bar that reduces a window to an icon.

**modem**   a device that converts computer signals to and from sounds that can be transmitted over phone lines.

**modem communication**   the process of transmitting information from computer to computer over telephone lines.

**mouse**   a device that rolls on a flat surface and has one or more buttons on it used to interact with a computer.

## N

**navigation buttons**   buttons in the Form view window that allow you to move among records.

**Next Record search**   a database operation that finds the first record after the highlight in which the specified data is present.

## O

**on-line services**   commercial modem communication services.

**open**   the process of loading a file from a disk onto the screen.

**operand** numbers, cell references, or field names used in calculations in the formulas of spreadsheets or databases. In a spreadsheet the operand will be a cell reference; in a database the operands are field names.

**operator** tells Works what to do with the operands in a spreadsheet or database formula (for example, +, -, *, and / )

**order of evaluation** sequence used to calculate the value of a spreadsheet or database formula amount.

**Overtype** an editing option that is toggled on and off with the Insert key which replaces existing characters on the screen with new characters as they are keyed.

## P

**page break** a manually inserted character used to keep text together.

**pagination** the process by which Works automatically breaks long documents into pages by inserting page breaks.

**pane** a section of a document window that appears with a set of separate scroll bars when a window is split.

**paragraph indent** an indent in which the first line of text is indented and the remaining lines are against the left margin.

**path** see *pathname*.

**pathname** the location of a file on a disk.

**percent format** displays numerical data followed by a percent sign.

**pie chart** a spreadsheet chart that shows the relationship of a part to a whole. Each part is presented as a "slice" of the pie.

**portrait orientation** refers to a page that, when printed, is longer than it is wide.

**Program Manager** the program in Windows that organizes your programs into groups and allows you to launch other programs.

## Q

**queries** database operations that display on the screen only those records that have certain qualities.

**Query view** a database view in which query criteria are specified. The view is similar to Form view except that the word *QUERY* appears at the right side of the status line.

## R

**range** a selected group of cells in a spreadsheet and entries in a database. A range in a spreadsheet is identified by the cell in the upper left corner and the cell in the lower right corner, separated by a colon (for example, A3:C5).

**record** a row of entries.

**record number** number on the left side of a screen that identifies the sequence of a record in a database.

**relative cell reference** adjusts to a new location when the cell reference is copied or moved. For example, if the formula =B2+A3 is copied or moved from B3 to C4, the formula will be changed to =C3+B4.

**report** see *database report*.

**Report view** screen appearance for the database in which a database report is created and changed.

**row labels** columns on the left side of the Report view of the database that determine the appearance of the database report.

**rows** appear horizontally in the spreadsheet and are identified by numbers on the left side of the spreadsheet window.

**ruler** the row of numbers at the top of the document window that displays tab stops and margin settings.

## S

**sans serif font** a font without serifs.

**save** the process of storing a file on disk.

**scatter chart** a spreadsheet chart that shows the relationship between two categories of data. Scatter charts are sometimes called XY charts because one category is represented on the vertical (*Y*) axis and the other category is represented on the horizontal (*X*) axis.

**scroll arrows** arrows at the end of a scroll bar.

**scroll bar** a device that appears on the edge of a window that allows you to move the window over the contents.

**scroll box** a small box in the scroll bar that indicates the position within the contents of the window.

**searching** the process of locating specific data in a database.

**selecting** highlighting a block of text.

**serif font** a font that has serifs.

**serifs** small lines added to the ends of characters.

**size** the measure of the height of characters in units called points.

**software** the lists of instructions that computers follow to perform specific tasks; a program.

**sorting** a database operation that arranges records in the database in a specific order (such as alphabetical or largest to smallest).

**spacing** the distance between lines of text or paragraphs.

**splitting** Works operation that permits you to view several parts of a file on the screen simultaneously.

**spreadsheet** a grid of rows and columns containing numbers and other information. The purpose of a spreadsheet is to solve problems that involve numbers.

**statistical functions** function formulas that describe large quantities of data in a spreadsheet or database. Examples include averaging, calculating the standard deviation, or calculating the variance of a range of data.

**status bar** the horizontal bar located at the bottom of the document window that displays short informative messages.

**style** see *type style*.

**subdirectory** a directory within a directory.

**T**

**tabs** mark the place that the cursor will stop when the tab key is pressed.

**terminal** a screen and keyboard used to interact with a host computer.

**text file** a file that does not contain any of the codes that control fonts, font size, and type style.

**Thesaurus** a Works feature that contains 190,000 synonyms of a variety of words.

**time/date format** displays text and numerical data as times or dates.

**title bar** the horizontal bar located at the top of every window that contains the name of the program or document in the window.

**Toolbar** the horizontal bar below the menu bar that contains buttons that give shortcuts for the most commonly used word processing commands.

**true/false format** displays the word *TRUE* for all nonzero number values and *FALSE* for zero.

**typeface** a different design of type; see *font*.

**type size** a measurement of the height of a typeface given in points.

**type style** certain standard changes in the appearance of a font. Boldface, italic, and underline are common type styles.

**U**

**Undo** a command that will reverse the effect of the most recent formatting change.

**W**

**wildcard** a character in a search that permits any character to be specified. For example, the search criteria *al\** will find *Alabama, already,* or *Albert*. In a database search, the asterisk (*) is the wildcard character.

**word processing** the use of computer software to enter and edit text.

**wordwrap** a word processor feature that automatically moves text from the end of a line to the beginning of the next line.

**WorksWizards** automated programs that help you create an address book, form letter, and mailing labels.

# INDEX